Blackjack: Play Like the Pros

BLACKJACK:
Play Like the Pros

JOHN BUKOFSKY

LYLE STUART
Kensington Publishing Corp.
www.Kensingtonbooks.com

LYLE STUART BOOKS are published by

Kensington Publishing Corp.
850 Third Avenue
New York, NY 10022

First printing: August 2006

10 9 8 7 6 5 4

Printed in the United States of America

ISBN 0-8184-0656-9

This book is dedicated to you, the Player.

———

According to my old man, gamblers get a bad rap. They're really a nice bunch of people. And he's right, as usual. Only, as he well knows, this book isn't about gambling.

Contents

Acknowledgments

Many great minds associated with this game have influenced me over the years, directly and indirectly. To the following I extend my thanks: Edward Thorp, the late Lawrence Revere, Stanford Wong, Don Schlesinger, the late Kenneth Uston, the late Peter Griffin, Arnold Snyder, Lance Humble, Julian Braun, and Ian Andersen.

Thanks are also in order to the many other players, authors, and experts who have done things like written short but valuable pieces in magazines or online, or have been involved "behind the scenes" in recent years with extensive computer simulations. It is indeed a long and growing list. You know who you are, as do advantage blackjack players everywhere.

In New York, from conception to revision to completion: Richard Ember, Sheree Bykofsky, Janet Rosen, Brian Rubin, Megan Buckley, and everyone at Kensington who touched this project deserve and are given my sincerest thanks.

I am indebted to Don Schlesinger for a painstaking review and commentary. Is any current blackjack book really a bona fide blackjack text if it hasn't undergone a proofread by this blackjack luminary?

Special thanks to Professor Robert Cammarata and Josh Lubin for reading an earlier version of the manuscript and offering many insightful comments. Bob, you really should think about doing stand-up.

My gratitude is extended to Norm Wattenberger. The computer simulations I ran to provide data for this text come right from his invaluable Casino Vérité software package.

A big thank you goes out to my father, John Bukofsky, for lending his artistic talent to this project. Your technical illustrative skill is second to none.

I owe a warm and fuzzy thank you to my wife, Kristen, for her patience and support. J.J. and Katie, thank you, too!

Last but not least, thank you, Dini Bin. From Laughlin to Ledyard to London, it has been quite a ride.

Introduction:
So You Wanna Be Rain Man?

You're watching Dustin Hoffman play blackjack, you've heard of card counters winning huge sums of money at the blackjack tables, and you say to yourself, "How amazing is it that these guys can remember every card that comes up? I could never do that."

Well, guess what? Card counters aren't autistic savants, and just like everyone else they don't (or for that matter can't) remember every card that's been dealt. That's Hollywood, or that's being lucky enough to have been born with a gifted memory. And although being a successful counter at times does lend itself to a little glamour and sophistication, playing blackjack at the professional level is no walk down Hollywood Boulevard. But it can be very rewarding, and at the same time lots of fun.

The pages that follow assume you're a mere mortal. You have trouble remembering directions. No matter how many times you dial the local Chinese takeout, you still aren't sure if the first three digits are 254 or 245. And in the long run you're behind in the casinos, even though your wife's friend and her husband never seem to have a losing trip to Vegas—and they've been doing Sin City West for as long as you can remember. (A little inside information: They're lying.)

Everyone loses in the end, with the exception of a small group comprising professional card counters and expert poker players, and that rare breed of gambler who wins big on a slot machine and then stops gambling altogether. That's because it's impossible to overcome the mathematics of playing at a disadvantage. Make no mistake about it, beating the casinos at their own game isn't easy, which is why professional card counters and expert poker players, even with an advantage, lose a little more often than you might think.

I'd be lying to you if I said that in all the years I've been playing blackjack, I never fantasized about walking up to a table and remembering every card that comes out. But that's neither what card counting is nor pretends to be. Being a counter means using a point count to keep a running track of what cards have been dealt, and then doing a bunch of "related calculations." The tricky part is that you have to do these other calculations simultaneously, and you have to do them quickly; things like (1) remembering the correct *basic strategy,* (2) converting the *running count* to what's called (3) a *true count,* (4) *deviating from basic strategy,* depending on the true count number just calculated, and (5) applying a correct *betting strategy.* Some advanced card-counting methods also involve keeping a side count of aces, because the ace is such a valuable card when it comes to betting strategy. And the entire effort should be orchestrated with the same relaxed air you used in ordering a cocktail at poolside the night before.

Sounds tough, doesn't it? Well, it's really not that bad. In fact, it's a lot easier than you might think. But that's what it takes to eke out an advantage, and that's precisely what a card counter does. The pages that follow will walk you through each and every step of the process, and then some.

No introduction would be complete without a few words of encouragement. If at first glance any task or procedure seems too difficult or complicated, take a short break, a deep breath, and then say, "I can do this." Say it again to yourself, and remember to remain optimistic as you begin to learn the process. Spend the necessary time in the beginning and what you will come away with is a lucrative talent that can be applied as long as blackjack games are offered. And from the look of the game's popularity, it appears blackjack will be around for a long time to come.

Remember that you don't have to eat, drink, and sleep mathematics to become a proficient card counter. As with so many other things in life, all you need is some determination and the will to succeed. Stay focused and give yourself and the process a legitimate chance to succeed. Learn at your own speed. Read and reread if necessary, and move onto the next task only when you have mastered the preceding one.

Oh, and one more thing: *Have fun.* Enjoy the challenge, and revel some in your accomplishment as the winnings start to accumulate, knowing that millions of people around the world gamble in casinos every day—some with surprising regularity—and you're one of only a select few who will actually end up ahead in the end.

Blackjack: Play Like the Pros

CHAPTER ONE

Ground Zero

This chapter begins with the very basics of casino blackjack. The object of the game, how it is played, and other fundamentals are covered so that a solid foundation is formed on which to build. The chapter concludes by explaining the role of the dealer and then taking the reader along for a bird's-eye view of an imaginary hand.

As with most any subject, a thorough understanding of the fundamentals is a prerequisite for learning advanced techniques. So if you're just starting out, you may, over time, want to revisit certain sections like Player Options (p. 4) until thoroughly familiar with the material. If you frequent a casino from time to time or plan to do so shortly, wander over to any blackjack table and observe the action from behind. There's no better experience than watching the real thing. And for those of you already familiar with the game, you can either skim these pages using the material as a refresher, or move directly on to Chapter Two. It's your choice.

So, are you ready?

Okay then, let's start right from the beginning.

The Basics

The Cards

Blackjack, or "21" as it is sometimes called, is a game played with standard playing cards, minus the jokers. As you probably know, a standard deck of cards contains a 2, 3, 4, 5, 6, 7, 8, 9, 10, jack, queen, king, and ace—each in one of four different suits. Suits include spades, hearts, diamonds, and clubs, but are irrelevant. Each card from 2 to 9 has a value equal to its number, or total spots. Tens, jacks, queens, and kings are all worth 10. Aces are unique in that an ace can be counted as 1 or 11, depending on which is more favorable to the player at the time of its usage. For some hands the ace may start out being considered as 11 only to be counted as 1 later in the same hand.

Object of the Game

The object of the game is to beat the dealer, as opposed to getting as close as possible to 21—a common misconception. Players compete solely against the dealer, or house, and not against one another as is the case in many other card games.

Number of Players

Typically, there are five to seven locations to place a bet on a standard table, and a game may be dealt to anywhere from one to seven players depending on the number of betting locations available. On rare occasion, usually at higher-limit games, table layouts with even fewer betting spots may be offered.

Number of Decks

While home games are generally played with one deck of cards, casino blackjack may involve using anywhere from one to eight decks simultaneously. Be aware that some variations in the rules of the game do go hand-in-hand with the number of decks in use, but for the most part, the game is played the same way.

Although not a rule per se, one very obvious difference relating to the number of decks used is how the game is dealt. Single- and double-deck games are traditionally dealt face down, requiring the player to physically pick up his cards in order to total them. Shoe games, or those played with four, six, or eight decks, are dealt face up, meaning all player cards are visible to everyone at all times. And unlike in single- and double-deck blackjack, players aren't allowed to physically touch the cards—even their own. For a number of reasons that will be discussed later in the book, multiple-deck blackjack has become far more popular than single- or double-deck blackjack. In fact, these days many casinos offer only the multiple-deck variety.

Win, Lose, or Tie?

Those are the three possible outcomes for any given hand. The player wins when his hand totals higher than the dealer's, or when the player remains in the game after the dealer has gone over 21. Exceeding 21 in blackjack is a common occurrence by both player and dealer, and is generally referred to as "busting." The player loses when his hand totals lower than the dealer's, or when the player busts. Since all players must receive or decline additional cards before the dealer finishes his hand, a player loses if he busts and the dealer subsequently goes on to bust as well. Ties or "pushes" occur when both the player and the dealer end up with the same total, excluding the instance just mentioned—when first the player busts and then the dealer busts. In casino blackjack, a tie neither wins nor loses, whereas in most charity or home-dealt games, the player loses when ending with a total equal to that of the dealer's.

Naturals

A "natural" is a blackjack and consists of an ace and any 10-value card dealt on the first two cards. All totals of 21 comprising cards received after the initial two are not considered "blackjack."

Hard Hands and Soft Hands

Because the ace can be worth either 1 or 11 depending on which is more favorable, special terminology is used to describe a hand that distinguishes how it is being used. Hands in which an ace is counted as 11 are known as "soft hands," while those hands without an ace or where any number of aces are counted as one are known as "hard hands." For example, a 17 comprising an ace and a 6 is referred to as a "Soft 17." Likewise, an ace and a 4 comprise a Soft 15. But what happens if we add a queen to a Soft 15, as might happen in play? With the presence of a queen, the value of the ace must now be counted as 1—otherwise our total would exceed 21. Counting the ace as 1, our total, now made up of an ace, a 4, and a queen, went from a Soft 15 to a hard hand of the same total.

Soft hands are usually very good hands for the player in that an opportunity exists to improve, at least initially, without the possibility of busting. There are some soft hand totals, such as 19, 20, and 21, where it's advisable for the player not to take additional cards, but more often than not, a soft hand means a "free" opportunity to improve.

Player Options

Hitting
"Hitting" in blackjack means asking for or "drawing" another card. A player hits when hoping to improve his hand. In single- and double-deck games, where the first two cards are dealt face down, the player requests another card by way of a quick, short scratch of the table with the two cards he is holding. In multiple-deck games, or when all cards are dealt face up, the player requests another by simply tapping the table with a finger.

A hand signal or some type of movement indicating intent is required. Simply asking for or declining another card verbally is almost universally unacceptable.

Standing

Once the initial deal is complete, the player has several options. One of those options is to "stand," or stay put when satisfied with the total of his cards. To "stand" or "stay" means to not take additional cards, whether that occurs after the initial deal or after several cards have been drawn. In handheld games, a player desiring to stand simply takes his initial two cards and slides them, facedown, beneath his wager. In shoe games, a quick shake of the hand in a back-and-forth motion signifies to the dealer that no additional cards are desired.

Doubling Down

A player may double his wager after the first two cards, and in doing so must take one additional card—and one only. To double down, the player must bet any amount *up to but not exceeding* his original wager. In handheld games, the player tosses his first two cards face up on the table, and then places an amount up to the equivalent of his original bet next to the original wager. In multiple-deck games the player simply adds the desired amount in a stack next to the original wager and confirms his desire to double down.

There are many situations when doubling down is very advantageous to the player. Just the same, there are numerous situations when it should be avoided. By the way, doubling down for any amount less than the original wager is known as "doubling for less."

Soft Doubling Down

This is a slight variation to the traditional double down in that the player elects this option when holding a soft total, or a hand in which an ace is counted as 11. In other words, doubling down with an ace and a 5 would be considered doubling down on a Soft 16, or soft doubling. As with the more traditional form of doubling down, there are times when soft doubling is advantageous to the player and times when it isn't. The same procedure is followed: The player simply doubles his bet (or bets any amount up to or equaling his original wager), and receives one additional card.

Splitting Pairs

If the player is dealt two cards that form a pair (e.g., two 9s), he may elect to split the pair. The player must then bet another amount equal to the original wager, and by doing so will signal his intent to split the pair. In hand-held games, the player tosses the pair face up on the table prior to doubling his wager. In multiple-deck games, just as with doubling down, a second bet equal to the first is placed next to the original wager. The dealer then begins by dealing a card to what becomes the first of two hands, moving to the second only when either the player has busted or indicated by hand signal that no more cards are desired on the first. In some casinos, the player may split again, or "re-split" if dealt a third card of equal value to the original two (e.g., in this case, another 9).

Because aces are such favorable cards for the player, special rules apply when splitting them. Whereas for normal splits, any number of cards may be drawn to each new hand, the player is allowed only one additional card for each ace—and the ability to re-split a third ace isn't usually an option in those instances when a third ace appears.

Like doubling down, splitting pairs—in many cases—is a very favorable player option when exercised in the right situation.

Doubling After Splitting

In some casinos a player may double down after splitting pairs. For example, two 9s are split, and on the first 9 the player receives a 2 for a total of 11. The player may then elect to double down on the 11. Just as in a normal doubling decision, the player simply puts out yet another bet (again, any amount up to or equaling the original wager) and is dealt one additional card on the first hand. The deal then progresses to the second 9, and goes from there.

Insurance

"Insurance" is an option in which the player may bet on whether or not the dealer has blackjack. Whenever an ace appears as the dealer's up-card, the player has the option to purchase insurance. Insurance may be taken for any amount up to or equaling half of the player's initial wager. The dealer then checks for blackjack. If the dealer has blackjack, the original wager is lost—but the insurance bet is paid at 2:1, which equals the amount of the original wager. So in the end the player breaks even, which supports the definition of traditional insurance—that of indemnifying the insured. If the dealer does not have blackjack, the insurance bet is collected as a losing wager, and the hand continues on like any other.

Surrender

"Surrender" is an option that allows the player to give up, or surrender, after the first two cards are dealt, and in doing so forfeit half of his original wager. There are two varieties of surrender: early surrender and late, or conventional, surrender. The notable difference is that early surrender allows the player to give up his hand *before* the dealer checks for blackjack—if the dealer's upcard is an ace or ten. Conventional surrender is the ability to bow out only *after* the dealer checks for blackjack. Depending largely on both the player's hand and the dealer's up card, the option to surrender, when available, can be a very advantageous one. For that reason, the option isn't always offered, and in fact is lessening in popularity. Surrender will be touched on in more detail in the Chapter Two section titled "Rules Variations."

Playing Multiple Hands

A player may elect to play more than one hand. This is done simply by placing another bet in a neighboring betting circle. Most casinos permit a single player to play two, three, or even four or more hands at the same time. However, some casinos require the player to make larger bets on each hand if playing more than one. For example, playing two hands might require each one to be at least double the table minimum.

"Checks Play"

Before a hand is dealt, each player who desires to be included in the deal must make a wager. Chips, also known as "checks," are placed in a small circle on the table layout, or often over a miniature version of the casino logo. Bets must be equal to or greater than the posted table minimum, and not exceed the table maximum.

All original bets that become winning wagers are paid at 1:1, otherwise known as "even money," with one exception: Blackjack pays 1½:1, or 3:2.

Other bets that may occur during the course of a hand, such as splitting pairs or doubling down, are also paid at even money. As mentioned earlier, in most casinos a player may elect to double down "for less"— which still results in even money, or a payoff equal to the original wager plus a payoff equal to the lesser amount—should the player end up winning the hand.

A rare exception to either even money for winning or 1½:1 for blackjack is 6 to 5 for blackjack, a rule now common on many single-deck games.

Keep in mind that in blackjack—unlike in poker, for instance—players compete only against the house and not in any way against one another. Thus any given hand can have more than one winner.

The Dealer

We've covered the fundamentals and the various options available to the player. Now let's take a brief look at how the dealer runs the game, what he uses to do so, and what rules and procedures he is forced to abide by. Let's start with the various objects found on a typical blackjack table, and follow with a description of what the dealer's responsibilities are once the cards are being dealt.

The Shoe

In four-, six-, and eight-deck games, cards are placed in what's called a "shoe," as it would be impossible for any dealer to hold four or more decks of cards and effectively run a game at the same time. In single- and double-deck games, shoes are generally not used, as dealers are trained to hold the cards while performing all of the duties necessary.

The Discard Tray

The discard tray holds those cards that have already been used, and accumulates cards both when players bust and at the conclusion of each hand. The discard tray is found next to the player sitting in the last seat, sometimes refered to as "third base," located to the dealer's right.

The Chip Rack

Each table's chip rack holds the many chips needed to either pay off winning hands or hold losing wagers after they're collected. All chip racks are arranged and maintained with the highest-denomination chips kept at center and those with lesser value on each side. Often, little plastic disks called spacers are used to maintain checks in stacks of twenty.

The Plunger

Just as the name implies, the plunger is used to push cash from player buy-ins into the lockbox located beneath each table.

Signage

Signage on the table includes the minimum and maximum bets allowed on a given hand, along with a brief description of the rules. Other signs may include special promotions, or advertise the fact that a particular table is a nonsmoking one.

Dealing the Cards

The start of every hand begins with the dealer giving each player a card. After dealing himself one, he deals a second round—again one to each player in a clockwise direction around the table. The initial deal ends with the dealer's second card placed face down, neatly below the first.

At this point, with only one dealer card visible, each player in succession is given the opportunity to hit, stand, or exercise any of the player options available. Remember that in single- and in most double-deck games, players' cards are dealt facedown, whereas in multiple-deck games using four or more decks, all cards are dealt face up.

After giving additional cards to those players who want them, the dealer flips over his down card, or "hole" card, and tallies the total. This is the critical juncture of every hand. At this point, unlike the player, who may decide whether or not it is beneficial to take additional cards, the dealer *must* abide by the rule printed on the playing surface of every table—and on which the entire game essentially rests:

Dealer must draw to 16, and stand on all 17s

Thus, the dealer is required to take additional cards and risk busting if his hand totals 16 or under, and stand with any total of 17 and above. It is only after reaching a total of 17 to 21, or busting, that the hand ends and the dealer begins paying or collecting winning and losing wagers.

The Shuffle

Shuffling occurs when the cut card is dealt, or in some hand-held games at the dealer's discretion, based on a rough estimate of how many cards remain unused. "Washing" is a term used to describe the initial shuffle, where the cards are manually spread out across the table's surface and randomly mixed together.

The Cut Card

The cut card often is a piece of plastic dealt to one of the players whose job it then becomes to cut the cards after the dealer has shuffled. The cut card is then placed back into the deck or decks by the dealer to signify when the cards should be shuffled again. In some cases the general placement of the cut card is left up to the dealer, while in other situations it reflects specific management policy.

The Burn Card

"Burning" the first card, a blackjack tradition, occurs at the beginning of a new deal, or in most casinos when one dealer relieves another. The card is simply taken off the top of the deck, or from the shoe, and placed in the discard tray. Some dealers automatically display the value of this card, while others do not. In the latter case, many players request to see the card, and almost always their wish is granted.

A Glimpse into the Future

We've touched on the various options available to the player. We've also discussed what functions the dealer performs, as well as what objects are found on a standard blackjack table. Now let's take a moment to walk through a typical hand. This should give you a feel for how the game is played and how everything we've covered so far interrelates.

Imagine a posh casino floor on the Vegas Strip. It's late at night and you can feel the electricity in the air, amplified by the frequent roar of a nearby craps game. You approach a $25 table—a multiple-deck game with five players facing an attractive blonde snapping out cards like she's been dealing blackjack since high school.

She finishes the deal by taking a second card for herself, and deftly buries it, facedown, beneath the first. Starting on her left, players must now decide whether or not to take additional cards or employ any of the variety of other options available. For this hand we note that the dealer's upcard is a 7.

THE DEALER (MICHELE, FROM COLBY, KANSAS): Seeing that she does not have a blackjack and Player Number Four does, her first order of business is to pay Player Number Four one and a half times his original bet. She does so in quick order, collects his two cards then turns to Player Number One.

PLAYER NUMBER ONE (BETSY, FROM SIOUX FALLS, SOUTH DAKOTA): The total of her first two cards is 11. Betsy puts out another bet equal in amount to her original wager—in order to double down—and receives a 6 for a total of 17.

PLAYER NUMBER TWO (PATRICK O., FROM WESTON, MASSACHUSETTS): The total of this player's first two cards is 19. Pat elects to stand "as is."

PLAYER NUMBER THREE (JIM, FROM TALLAHASSEE, FLORIDA): Jim has a total of 9, and subsequently draws a 5 for 14, followed by a 2 for 16, followed by a 10 for 26. This player has busted, and automatically loses. Like those of the player with blackjack, Jim's cards are removed right after his chips are taken away.

PLAYER NUMBER FOUR (GLEN, FROM REDONDO BEACH, CALIFORNIA): This player is skipped. Glen had an ace and a queen on his first two cards—a blackjack, and was previously paid.

PLAYER NUMBER FIVE (NANCY, FROM ALEXANDRIA, VIRGINIA): This player has two 3s, and decides to split them. She puts out a bet equivalent to her first, and the dealer separates her cards. On the first 3 Nancy is dealt a 10. She hits again and receives an 8 for 21. On the second 3 Nancy is dealt a 7. This prompts her to put out a third wager, again equal to her original bet, in order to double down on the second hand—on what now totals 10. She receives a king for 20.

Our dealer then flips over her hole card, revealing a 6 for a total of 13. As 13 is below 17, she must draw another card and does—a 5 for a total of 18. According to the rules of the game, she must now stand, and proceed to pay off or collect winning and losing wagers.

Where does a dealer 18 leave our players? Player Number One made the correct move by doubling down, but unfortunately the dealer ended with a higher total. Betsy loses both her original bet and her second wager, the double down. The dealer loses to Player Number Two, and pays Patrick an amount equivalent to his original bet. Jim from the Sunshine State had previously busted. His cards and wager were removed at the time that occurred. Likewise, Glen had been dealt a blackjack—his cards were removed and a payoff had been made earlier in the hand. Our last player, Nancy, is the big winner this round, with a payoff equal to three times her original bet for two hands that both totaled higher than the dealer's. The stand-alone 21 gets paid even money, as does the second 3, which then became part of a double down.

There are endless variations to the above, but that's the general flow for how a typical hand might unfold. After the dealer's cards are totaled, wagers are paid, taken away, or left on the table, depending on whether the player has won, lost, or tied the dealer.

Let's again summarize the three possible outcomes, keeping in mind two very important points, the first of which we've covered earlier:

- The dealer must draw with a total of 16 or less, and stand with any total of 17 and above. These are the rules of the game. Whereas a player can decide on whether or not to draw additional cards, the rules of the game force the dealer to draw or stand based on the total of his cards.

- The dealer goes last. By the time the dealer completes his hand, all players are either content with their totals, or have previously won with a blackjack or lost by going over 21.

WINNING: A player's hand totals higher than the dealer's, or he has a blackjack and the dealer does not, or he remains in the game with any total and the dealer subsequently goes on to bust.

LOSING: A player loses when he busts, or when the dealer's hand ultimately totals higher if the player has remained in the game.

TYING: A player ties, or pushes, when his hand and the dealer's hand total the same amount.

Remember that a player loses immediately upon busting. So if a player busts and the dealer subsequently goes on to bust as well, the player loses.

Along about now you might be asking yourself why anybody would ever take another card if the possibility of going over 21 exists? The reason for doing so in some situations is that reliable computer-tested blackjack strategy has proven that it is to the player's advantage to sometimes risk the possibility of busting in an attempt to improve a relatively poor hand. Not risking the possibility of busting in some situations is by far the single most common "beginner" error.

Double Exposure and Other Forms of "Exotic" Blackjack

No chapter on blackjack basics would be complete without a brief mention of Double Exposure and other, newer forms of "exotic" blackjack that involve various side bets and special bonuses.

Double Exposure has been around for years and is a form of the game in which both dealer cards are exposed. However, in double exposure the house wins ties. Although it may seem highly advantageous to know the value of both dealer cards at the beginning of every hand, do understand that losing ties is extremely unfavorable.

In other forms of exotic blackjack, what may seem like a very attractive bet at first glance is often, in reality, mathematically unfavorable to the player. The advice here is to exercise extreme caution. In fact, any and all forms of "untraditional" blackjack should be avoided unless some special facet of a particular game with a particular set of rules can be exploited, and reliable computer simulations along with a predetermined change in playing strategy has proven it.

CHAPTER TWO

Jellybeans, Rules Variations, and Card Counting

Why Blackjack Is "Beatable"

It's very important for the student to understand why the game of blackjack can be beaten. Over the years, many people have asked me about card counting, and in the beginning I used to delve right into explanations on running count conversions and variations to the Basic Strategy. Until I realized all that really doesn't mean much to the occasional player, because the occasional player simply lacks the experience or understanding to appreciate why those things are important.

What makes blackjack a game you can beat, plainly and simply, is the fact that *what has happened in the past will affect what is to happen in the future.* Nothing more—nothing less. Just think of it in this way: What horse track gambler wouldn't like to have tomorrow's newspaper today?

To bring this concept into focus, let's compare blackjack to some other popular games typically found in most casinos. Take craps, for example. Let's assume the shooter rolls an 8, composed of a 5 on one die and a 3 on the other. The dice are returned to the shooter, who is about to roll again. Obviously the 5 and the 3 contained on each die could easily come out again. And, in fact, the odds of that happening are no different than were the odds of a 5 or a 3 being rolled the first time. In roulette the same logic applies. Let's say the croupier spins the ball and it ends up falling into number 15. The physical pocket corresponding to number 15 always remains in the roulette wheel. So when the dealer spins again a few minutes later, number 15 has as much chance of coming out again as it did the first time. In simple terms this concept is called "replacement," or in probability theory, the "Law of Independent Trials."

Now on to blackjack, and notice the difference. When the dealer finishes dealing a hand, the used cards are placed in the discard tray—*not to be used again until after the next shuffle*. (Obviously, the shuffle at the beginning of each deal or "shoe" represents "ground zero.") For this example let's say the 3 of diamonds was among those cards just dealt in a single deck game. A hard fact has just been established. The 3 of diamonds *cannot* be dealt again until after the next shuffle. Think about it. In no other game does such an absolute present itself, where knowledge of the past can and will have a direct effect on the future. The same logic holds true for multiple-deck games, only on a lesser scale. In a six-deck game where there are a total of 24 3s, after one hand in which a 3 is dealt, you can rest assured that only 23 3s are left in the shoe. Although such specific information as knowing exactly how many of any particular card remains in the deck or decks at any given moment isn't humanly possible to track and process to one's advantage, nevertheless, this represents the basic premise on which all responsible card counting methods are based.

So where and from whom did all of this originate?

Card counting was first developed and proven to be a viable method by Dr. Edward O. Thorp, then a professor of mathematics at the Massachusetts Institute of Technology (MIT). The year was 1960, and using the University's IBM 704 computer, Dr. Thorp was able to formulate and test his theory that a significant advantage could be obtained by a blackjack player able to follow a predetermined strategy and keep some sort of track of high and low cards as they were being dealt. His research began three years after a technical paper appeared in the "Journal of the American Statistical Association" entitled, "The Optimum Strategy in Blackjack," written by Roger R. Baldwin, Wilbert E. Cantey, Herbert Maisel, and James P. McDermott of the U.S. Army's Aberdeen Proving Ground. "The Optimum Strategy in Blackjack" outlined the first bona fide version of a "basic strategy," but it was Dr. Thorp and his exhaustive computer simulations that led to the first comprehensive playing and card counting strategy that could successfully beat the game. A year after proving his method in live casino play, the first edition of Thorp's 1962 best-selling book *Beat the Dealer* was published, and revealed to the masses just how blackjack could be beaten.

Ultimately, the bottom line result of knowing something about the future (and implementing all the facets of a sound card counting method) enables the counter to play at what's called a "positive expectation." Don't confuse positive expectation with a confident or optimistic outlook on the idea of winning money. What positive expectation means is that over the long run the odds of winning exceed the odds of losing. In a sense, card counters switch the traditional role of casino and player. The card counter with his advantage—believe it or not—assumes the role of the casino (normally holding the advantage), while the casino becomes the ordinary gambler, typically playing at a disadvantage and destined to lose in the long run.

So, how much of an edge is obtainable? A proficient counter can garner about a 1.0 percent to 2.0 percent advantage over the house. What's a 2 percent edge? Consider the following: A jar is filled with one hundred jellybeans. Fifty-one are red. Forty-nine are black. Let's blindfold that casino know-it-all every one of us knows, and ask him to select one jellybean from the jar. After each selection, he's allowed to throw the jellybean back into the mix. When blindfolded, are his chances better to pick out a red jellybean or a black jellybean? Obviously, with more red jellybeans present, the odds of his picking out a red jellybean are greater than the odds of his picking out a black jellybean. And, in fact, if he were to make one hundred picks, red jellybeans should outnumber black jellybeans by two. That's the equivalent of a 2 percent advantage. Think of the red jellybeans as the advantage player's chances of winning and the black jellybeans as the advantage player's chances of losing. Since the red jellybeans outnumber the black jellybeans, the proficient card counter *must* come out ahead in the end.

But could he pick out a black jellybean on any given grab? Certainly. And, in fact, forty-nine isn't a very small number in comparison to fifty-one, so there will be many instances when our friend will indeed pick a black jellybean out of the jar. But it won't happen as much as it would to the really uninformed or even Basic Strategy player—picking jellybeans from jars holding perhaps forty-eight and fifty red jellybeans respectively. In fact, have our three players pick one hundred jellybeans a day out of their respective jars for a period of a year and you would no doubt see quite a difference between the card counter's results and those of the other two.

Rules Variations

In a perfect world the rules of blackjack would be exactly the same no matter where one played, from Australia to the Caribbean to the smallest of casinos located in rural areas like Northern Minnesota. But unfortunately that's not the case, and for the long-term player it's essential to interface only in games where certain rules don't negate too much of the edge otherwise obtained through advantage play.

The differences that exist are largely dependent on locale, although variations do exist from casino to casino in the same city. The classic example of this is the difference in how blackjack is played between casinos in downtown Las Vegas and those located out on that amazing stretch of pavement known as the Las Vegas Strip. Downtown, dealers hit on Soft 17—somewhat of a departure from that old saying we read about in Chapter One: *"Dealer must draw to 16, and stand on all 17s"*. A change in rules usually means a slight change in the player's overall advantage or disadvantage. In this case, that's a slight increase in house advantage, because in those situations where the dealer would have otherwise stood with 17, he instead will get another chance of improving his hand without the possibility of busting (since the ace can be totaled as "1" if totaling it as "11" ends up exceeding 21). In this case, the house advantage increases by about 0.2 percent, which in the long run will end up costing the player a couple of dollars in expected value.

In this section we'll touch on some common rules and the corresponding effects on player advantage. Keep in mind that a player using perfect Basic Strategy in a game with a typical set of rules plays at only a very slight disadvantage. And a proficient card counter, under those same circumstances, garners about a 1.5 percent advantage. As mentioned earlier, it's imperative for the serious player to find a game with rules that don't negate too much edge. Otherwise, all that is really happening is the passage of time. And why go through the effort of counting, proper bet sizing, and all the other facets of professional-level play if the rules of the game reduce your advantage to a level on which playing becomes an exercise in futility? Thankfully, in more instances than not, card counting can overcome the negative effects of rules that are unfavorable to the player. But regardless, the first order of business should be an assessment of the game and what rules apply.

Aside from the number of decks used, there are essentially five major rules variations that the player will encounter:

DOUBLING DOWN ON 10 AND 11 ONLY: This is common throughout Northern Nevada, and restricts the player's ability to double down to only hands in which the player's cards total 10 and 11. This increases house advantage since there are many advantageous opportunities to double down with totals other than 10 and 11.

SURRENDER: Offering surrender is becoming less and less popular. Casinos that once offered this favorable rule, such as those in Atlantic City, no longer do so. Surrender is a very advantageous rule for the card counter, because those situations that call for surrender often occur when the advantage player has a larger-than-normal bet on the table.

DEALER HITS SOFT 17: As mentioned earlier, dealers' drawing on Soft 17 is standard operating procedure for casinos in downtown Las Vegas, as well as those in Northern Nevada. Hitting Soft 17 carries a .2 percent house advantage.

DOUBLING AFTER SPLITTING: In some casinos this is allowed, in others it isn't. Since doubling down is a favorable player option, a small advantage is lost during double down opportunities that arise after splitting pairs.

RE-SPLITTING PAIRS: Years ago, no limit existed on how many pairs could be split. Nowadays, though, that's rarely the case. Casino rules usually allow the player to split a pair, and then split again only once or twice. When casinos realized re-splitting of pairs was advantageous to the player (and especially the card counter in some cases), rules were modified to limit the number of splits allowable on any given hand.

The following table lists the effects of these rules variations, plus a few more. The figures shown are percentages that affect the Basic Strategy player, and are listed from most beneficial to most detrimental. The percentages are close approximations. Note that no single variation exceeds 1 percent individually, but in many cases several will apply. To determine how good or bad a game is from a Basic Strategy perspective, simply ascertain what rules apply and then add or subtract accordingly. When more than one number appears in the "% Change" column, the first number applies to single deck, the second number to multiple deck.

Table 2.1: Effects of Common Rules Variations

RULE	% CHANGE	
Early Surrender	0.6	
Doubling Down After Splitting Pairs	0.14	
Conventional Surrender	0.02	0.08
Split Aces More Than Once	0.03	0.08
Dealer Hits Soft 17	-0.2	
Doubling Down on 10 or 11 Only	-0.28	-0.18
Double Deck	-0.3	
Four Deck	-0.5	
Six Deck	-0.55	
Eight Deck	-0.6	

Clearly, the two most common favorable rules are the Early Surrender option and the ability to double down after splitting pairs. The two most common unfavorable rules, other than an increase in the number of decks in use, are doubling down restricted to 10 and 11 only, and games in which the dealer draws on Soft 17.

On the Strip, rules vary from casino to casino. In some places doubling after splitting is allowed, while in others it isn't. Likewise, surrender can be a "yes" or "no" depending on location. In the same casino, rules at single deck are likely to be a little more restrictive than rules for multiple deck. All in all, the Las Vegas Strip with its single-, double-, and multiple-deck games is one of the more favorable locations in the world to play blackjack, but differences among casinos do exist in terms of what blackjack rules apply. So it's prudent for the serious player to shop around some for the best game available.

Downtown Las Vegas is known for its similarity to Northern Nevada, in that the dealer draws on Soft 17. However, unlike their northern counterparts, downtown players may double down on any two cards. Casinos on Fremont Street are smaller than most Strip casinos, but proportionately offer many more single- and double-deck games.

Although casinos exist all over the state of Nevada—in towns such as McDermitt, Wendover, Ely, and Mesquite, to name just a few—in the blackjack world "Northern Nevada" has become synonymous with Reno and Lake Tahoe. Casinos here are known for restricting the player from doubling down on any total other than 10 or 11, in addition to the dealer hitting Soft 17s. The double down restriction adds an additional -0.18 to -0.28 to the already-present -0.20 (for hitting Soft 17s), for a Basic Strategy starting disadvantage of about -0.38 to -0.48 off the top.

Atlantic City rules include doubling down on any two cards, doubling down after splitting, and the more traditional game wherein the dealer stands on all 17s. These rules are enforced by the Casino Control Commission—the authority having jurisdiction up and down the boardwalk and out on the shores of Brigantine Bay. The vast majority of AC casinos offer eight-deck games, although several houses have high-limit pits offering the six-deck variety. As of this writing, only one Atlantic City casino offers a six-deck game throughout.

Indian reservation and riverboat casinos are difficult to summarize because they exist in so many places, and vary from locale to locale. For the most part, players are allowed to double down on any two cards and the dealer must stand on Soft 17. Multiple-deck games are far and away the standard, although here and there one may come across a hand-held game—albeit most likely of the 6:5 for blackjack variety.

With regard to rules, a few closing thoughts: First and foremost, be proactive. The first thing you should do before sitting down at a table in a casino you've never played in before should be to ask about or find out what the rules are. Sometimes signage on the table will mention all or some of what applies. If you're uncertain about something, don't be afraid to ask. Most casino personnel will be more than happy to answer any questions you may have about the game. Of course, be discerning. Ask only a question any normal player might ask, in the way any normal player might ask it. The last thing you want is to be scrutinized as a possible advantage player even before you sit down.

In the beginning or for low stakes, I would encourage you to play only in games with the most advantageous sets of rules. But as time goes on you will find that sometimes the necessity of remaining anonymous becomes a higher priority than the attractiveness of a game offered in any particular casino. In other words, even though a mathematically better game may be had in Casino A than in Casinos B through Z, for longevity purposes the pro will instead spread himself around and thus stand a better chance of remaining undetected.

If you come across an unusual rule that seems too good to be true in a casino that's been around for a while, then it's probably just that—too good to be true. Often, new games or rule changes to existing games aren't as advantageous as they first appear to be. In fact, many harbor a mathematical disadvantage. Casinos in general rarely come along and make it easier for the player to win. If you encounter a new rule in any casino, there's really nothing you can do but abstain from play or rely on your own best judgment as to whether the rule is perhaps advantageous or not. Then, later, a visit to one of the reputable blackjack websites that list new rules and their corresponding advantage/disadvantage might prove helpful in determining whether or not to take advantage of it. After reading this text, odds are you'll be more than knowledgeable enough to draw a reasonable conclusion, at least for the time being.

Ultimately, use the rules of a game as your starting point. I've played in hundreds of casinos all over the world, and the very first thing I do in any house I've never been in before is determine how many decks are in use and ascertain what the rules are. Consider this the necessary initial assessment that allows you to determine whether or not the game is "beatable," how "beatable," and whether or not it's worth your time to put on the gloves and get into the ring.

Why Keep Track of the Cards?

The better question might be, *why not keep track of the cards?*

In the Introduction, I touched briefly on what is required to play blackjack at the professional level. And earlier in this chapter, we talked about how slightly more red jellybeans than black jellybeans represents the card counter's advantage over the casino. But let's not forget about the basics. Learning the best possible way to play each hand, otherwise known as Basic Strategy, is the first step on the road to becoming a pro. The next step involves learning how to actually count the cards by assigning a point value to each, and then keeping a running total.

Before we go on, let's tackle somewhat of a misnomer. Card counting isn't *that* difficult. What it does take is perseverance, along with a good deal of practice. In college, I went through four years of electrical engineering. Now *that* was difficult. (At least to me it was.) But card counting? In fact, if I had to guess, I'd say that most people have the mental capacity necessary to become professional-level players—and good ones at that. Whether or not these same people have the perseverance or discipline necessary is probably the bigger question.

So why not keep track of the cards?

To be honest, I don't understand why more people don't. What I find amazing is the number of players who have obviously mastered Basic Strategy, but do nothing to further improve their game. Over the years I've had the pleasure of playing alongside physicians, entrepreneurs, investment bankers—businessmen and -women of all types—bright people definitely capable of winning in the long run. And yet when the count goes negative, these same people often are, unknowingly, "betting the ranch." I see it time and time again. And, of course, when the count goes through the ceiling, they're usually betting the table minimum. It never fails: a classic example of just not being aware of what's going on behind the scenes.

So why not keep track of the cards?

Here's yet another reason: It looks like casino gambling is here to stay. On May 26, 1978, Atlantic City, New Jersey, became the eastern home of legalized casino gambling. And casino gambling outside of Nevada hasn't stopped expanding since. Speaking of Nevada, have you been to Las Vegas lately? From casinos with mountains to virtual reality to Celine Dion, Vegas is (and always will be) the cutting edge. And they're still building. Wynn Las Vegas, the newest megaresort, recently came in with a price tag of over $2 billion, surpassing the likes of the Venetian, Bellagio, Mandalay Bay, and several other hotel-supermodels lining the world-famous Las Vegas Strip. With that kind of investment going down, you can rest assured Sin City plans to leave the lights on for many years to come.

Indian reservations? There's another phenomenon. Twenty years ago gaming on Indian reservations was just a gleam in a young tribal chief's eye. Now casinos are on a multitude of reservations all over the United States. I'm willing to bet that there's an Indian casino near you.

Riverboat casinos? Need I say anymore?

The point I am making is that casino gambling is everywhere nowadays, and no doubt isn't going away any time soon. And lots of people are "doing it," including many of those same people who frowned on casino gambling years ago. Even if you don't see yourself sitting at a blackjack table with regularity, that's all right. Make it a long-term investment—a "life game"—and apply it whenever you do play. In fact, for occasional players there are several inherent advantages to not playing too often, touched on in more detail in Chapter 13.

In conclusion, I know there are many people out there who already play blackjack with great regularity. What's hard to understand is why anyone would do so and not attempt to take their game to the highest level possible? Serious blackjack for the "regular" player has long ago evolved to a level higher than that of just "Basic Strategy." For the occasional player, I must wonder at what point or after how many years of play does the amount of hours logged at a blackjack table become large enough such that keeping track of the cards might have been well worth the effort to begin with? A question you, the occasional player, might want to consider with every new trip to Vegas, or foray into Indian country. And finally there are the newbies, for whom blackjack presents a wonderful opportunity to "beat the casinos at their own game" right from the start. You're not alone these days. With casino gambling so popular, it's not surprising that more and more players are becoming informed players—players who gravitate to a game like blackjack because it requires skill and offers a mental challenge, and most important, *can be beaten* by the player who takes the time to master a winning method.

CHAPTER THREE

Casinos: Love 'Em or Leave 'Em

Like it or not, it's hard to go anywhere in this country, or in the world for that matter, and not be within striking distance of a casino. As touched on in the last chapter, that wasn't the case ten or fifteen years ago, at least in the United States. But it certainly is now.

So what are these places really all about? What goes on behind the scenes? And now that you're going to be part of an elite group of players that actually wins money in the long run, what will you need to know?

Let's take a chapter to talk about casinos—where they are, what's in them, how you'll interface, and some other interesting things to know about an environment truly unlike any other.

Where Are They, and What's With the Mountain?

What city is home to more casinos per square mile than anywhere in the world, and also happens to be mecca for the modern-day card counter? If your answer was "Las Vegas," you're right. Sin City has turned up the volume yet again. And that was a good business decision, because with the popularity of casino gambling exploding across the United States, some place had to emerge as the crème de la crème of gambling towns. And that somewhere remains, indisputably, Las Vegas, Nevada.

Okay, enough about Vegas. Where else can I find casinos to throw my 1½ percent at?

In the United States, try Atlantic City, Northern Connecticut, Gulfport/Biloxi, Reno/Lake Tahoe, Chicagoland, Minnesota, Michigan, St. Louis, New Orleans, Niagara Falls—the list goes on and on, and includes hundreds of riverboats and Indian casinos all over the United States. By the way, unless you're from the Upper Midwest, I'll bet you didn't know that the state of Minnesota alone has about nineteen operating casinos.

On the international front, casinos can be found in many countries all over the world. They're just a little more low-key than those in America. Don't expect mega-structures with 6,000-room hotels overlooking a volcano. In fact, in some European countries it's very possible to pass a casino on the street and not even know of its existence behind the glass doors of what could easily be mistaken as a private club or office. Serious players find out where the games are and what rules apply—without the aid of blinking lights or garish advertisement. It's a whole different kind of interface—you'll know what I mean if you ever play in other countries.

Some better-known international destinations offering casino gambling include the Caribbean, Canada, London, Amsterdam, Monte Carlo, and all over the Pacific Rim, including the major cities in Australia.

The Advantage Player Interface

Casinos come in all shapes and sizes: big ones, small ones, those plainer than plain, and those lavish beyond your wildest dreams. But remember casinos are businesses like any other, and whether big or small, the bottom line for any operating business is to make a profit.

From your experience to date, is it hard to imagine a pit full of friendly casino personnel suddenly turning against you? It probably is, and it's probably also hard to imagine a multi-million dollar corporation "sweating" the action of a single card counter varying his bets between $10 and $200 per hand. But that happens too. Why? Because you, as an advantage player, are taking up space at a blackjack table otherwise

worth "x" dollars per hour to the house. And losing money to one customer when a casino would otherwise stand to make money from another is the last thing any good company wants to do on a consistent
basis. Which is what would happen if casino management allowed you
to play.

So how bad does it get? That depends where you are and what rules
are in effect for the particular jurisdiction you're playing in. I've been
both backed off and barred in my playing career and, believe me, it's no
fun. In Las Vegas, for instance, casinos can still prevent card counters
from playing blackjack by throwing them off the premises, often referred to as being barred, or in casino lingo, being "86'd." Whereas in
Atlantic City, for example, regulations enforced by the Casino Control
Commission prevent any casino from actually barring someone from
the premises. But the flip side (and there's always a flip side) is that the
casinos in AC can suddenly impose procedures or rule changes that nullify the card counter's advantage, thereby making it pointless for a skilled
player to keep playing. Barrings and other casino countermeasures are
covered in more detail in Chapter 12.

But you're not doing anything wrong, you say? Tell me about it. It's an
age-old dispute that has existed since the days of Dr. Edward Thorp and
company. You're simply using your head, aren't you? What right does the
casino have to change the rules, or worse, prohibit you from playing?

Thankfully, most people aren't advantage players. They show up at
their favorite casino—eat, drink, laugh, cry, and in the process usually
drop a few dollars at the tables. That keeps the casinos happy—at least
most of the time. But you are soon to become *persona non grata,*" an ex-
pression commonly used to describe the absence of a welcome mat for
modern-day card counters. Not because you're a threat to wander in off
the street and take any casino for $100,000 on one afternoon, but be-
cause you're playing with an advantage *every time you sit down at a
blackjack table.*

As auspicious as that sounds, there are still many bosses who don't
understand that counting is a long and difficult undertaking—and that
the greatest counter in the world still loses four out of every ten times he

sits down at a blackjack table. In a world where knowledge of percentages should ooze from the corners of every blackjack pit, this mistaken belief in how easy it is to win by counting cards continues to prevail for some reason. And that makes life for card counters a lot more difficult than it should be.

The purpose of this section was to simply make you aware, if you weren't already, that becoming an expert at blackjack involves a whole lot more than simply mastering the mechanics of the process. The reality of the situation is that playing in any casino as an advantage player is an art form all to itself. Whether owned by a large gaming corporation like MGM Mirage or a smaller independent like the Golden Nugget in downtown Las Vegas, the casinos are in business to make money just like any other business. And if you're not adding to their bottom line like everyone else is, then you're really not a welcomed customer.

What Are the Odds?

The modern casino offers a variety of different games. The following table lists the more popular ones and the corresponding house advantage. Keep in mind as you read the table that the Basic Strategy player is playing a little under even with the house, and the proficient card counter at about a 1.5 percent advantage.

Table 3.1: House Advantage for Various Casino Games

GAME	BETS	HOUSE ADVANTAGE
Craps	Pass/Don't Pass	1.40%
	Pass/Don't Pass w/Odds	0.80%
	Pass/Don't Pass w/Double Odds	0.60%
Baccarat	Player	1.36%
	Banker	1.17%

GAME	BETS	HOUSE ADVANTAGE
Roulette	(Single Zero Wheel)	2.70%
	(Double Zero Wheel)	5.26%
Pai Gow		2.50%
Three Card Poker		3.40%
Let It Ride		3.50%
Big Six		~17.0%
Slot Machines		~2.0% – ~25.0%
Keno		~25.0% – ~40.0%
Video Poker		Varies to ~0%

As shown in the table, certain craps bets that include "giving" and "taking" odds represent independent trials with the lowest possible house advantage. Other bets like the field, hard ways, and place-bet wagers yield a higher house advantage.

In baccarat the house advantage is between 1 percent and 1½ percent for bets on both player and banker, with banker coming in a little lower than player. Baccarat is often viewed as the high-rollers' game, with tables beneath chandeliers in posh rooms off the main casino floor. But no matter how or where it's dealt, the player is still playing at a disadvantage.

Roulette players, who must play a game with a negative expectation, should stick to one-zero wheels only, due to the tremendous reduction in house advantage. Yet you will often see the one-zero wheel empty while throngs of gamblers reach over one another to place bets at the double-zero wheels. That makes little sense. Someone please tell these folks that if you're getting 35:1 in both cases, there's no point to doing battle with 38 numbers when it's possible to reduce the number of possible outcomes to 37. The down side for many roulette players, though, is that often one-zero tables are kept at much higher minimums.

Pai Gow, "Three Card™," and Let It Ride™ all come in at between a

2½ percent to 3½ percent advantage for the house. Of the three, Pai Gow poker offers the lowest house edge.

The Big Six Wheels are those vertical wheels with stoppers that are popular at carnivals and, yes, *fund-raisers*—which says it all without the need for further analysis.

Slot machines can vary greatly, depending on the type. The house advantage generally ranges from 2 percent to 25 percent. That means, for machines considered the most advantageous for the house, a player might expect to get back, on average, only $75 for every $100 dropped in. Likewise, those that advertise "98 percent payback" do just that—over the long run.

Keno is essentially an "all or nothing" proposition. If you must try your luck at keno, I'd advise trying to win $100,000 for a dollar and then quitting after you lose the dollar.

And last but not least, video poker, which when played correctly on certain machines nullifies the house advantage altogether. In fact, on some machines, players can obtain a very slight positive expectation due to the payoff odds given on certain hands.

In summary, blackjack remains the only casino game (other than poker, and in a few select cases video poker) in which the player can obtain an advantage and win in the long run. It's not easy, as soon you will see, but it's definitely the one game where at worst you won't lose a fortune in the long run even if you aspire to learn only Basic Strategy and nothing more.

Surveillance

Casino surveillance has come a long way in the last twenty-five years. In fact, it has advanced so much that it seems like every television show about casinos or casino gambling dedicates at least some portion of the program to surveillance technology. In earlier days, surveillance used to consist of a few guys in suits, smoking cigarettes and walking catwalks—looking down on the action from above through ceiling-mounted one-way mirrors. Now, casinos have control rooms with games analysts or surveillance specialists who watch over an entire array of monitors. Behind all those bubbles on the ceiling are cameras, and with a flick of a switch, anyone in the control room can watch with great detail the goings-on at any one table game or slot machine.

The guys dressed in uniform stationed near the casino entrance, or delivering chip rack refills, are the members of the security team you can see. But it's those you can't see, or those in the control room mentioned above, who can focus in on your play and even record it for analysis later on. If you're suspected of being a card counter, there's no doubt that at some point the cameras will be focused on you. Often it's the control room in conjunction with a games analyst, and not the suits clustered around the podium, that assess the strength of your game.

In the old days, the lights used to dim for a second when pictures were being taken. But with today's technology, the counter will likely never even know that he's being filmed. One clever casino ploy involves letting the card counter "hang himself." This can occur if you're suspected by pit personnel of card counting, and then all interest in you suddenly ceases. Sometimes the pit even seems deserted. What's really going on is that surveillance is recording your every move and play, and local personnel are giving you free rein to show them everything you're made of before the hammer comes crashing down. Just because a suit isn't watching your game doesn't mean ten pairs of electronic eyes don't have your face, your cards, your bets, and your eyes plastered across seven thirty-one-inch television screens in the surveillance room.

No section on casino surveillance would be complete without a brief mention of Griffin Investigations, Inc., of Las Vegas, Nevada. This is an outside agency that casinos can contract for assistance in combating cheats, crooks, and other undesirables. So why is it being mentioned here? Because, as ridiculous as this sounds, in most cases card counters are lumped right alongside these criminals. Griffin maintains an extensive electronic database, and can be contacted at any time to help the casino identify an individual considered a threat to its bottom line. More on the Griffin Agency can be found in Chapter Twelve, "Casino Countermeasures."

Casino Personnel

The all-around professional is knowledgeable about every aspect of the game, including the roles of the various casino personnel he is forced to interact with. This knowledge is largely needed to better understand how casino "heat" originates, and what you may expect to encounter as a result.

What follows is a listing and description of some of the duties of all those people wearing formal business attire on the other side of the table. In your mind a casino should start to look and feel more like a place of business than a place for recreation, with your office being the blackjack table you're sitting at, and your customer the casino you're sitting in.

- Floorperson: This individual is responsible for supervising several tables. It is the floorperson's job to ensure the games are running smoothly, catch dealer mistakes, and settle any disputes that may arise between players and the house. The floorperson will also take cards for player rating purposes, and track each player's buy-ins, wins, and losses.

    Your interaction with the floorperson will be significant. Often, these people will drift from table to table observing the flow of a game, or even once in a while engage a player in conversation. Since floorpeople are not actually dealing, their perspective sometimes allows them to evaluate you with a little more discretion than can the dealer, whose responsibilities include dealing to other players at the table. Oftentimes it's the floorperson who may alert the pit boss or surveillance to the possible presence of a card counter.

- Pit Boss: As the title implies, the pit boss is responsible for all table games in his or her pit. Just as the dealers report to their respective floorperson, the floorpeople report to the pit boss. The duties of the pit boss vary and can include everything from determining table minimums to settling disputes between players and the house.

Generally, your interaction with the pit boss will probably be less than that of any with the floorperson. But interaction can occur if a floorperson refers a particular situation to the pit boss, or asks for assistance. If you notice a pit boss watching your every move, be on high alert.

- Shift Manager: The shift manager is the next level up the ladder. Pit bosses report to the shift manager, who is the highest decision-maker for all table games on a given shift.

  If you're a smaller-stakes player, you generally won't be dealing with the shift manager. Upper-limit players may have interaction, especially if the shift manager puts on his or her marketing hat. If you're thought to be an advantage player, there is no doubt that the shift manager will be alerted.

- Casino Manager: This person is the highest level "hands-on" operations manager. Shift managers report to the casino manager, whose authority spans all operating shifts.

  Other than having a friendly conversation if the opportunity presents itself, it is unlikely that you will ever see, or speak to, the casino manager. Of course, all bets are off if you're discovered as an advantage player, and you're playing for high stakes.

- Counter Catcher: The name says it all. Some casinos have roving personnel whose job includes, among other duties, identifying and dealing with card counters. The counter catcher may be summoned by a floorperson or pit boss to evaluate a particular player suspected of being a counter. The counter catcher is usually most familiar with counting methods, betting, and camouflage techniques employed by advantage players.

  Your interface with this person should be nonexistent. If you're chatting with the counter catcher, you'd better be sure he has no idea you're a card counter, and you should

be chatting about something like the UNLV basketball team or
what specials are running tonight at the casino's finest seafood
restaurant.

- Cocktail Waitress: Cocktail waitresses are usually assigned
  one or two pits to service. Orders are usually taken on one go-
  around, and the drinks arrive on the next.

    Your interaction with cocktail waitresses might entail part of
  "your act," such as ordering drinks and making casual conversation typical of most players simply having a good time in a casino.

Ultimately, the goal during any interaction with casino personnel
should be to come across like any other players—there to enjoy themselves with the hope of making a few bucks in the process. Friendly conversation is encouraged—even though reciprocation may not occur if
you've been identified as an advantage player. In fact, it can get pretty
testy, depending on where you are or what level of professionalism those
who've discovered you choose to act with. I'm sorry to say I've been on
the receiving end of some pretty harsh treatment, bordering on harassment, and it took everything in my power to remain both cool and collected. In any event, the goal should be to ingratiate yourself with all
casino personnel, whenever possible, with the hope that their positive
outlook on you and your play will ultimately earn you bonus miles in
the "ability to get a game" department. The counter must remember that
retaliation to heat in any form does nothing to promote future playing
conditions remaining attractive to you as an advantage player. *As long as
you have a game, and the game can be beaten, you should do everything in
your power to preserve your longevity.*

A Virtual Tour

Just as we did in Chapter One, let's take a look at things up close. Only
this time, instead of looking down from above at the action on a single

blackjack table, I'll be your tour guide as we take in the sights and sounds of a modern-day casino at ground level. As we walk, I'll try to add as much commentary as possible on how what we see relates positively or negatively to the advantage player interface.

Imagine it's a warm, balmy night in late August. Seagulls are flying high in the air above—white dots against the dark backdrop of a clear sky interrupted only by a large superstructure rising up out of the marshland before us. A slight breeze blows in off the ocean. Did I say "ocean"? Where else can we be but in Atlantic City, New Jersey, right?

As we walk through the doors of AC's newest casino, the first thing that captures our attention is the décor. Indirect lighting, columns, and a spacious landscape combine to offer a cutting-edge, post-modern blanket of visual stimuli.

Then we see them—rigid shapes aligned in rows, military style. Solid forms with blinking lights and colored glass. Steadfast soldiers in waiting, with anxious people standing before them. The mechanical sound of moving levers gives way to a whimsical melody as reels with bars and fruit and various logos spin and then stop in programmed succession.

We venture into a sea of one-armed bandits—our destination of course, the higher-limit blackjack tables. More and more, though, slot machines are taking over the landscape. In this business square footage means money, and the casino will make more money from a few slot machines than from the equivalent amount of space occupied by anything else. That's bad news for card counters because that means fewer tables to choose from—which means more-crowded tables among those that remain, which means fewer hands per hour and fewer tables to jump to if the count on one table suddenly goes negative.

A cocktail waitress steps in front of us. She's dressed in a black outfit that somehow combines stylish with skimpy. The drinks on her tray are free. Imagine that? Of course, the casino is providing this form of hospitality with the hope that gamblers will then have too good of a time to think twice about reaching for another Franklin.

It suddenly dawns on you that windows are nonexistent. Although once in a while an architect comes along who lets in the good old-fashioned light of day, for the most part, the vast majority of casinos keep the inside world in and the outside world out. I point out that clocks are nowhere to be found either. Let's not forget that whenever one is playing with a positive expectation, time means money, and in virtually all cases (except yours very shortly) the casino is playing with a positive expectation. So no one needs to know how late it is or, more precisely, how early.

We finally reach a row of blackjack tables, all at $25 and $50 minimums per hand. In the pit are a number of dour-looking men and women dressed in suits and conservative business attire. These are casino personnel mentioned in the last section. It's a good thing I'm wearing my Jets hat and fake prescription glasses, because I recognize one of them as a boss whom I had gotten heat from several months earlier when he was employed by another casino in town. Casino personnel move around a lot—that's good and bad, depending on where the most advantageous games are located.

We come up behind one table in particular, a table with three players betting from two green to several black per hand. Chips have different value, depending on color—and do note that variations exist between houses, especially involving the higher denominations. Here's the lowdown on the value of casino checks and their colors, which apply at most but not all casinos:

Table 3.2: Chip Values

COLOR	VALUE
White	$1.00
Pink	$2.50
Red	$5.00
Green	$25.00
Black	$100.00
Purple	$500.00
Orange	$1,000.00
Brown	$5,000.00

Higher denominations exist, but colors and even the size and the shape of these chips may vary. Chips that are valued at $5 are commonly referred to as "nickels," and $25 chips as "quarters." Also, $1 chips, depending on locale, may be coinage. For instance, in Nevada, tokens that look like silver dollars and often bear the casino logo or another picture serve as $1 chips.

We move on and a few minutes later come upon a full table that captures your attention. The minimum bet is $25 per hand. Table minimums and maximums, along with some common rules such as the number of times you can split a pair or what the player may double down on can typically be found on those small rectangular signs in the corner of each table.

Following are typical table minimums, which—if I might add—have a lot to do with where you are playing. For example, $2 minimum blackjack is nonexistent here in Atlantic City, but can be found in most casinos throughout Northern Nevada. Table minimums are typically one of the following:

Table 3.3: Common Table Minimums

$1, $2, $3, $5, $10, $15, $25, $50, $100, $500, $1000

In some jurisdictions, tables marked with a sign that reads "reserved" can be set to any minimum, often at the discretion of the high roller for whom the table is being reserved.

Someone at the table leaves, and almost immediately a middle-aged man sits down. The floorperson comes over as the dealer fans $500 in $100 bills across the table. The man gives the floorperson a little plastic card. This card is called a "comp card," or player-rating card, and is issued to any customer who desires to earn comp points based on the amount of "action" he or she gives the casino. The casino uses it to track the average bet made by the player along with, as accurately as possible, the total amount won or lost. Casinos then reward their valued customers by issuing complimentary meals, show tickets, rooms, etc. For the duration of their stay, "high rollers" typically expect "RFB"—meaning complimentary room, food, and beverage. A "whale," or the highest of high rollers, will often get the top-level suite the hotel has to offer, free of charge for however long he wants it—including all transportation expenses incurred in getting him to that casino, whether those expenses involved plane tickets, limousines, or even helicopters.

Although it is completely up to the individual to accept or decline a player rating, or use of a player's card, the modern-day card counter is almost forced to get one and get rated for play just because of how popular getting rated is. In fact, it's so uncharacteristic to deny a rating that nowadays doing so often attracts more attention from the pit than being rated like a normal player. For that reason, the counter should get a player's card (under an alias) in any casino that he or she plans to play in with regularity.

Our attention wanders from the blackjack table in front of us. You're amazed at how much money is being placed into action. In most cases, as the crowds increase, so do the table minimums—purely a case of supply and demand. And with virtually everyone playing at a negative expectation, the more money the casino can get players to wager, the more money the casino stands to make. To that I say that a card counter spreading $25 to $400 per hand would have a decent shot at blending in fairly well at a casino like this one. That's a good thing. The larger casinos catering to "bigger action" allow a counter playing quarters or even black to spread ten to one or more without seemingly standing out—at least for a little while. The flip side for lower-level counters is that the $10 tables are usually mobbed because, although everyone wants to play at the "in" casino, not everyone is willing to ante up to the table minimums typically found at the newer houses. That means fewer hands per hour, and of course that's only if a seat becomes available. A smaller, less fancy casino would probably have a greater abundance of lower-limit tables. In fact, it pays for a card counter to play wherever he blends in best with the general population.

You notice an elevated room with a sign that says "Baccarat." But it looks like—from where we are standing—there are blackjack tables in that room as well. You are correct. Almost always there are several high-limit blackjack tables in the baccarat pit, or the "high limit pit" as it is sometimes called. These tables are likely minimum $100 per hand and up. The good: more hands per hour because of fewer players, and often games that use fewer decks, such as four or six, in a casino that normally offers only six or eight. The bad: the amount of scrutiny from casino personnel you are forced to play under. As you can imagine, they watch the $100 and $500 tables pretty closely. As a general rule, I try to avoid blackjack in the high limit pit for exactly this reason. But sometimes the lack of seats in the main casino or the lure of an empty six-deck game with great penetration (how far into the deck or deck the dealer deals) makes playing among the masses in the main casino almost impossible to endure. This is a case-by-case scenario. And, of course, if I'm playing in the bac pit, my "act" is nothing short of an art form.

You notice the gleam of a spinning roulette wheel behind us, and we wander over to the nearest table—one packed with a crowd of onlookers. The electronic display shows that the last nine numbers that have come out have all been red. On the table layout, there's a mountain of chips on black. Happens every time. A bunch of one color comes out, and the opposite color fills with chips. One guy even has several purple crammed on one corner of the betting square. A young man with a baseball cap is saying to his buddy how black *has to* come out. Unfortunately, nothing could be further from the truth. As we now know, in no other casino game beside blackjack (and poker) does past history influence the future. The tenth spin has just as good a chance of being red again as it does black, since there are as many red numbers in the roulette wheel as there are black. Yet everyone at the table seems convinced that sooner or later a black number will come out. And they're right. Only there's no way of knowing when "sooner" or "later" will be—unlike blackjack, of course, wherein a preponderance of low cards usually results in a preponderance of high cards at some later point in the deal.

The ball lands in number 26, black. Wonderful. Today everyone wins, including the guy with $1,500 on the table. I'm happy for them all, but unfortunately this experience will probably end up fooling at least one of these players into thinking they've got a winning system when, in fact, they don't.

We wander along a row of roulette wheels until raucous laughter and shouting attract us to a nearby craps table. A man in a cowboy hat is throwing black chips around like M&M's, and on one arm is a blonde who couldn't seven-out with three crooked dice. Before every roll she goes through a gyration that includes rubbing the dice on the table, turning one or two over and over again until a certain combination faces skyward, shaking her hands back and forth before picking them up, covering them with her hand, tapping one with a long, pink fingernail, and then finally tossing the pair with a wild, flailing motion that continues long after the dice are airborne. One flies off the table down at the other end, and the stick man almost reluctantly offers her four new dice to choose from. The man with the cowboy hat delays her long enough to bet a little more, and as he does so she goes through the same rigmarole as before. The dice fly, bounce off the far wall, and come bouncing back almost to the point of origin.

"Seven out, line away," the stick man says softly.

I estimate our cowboy just lost about $3,200 on that one roll of the dice, but he doesn't seem fazed. He gives the blonde a kiss and begins betting again as the stick man prepares for a new shooter. The only comment I offer is that craps players are a colorful bunch.

We circle back around to our favorite pit of blackjack tables, and come upon a young Asian betting between $500 and $2,000 per hand. Back to business. Both the floorperson and the pit boss are watching intently. That's a great situation for the card counter—playing a game in which you are far from the biggest player on the table, or in a pit with really heavy action at a table other than yours. In that scenario, attention almost solely focuses on the bigger player and not on you—a great opportunity to ply your trade as anonymously as possible.

Another cocktail waitress passes, offering up coffee, tea, and soda. As your camouflage efforts increase, your orders for the cocktail waitress may change from coffee and bottled water to gin and tonic or vodka and Seven. By the way, you don't actually drink the stiff ones—you're just ordering them for the subtle image it plants, perhaps at an opportune moment like when a suspicious pit boss is observing your game. You can dump the contents of the glass a little later on, when outside or in the restroom, and refill it with water.

"You've actually done that?"

"Many times," I say. "My drink of choice is a gin and tonic, something that simulates water."

Just then the pit boss who had given me heat in the past looks right at us, then looks away. For a minute I think he has recognized me. But apparently he hasn't, thanks in part to a large man whom I've been sort of standing behind since we pulled up at the table. It's a good thing I had spotted him first, otherwise I might not have been as prone to move among the shadows of others as it often becomes prudent to do—especially after you've been around the block a few times.

A roar erupts a few tables down, which is a little farther away from our friendly pit boss, and so I'm more than glad to meander in that direction. We go over to see what the commotion is about, and find a table in which it took the dealer seven cards to bust. The hand had involved several player double downs and splits, with lots and lots of money on the table. A young woman hugs her boyfriend as he pulls back two stacks of green. An older man sitting in the anchor seat appears to be chatting with the dealer about the Outer Banks of North Carolina as the dealer finishes paying off the table. If possible, that's exactly what a counter should be doing—periodically chatting with the dealer or another player at the table. Although I'm not the biggest extrovert in the world, I try to make small talk whenever possible, because to sit there and say nothing *and* watch the cards with noticeable interest is a dead giveaway that something else might be going on.

The next table is a somber-looking bunch. From the looks of things, the dealer is hammering these poor people into oblivion. The guy at first base has a total of 20, and as we watch the dealer snaps out a five-card 21. Probably not the first time that's happened here in the last ten minutes.

The guy in seat number four slams the table with his fist. We move on. Nobody likes being watched while getting massacred.

The lesson here is that emotions run high at the tables. So to best blend in you must smile and "celebrate" a decent win, and likewise show obvious disappointment upon losing. As ridiculous as this might sound, when I first started playing, I didn't get "mad enough" at times, probably because I knew that in the end I'd end up a winner. That's a common mistake made by rookie card counters. Get mad when you lose and smile when you win. Look around for examples of how to act—good ones are everywhere. Of course, don't overreact. Nothing bombs more than someone pretending to be either elated or disappointed.

Actually there is one thing more detrimental than a phony act. And that's hanging around for longer than you should, otherwise known as "wearing out your welcome." Had we actually been playing all this while, it might have been time to move on—for any number of reasons ranging from how many units we were up or down to the sudden interest of our friendly pit boss in the way our bets seem to rise and fall. Nothing is better than preserving your longevity. And that's exactly what we decide to do.

We leave in the same relaxed way we strolled in. More than anything, we want there to be a next time just like this one.

CHAPTER FOUR

Basic Strategy

This is where it all begins, or should begin for every player. Independent of card counting, Basic Strategy is the name given to the set of rules that represent the best possible way to play each hand.

Before learning an advanced technique, the aspiring counter must have Basic Strategy committed to memory, which means the ability to instantaneously recall the correct move to make based on (1) the total of his hand, and (2) the dealer's upcard. Consider Basic Strategy as the tool that minimizes the house advantage. Alone, it's not enough to win in the long run. But it's the essential foundation for allowing card counting to do just that. In short, consider Basic Strategy as getting you playing at about even with the house—and card counting as putting you over the top.

Where Does It Come From?

Basic Strategy exists thanks to a very large number of computer simulations run for every possible player and dealer combination, such as a player's total of 12 against a dealer's upcard of 2, a player's total of 13 against a dealer's upcard of 2, a player's total of 14 against a dealer's upcard of 2, and so on. Card values are either randomly generated, or, even more precisely, an exact combinatorial analysis is performed. The results are analyzed to determine which decision is most advantageous (or least detrimental) to the player, and the result becomes known as the correct Basic Strategy decision.

From time to time I meet people who claim to know "Basic" inside and out, when in fact they really don't. The explanation I hear most often when their lack of knowledge of Basic Strategy becomes apparent is that some decisions are better made based on "how the cards are running." Unfortunately, there is no way to tell "how the cards are running," because patterns or tendencies or whatever else you may want to call an overall assessment of "the present state of affairs" are nothing more than a summary of the past. Basic Strategy is pure mathematics founded on computer simulation. Hunches should be avoided, and Basic should be so well committed to memory that you should never find yourself in the position of not knowing exactly what to do at any given moment.

You'll find that the majority of blackjack players know some degree of Basic Strategy. Generally, although not always, the higher minimum tables are where you'll see it played with more precision. That doesn't mean you won't see a fair share of players at all levels making moves to the contrary. Bear in mind that there will be instances when non-counters (let's call them normal players) deviate from Basic Strategy and win. For instance, you might see a player standing on 16 against a dealer's 10. The dealer turns over a 5 for 15, and then goes on to draw a 9 for 24. Yes, wins and losses like this will occur, where using the correct Basic Strategy results in a loss, whereas deviating would have resulted in a win. But remember that we're not in this game for the short run. We're in it for the long run, and the computations that were used to determine the mathematically best way to play each hand were based on a very, very large number of trials—no doubt more hands than the average player will play in a lifetime. In the long run correct Basic Strategy will prevail. And although some plays may at first seem questionable—and actual short-term experience may yield what seems like a disproportionately high number of losses for a given situation—remember that any variation to Basic Strategy will, over the long run, end up costing the player money. It's that simple.

As a final note, it might be of interest for you to know that later you'll actually deviate from Basic Strategy based on the count. That's right, you'll be doing exactly what I've been thus far preaching not to do—only as a card counter you'll be deviating when it represents the mathematically correct move to make. Again, computer simulation has shown that under certain conditions relating to the content of the remaining cards, it's in the counter's best interest to do the opposite of what Basic Strategy recommends. The key words to remember, though, are *under certain conditions relating to content,* which represents information the non-counter isn't aware of. That's why the normal player should never deviate from Basic Strategy, whereas it remains in the best interest of the card counter to do so in certain circumstances. Is that confusing? Not to worry. We'll get into all of that in much greater detail a little later on. Right now though, your mission is to learn Basic Strategy to a T—and I mean stone-cold perfect.

The Tables

Unfortunately, there isn't one Basic Strategy that applies to all games everywhere, because all games everywhere aren't the same. For that reason, the proficient player must make slight adjustments depending on the rules in effect or the number of decks used on a particular game.

In today's world, multiple-deck games are by far more prevalent than their single-deck counterparts. This is true for a number of reasons ranging from house advantage to supply and demand to what the general public has come to accept. For starters I would recommend that you focus more on learning Basic Strategy for the multiple-deck game. For one thing, multiple-deck exists everywhere, and where single-deck does exist, many houses have made the game even more difficult to beat than it was just a few years ago. One recent rule is to pay blackjack 6:5 instead of the more traditional 3:2, which represents a significant change for the worse. In addition, multiple-deck games receive far less scrutiny than their single-deck counterparts. Later, after you've acquired some experience, branch out into the world of single-deck when the rules of the game still allow you to garner a positive expectation. Whichever you choose, my advice would be to become totally proficient in one before taking on the other.

There are a number of ways to present the following information, which can be a little confusing or somewhat hard to follow because in some instances the variations aren't major and can go easily unnoticed. Since the number of decks and whether or not the player is able to double down after splitting pairs are the two most common reasons for why variations to Basic Strategy apply, the following pages contain several tables.

Tables 4.1 and 4.1a illustrate the correct Basic Strategy for multiple-deck blackjack when doubling down after splitting pairs is allowed and when it's not allowed, respectively. Likewise, Tables 4.2 and 4.2a illustrate the correct Basic Strategy for the single-deck game with regard, again respectively, to whether or not doubling after splitting is allowed. Finally, Table 4.3 at the end of the chapter illustrates Basic for the European game, wherein the dealer does not check for blackjack until after all players have acted upon their first two cards.

Later in this chapter is a section that delves into the logic behind many Basic Strategy moves, and following the tables are some suggestions for developing mnemonic-like tricks to help commit some of this data to memory. Learning why certain moves are made and paraphrasing the contents of the table into sentence form should make the entire process of learning Basic Strategy a whole lot easier.

Table 4.1: Multiple-Deck Basic Strategy—Doubling After Splitting Allowed

PLAYER'S HAND	DEALER'S UPCARD									
	2	3	4	5	6	7	8	9	10	A
8 or Less	H	H	H	H	H	H	H	H	H	H
9	H	DD	DD	DD	DD	H	H	H	H	H
10	DD	DD	DD	DD	DD	DD	DD	DD	H	H
11	DD	DD	DD	DD	DD	DD	DD	DD	DD	H

PLAYER'S HAND	DEALER'S UPCARD									
	2	3	4	5	6	7	8	9	10	A
12	H	H	S	S	S	H	H	H	H	H
13	S	S	S	S	S	H	H	H	H	H
14	S	S	S	S	S	H	H	H	H	H
15	S	S	S	S	S	H	H	H	SUR	H
16	S	S	S	S	S	H	H	SUR	SUR	SUR
17 or More	S	S	S	S	S	S	S	S	S	S
A2	H	H	H	DD	DD	H	H	H	H	H
A3	H	H	H	DD	DD	H	H	H	H	H
A4	H	H	DD	DD	DD	H	H	H	H	H
A5	H	H	DD	DD	DD	H	H	H	H	H
A6	H	DD	DD	DD	DD	H	H	H	H	H
A7	S	DD	DD	DD	DD	S	S	H	H	H
A8	S	S	S	S	S	S	S	S	S	S
A9	S	S	S	S	S	S	S	S	S	S
2,2	SPL	SPL	SPL	SPL	SPL	SPL	H	H	H	H
3,3	SPL	SPL	SPL	SPL	SPL	SPL	H	H	H	H
4,4	H	H	H	SPL	SPL	H	H	H	H	H
5,5	DD	DD	DD	DD	DD	DD	DD	DD	H	H
6,6	SPL	SPL	SPL	SPL	SPL	H	H	H	H	H
7,7	SPL	SPL	SPL	SPL	SPL	SPL	H	H	H	H
8,8	SPL	SPL	SPL	SPL	SPL	SPL	SPL	SPL	SPL	SPL
9,9	SPL	SPL	SPL	SPL	SPL	S	SPL	SPL	S	S
10,10	S	S	S	S	S	S	S	S	S	S
A,A	SPL	SPL	SPL	SPL	SPL	SPL	SPL	SPL	SPL	SPL

H = Hit
S = Stand
DD = Double Down
SPL = Split Pair
SUR = Surrender

Note: If surrender is not allowed, then hit.

For multiple-deck games when doubling after splitting is not allowed, substitute the Basic Strategy decisions shown in Table 4.1a, opposite, for those shown in Table 4.1.

Table 4.1a: Multiple-Deck Basic Strategy—Doubling After Splitting Not Allowed

PLAYER'S HAND	DEALER'S UPCARD									
	2	3	4	5	6	7	8	9	10	A
2,2	H	H	SPL	SPL	SPL	SPL	H	H	H	H
3,3	H	H	SPL	SPL	SPL	SPL	H	H	H	H
4,4	H	H	H	H	H	H	H	H	H	H
5,5	DD	DD	DD	DD	DD	DD	DD	DD	H	H
6,6	H	SPL	SPL	SPL	SPL	H	H	H	H	H
7,7	SPL	SPL	SPL	SPL	SPL	SPL	H	H	H	H
8,8	SPL	SPL	SPL	SPL	SPL	SPL	SPL	SPL	SPL	SPL
9,9	SPL	SPL	SPL	SPL	SPL	S	SPL	SPL	S	S
10,10	S	S	S	S	S	S	S	S	S	S
A,A	SPL	SPL	SPL	SPL	SPL	SPL	SPL	SPL	SPL	SPL

H = Hit
S = Stand
DD = Double Down
SPL = Split Pair

Tables 4.2 and 4.2a represent Basic Strategy for the single-deck game. Table 4.2 illustrates Basic Strategy when doubling after splitting is allowed, and Table 4.2a illustrates correct Basic Strategy for when doubling after splitting is not allowed.

Table 4.2: Single-Deck Basic Strategy—Doubling After Splitting Allowed

PLAYER'S HAND	DEALER'S UPCARD									
	2	3	4	5	6	7	8	9	10	A
7 or Less	H	H	H	H	H	H	H	H	H	H
6,2	H	H	H	H	H	H	H	H	H	H

PLAYER'S HAND	DEALER'S UPCARD									
	2	3	4	5	6	7	8	9	10	A
4,4	H	H	SPL	SPL	SPL	H	H	H	H	H
5,3	H	H	H	DD	DD	H	H	H	H	H
9	DD	DD	DD	DD	DD	H	H	H	H	H
10	DD	DD	DD	DD	DD	DD	DD	DD	H	H
11	DD	DD	DD	DD	DD	DD	DD	DD	DD	DD
12	H	H	S	S	S	H	H	H	H	H
13	S	S	S	S	S	H	H	H	H	H
14	S	S	S	S	S	H	H	H	H	H
15	S	S	S	S	S	H	H	H	SUR	H
16	S	S	S	S	S	H	H	H	SUR	SUR
17 or More	S	S	S	S	S	S	S	S	S	S
A2	H	H	DD	DD	DD	H	H	H	H	H
A3	H	H	DD	DD	DD	H	H	H	H	H
A4	H	H	DD	DD	DD	H	H	H	H	H
A5	H	H	DD	DD	DD	H	H	H	H	H
A6	DD	DD	DD	DD	DD	H	H	H	H	H
A7	S	DD	DD	DD	DD	S	S	H	H	S
A8	S	S	S	S	DD	S	S	S	S	S
A9	S	S	S	S	S	S	S	S	S	S
2,2	SPL	SPL	SPL	SPL	SPL	SPL	H	H	H	H
3,3	SPL	SPL	SPL	SPL	SPL	SPL	SPL	H	H	H
4,4	H	H	SPL	SPL	SPL	H	H	H	.H	H
5,5	DD	DD	DD	DD	DD	DD	DD	DD	H	H
6,6	SPL	SPL	SPL	SPL	SPL	SPL	H	H	H	H
7,7	SPL	SPL	SPL	SPL	SPL	SPL	SPL	H	SUR	H
8,8	SPL	SPL	SPL	SPL	SPL	SPL	SPL	SPL	SPL	SPL
9,9	SPL	SPL	SPL	SPL	SPL	S	SPL	SPL	S	S
10,10	S	S	S	S	S	S	S	S	S	S
A,A	SPL	SPL	SPL	SPL	SPL	SPL	SPL	SPL	SPL	SPL

H = Hit
S = Stand
DD = Double Down
SPL = Split Pair
SUR = Surrender

Note: If surrender is not allowed, then hit.

For single-deck games when doubling after splitting is not allowed, substitute the Basic Strategy decisions shown in Table 4.2a below for those shown in Table 4.2.

Table 4.2a: Single-Deck Basic Strategy—Doubling After Splitting Not Allowed

PLAYER'S HAND	DEALER'S UPCARD									
	2	3	4	5	6	7	8	9	10	A
2,2	H	SPL	SPL	SPL	SPL	SPL	H	H	H	H
3,3	H	H	SPL	SPL	SPL	SPL	H	H	H	H
4,4	H	H	H	DD	DD	H	H	H	H	H
5,5	DD	DD	DD	DD	DD	DD	DD	DD	H	H
6,6	SPL	SPL	SPL	SPL	SPL	H	H	H	H	H
7,7	SPL	SPL	SPL	SPL	SPL	SPL	H	H	S	H
8,8	SPL	SPL	SPL	SPL	SPL	SPL	SPL	SPL	SPL	SPL
9,9	SPL	SPL	SPL	SPL	SPL	S	SPL	SPL	S	S
10,10	S	S	S	S	S	S	S	S	S	S
A,A	SPL	SPL	SPL	SPL	SPL	SPL	SPL	SPL	SPL	SPL

H = Hit
S = Stand
DD = Double Down
SPL = Split Pair

Some casinos, such as those in Reno and throughout Northern Nevada, prohibit the player from doubling down on totals other than 10 and 11. *When this rule is encountered, instead of doubling down on those other totals (like soft hands or on 9, for example), the player should hit in all instances except as follows: with a Soft 18 against a dealer's 3 through 6 (for single- and multiple-deck) and a Soft 19 against a dealer's 6 (for single-deck), the player should stand.*

In addition, if the dealer hits Soft 17, Basic Strategy should be refined as follows:

Hit Soft 18 against an ace ("SOP" for multiple deck blackjack)

Surrender 17 against an ace, if surrender is available.

Surrender 15 against an ace, if surrender is available.

One thing to notice about the tables is that large areas or sections of each recommend similar plays. For example, there are many SPLs and DDs grouped together. Make use of these similarities to make easy-to-remember phrases. For starters, consider the following Basic Strategy rules, which apply to virtually every form of the game:

- With Hard 17 or more, stand.

- With 12 through 16, hit if the dealer shows 7 through ace (except where surrender is applicable).

- With a 12, hit against a dealer's 2 or 3, stand against a dealer's 4, 5, and 6.

- With 13 through 16, stand against a dealer's 2 through 6.

- Always split aces and 8s.

- Never split 5s and 10s.

Think about where you will be doing most of your playing, and learn the Basic Strategy that applies to the game most prevalent at that locale. Again, look for ways to summarize data in sentence form. Be creative. For instance, if you're learning multiple-deck "double after splits allowed," notice how the "DDs" form something of a stepladder leading up and to the right. Make use of that in the process of memorizing this information. "For A,2 and A,3 the player doubles on a dealer's 5 or 6. For A,4 and A,5 the player should double on a dealer's 4, 5, and 6. And for A,7 and A,8 the player should double down on a dealer's 3, 4, 5, or 6." Just remember that the span of cards against which to double down increases by one for every two soft doubles, starting with a A,2.

Here's another: "Split 2s, 3s, and 7s against a dealer's 2 through 7, and split 6s against a dealer's 2 through 6." An equivalent for single-deck "double after splits allowed" might go something like this: "Split 2s, 3s, 6s, and 7s against a dealer's 2 through 7, except for 7s make it 2 through 8." Every part of each table can't be memorized in this fashion, but some areas certainly lend themselves to this mnemonic-like shortcut.

Insurance

The normal player should never take insurance, although you will run into many who will advise taking it when possessing a strong hand like 19 or 20, or especially when having a blackjack. The problem with that logic is that the value of your hand is meaningless, because the wager is all about whether or not the dealer has blackjack, and nothing more. Keep in mind that the insurance wager is a completely independent wager. And the non-counter, or normal player, is only guessing as to whether or not the dealer has blackjack. Because in a standard deck of cards there are only 16 that can result in a dealer having blackjack, and 36 that can result in the dealer not having blackjack—and insurance pays only 2:1—to take insurance at any time is a losing proposition. For now, ignore it completely, even if you have a blackjack. Only when card counting can you benefit from knowing when to take insurance, and as with deviations to Basic Strategy, we'll cover that in a lot more detail later on. (By the way, losing half of your bet every time the dealer doesn't have blackjack adds up to a lot more in losses than most people realize.)

Basic Strategy Logic

In this section we'll discuss some of the reasons behind several Basic Strategy decisions. Knowing the logic instead of blindly following the tables will help you to become a better player overall. As mentioned earlier, it should also reduce the amount of time needed to commit Basic Strategy to memory.

Doubling on 9, 10, and 11

These are great totals to draw on since so many cards (16 out of every 52) have a value of 10. Thus, the player will end up with a strong hand of either 19, 20, or 21 a good proportion of the time—not to mention "weak draws" that sometimes end up as winners too. Notice how doubling down on 11 applies almost always, on 10 a little less than always, and on 9 even a little less. And the player will tend to double down with these totals a little more often in single-deck than in multiple-deck. The reason why this exists is that the two small cards that comprise the hand on which you are doubling have greater significance in a single-deck game (in terms of their removal from the cards you could possibly draw) than in a multiple-deck game.

Double downs are the hands that will often mean the difference between a winning session and a losing one. Although occasionally you'll draw what seems like an inordinate amount of low cards, or garbage, doubling down should always be viewed as a golden opportunity and taken advantage of whenever possible.

Hitting 12 Against a 2 or 3

Damned if you do, damned if you don't. Actually, it's really not that bad, but you'll hear that over and over again from other players who remember only the times this hand doesn't end favorably. Hit it all the time. With a 12, only a ten-valued card will result in a player bust. Even against a 3 the player should hit because both dealer and player will ultimately result in a pat hand quite often. So it's a shoot-out, and it's better to shoot first and hope for the best rather than not shoot at all.

Soft Doubling

You can't bust when you soft double down, because the ace can always revert to being counted as 1. And when you catch the perfect low card, soft doubling becomes a powerful weapon. Notice from the tables that soft doubling occurs always when the dealer shows a stiff. So often even the not-so-good draws end up having a positive cash flow.

Splitting Low Pairs

These also should occur only against a lot of dealer stiffs, which means the perfect ending is a dealer bust no matter what either of the hands ends up totaling. Since you're splitting against mostly low cards, low splits don't usually end up as busting hands, except for those instances against a dealer 2 or 7 when, let's say, a 12 or 16 requires another hit. An added bonus with low splits is being able to double down if the opportunity presents itself. But do notice that when doubling down after splitting is not permitted, the amount of advantageous low-pair splitting opportunities is less for both single- and multiple-deck.

Doubling on 5,5 Instead of Splitting

Splitting 5s is the equivalent of committing blackjack suicide. Don't do it, unless you like totals of 15. The flip side, as mentioned earlier, is that you should be salivating at the opportunity to double down with a total of 10.

Splitting Aces and 8s.

This is the opposite of blackjack suicide. One is a godsend, the other a doorway to salvation. The godsend (splitting aces) is being able to double your bet with the opportunity of drawing on 11 (twice). The doorway to salvation (splitting 8s) is not having to deal with a 16. Taking either one of those 8s and making a good hand often results in an overall push—as opposed to losing with your original 16. That's what a lot of players don't realize. In some cases, you're not playing offense as much as playing good defense, or clever loss control.

Splitting 4s

Splitting 4s is beneficial under only the most ideal conditions, such as a dealer showing a 5 or 6 in multiple-deck games where doubling after splitting is allowed or against a dealer's 4, 5, and 6 in single deck blackjack where doubling after splitting is allowed. In these games, it can also lead to a nice double down opportunity if dealt a 5, 6, or 7. And when doubling after splitting isn't permitted, forget about splitting 4s altogether.

Splitting 9s

Splitting 9s is an interesting one. Nines are split against everything but aces, 10s, and 7s. Nines should not be split against a dealer's 7 because (and here's an easy way to remember this) two 9s total 18, and an 18 beats a presumed dealer 17.

Nines are split against a dealers 8 because catching a 10 on either 9 will result in at least a 19 on one of the hands, which guarantees at least one win if, in fact, the dealer has the 18. An added plus is catching a two for an advantageous double down on either hand. Even busting on one hand (with the other one totaling 19) still ends up with an overall push against a dealer's 18, the same result you might have ended up with by just standing on 18 to begin with. But the latter method is still more advantageous for what possibilities it affords.

Against a dealer's 9, catching a 10 on either hand gives you 19, which will result in a tie in those instances when the dealer does, in fact, have 19. And losing just one hand of the two is the equivalent of what you would have lost had you not split the original 9s to begin with. So this move looks a lot more formidable than it really is.

Surrendering

When it's allowed, surrender a 15 against a 10, and a 16 against a 9, 10, or ace. Your chances of losing these hands are more than triple your chances of winning. Therefore, you'll lose less if you simply surrender, and give up half of what you've bet. This represents another good example of smart loss control.

Hitting Soft 17s and Soft 18s

It's a must-do, in the situations that call for it. Remember that you can't break with a soft hand. So in essence you have two shots at improvement. Get an ace, 2, or 3 and you're golden. If you draw garbage and end up with something like a 16, you have another chance at improving your original hand by drawing again. Let's not forget that Soft 17s and even Soft 18s aren't the strongest hands in the world to begin with. The telltale sign of a player who doesn't know Basic Strategy inside and out is the player who doesn't play soft 18s correctly.

Single-Deck Doubling Involving 4,4 and 5,3

This is a quirk of sorts in that doubling down with these totals has more to do with the fact that the single deck being used is somewhat depleted of those cards that can do you the most harm—and the dealer the most good. This principle was touched on earlier in this chapter, in the section involving doubling down on 9, 10, and 11.

What Games Are Found Where?

Nowadays, games of any kind can be found anywhere. The advent of riverboats and of casinos on Indian reservations essentially made learning the rules at every casino a case-by-case endeavor. So the message here is that the serious player needs to do a little pre-game prep before sitting down to play. Of course that doesn't mean you should belly up to the pit and ask a floorperson point-blank if surrender and doubling after splitting is offered—especially if you're an advantage player. No, your approach should be reserved. If the posted rules aren't thorough enough, perhaps a casual question to someone who looks like a serious player might be in order. Another option is to ask an idle dealer on the other side of the casino—with perhaps some ready-to-tell story about the guy you once saw in Vegas giving up half his bet on every hand? (I didn't know you could do that!)

To summarize, here are the "Big Five" that should pop into your head upon first walking into a casino:

- How many decks are in use?

- On what totals may the player double down?

- Is doubling after splitting permitted?

- Is surrender an option?

- Does the dealer hit on Soft 17?

Refer back to Table 2.1: Effects of Common Rules Variations for a quick check on how advantageous or detrimental a specific rule can be. By the way, the answer to the first question above will be apparent after learning the material in subsequent chapters. And the answer to the last question should be printed right on the table layout. Any one of the other three may or may not be posted, requiring a cautious inquiry.

Multiple-Deck Basic Strategy with doubling after splitting applies in Atlantic City. It also applies in some Las Vegas casinos, Indian casinos, and on some riverboats—which means it doesn't apply in some Las Vegas casinos, Indian casinos, and on some riverboats. Get the idea? Multiple-deck games that don't allow doubling after splitting are common. So inquire within.

Single-deck blackjack may be found in Las Vegas and throughout Northern Nevada. Rules can vary and sometimes change, so there's no point in saying what may or may not exist inside the walls of any particular casino.

European Multiple-Deck Basic Strategy

European-style blackjack is unique in a way because the dealer does not check his hole card (when the upcard is a ten or ace) until after the last player has finished playing his hand. This is a disadvantage since player decisions for doubling down and splitting pairs, for example, must be made before the dealer checks for blackjack. If the dealer has a blackjack, the player loses the entire amount wagered. Thus, correct Basic Strategy for this game is a more conservative approach in terms of doubling down and splitting pairs in those situations when the dealer's upcard is a ten or ace.

Blackjack abroad also typically restricts doubling down to 9, 10, and 11 only. Table 4.3 summarizes Basic Strategy applicable to the European game.

Table 4.3: European Multiple-Deck Basic Strategy—Doubling After Splitting Not Allowed

PLAYER'S HAND	DEALER'S UPCARD									
	2	3	4	5	6	7	8	9	10	A
8 or Less	H	H	H	H	H	H	H	H	H	H
9	H	DD	DD	DD	DD	H	H	H	H	H
10	DD	DD	DD	DD	DD	DD	DD	DD	H	H
11	DD	DD	DD	DD	DD	DD	DD	DD	H	H
12	H	H	S	S	S	H	H	H	H	H
13	S	S	S	S	S	H	H	H	H	H
14	S	S	S	S	S	H	H	H	H	H
15	S	S	S	S	S	H	H	H	H	H
16	S	S	S	S	S	H	H	H	H	H
17 or More	S	S	S	S	S	S	S	S	S	S
A2	H	H	H	H	H	H	H	H	H	H
A3	H	H	H	H	H	H	H	H	H	H
A4	H	H	H	H	H	H	H	H	H	H
A5	H	H	H	H	H	H	H	H	H	H
A6	H	H	H	H	H	H	H	H	H	H
A7	S	S	S	S	S	S	S	H	H	H
A8	S	S	S	S	S	S	S	S	S	S
A9	S	S	S	S	S	S	S	S	S	S
2,2	H	H	SPL	SPL	SPL	SPL	H	H	H	H
3,3	H	H	SPL	SPL	SPL	SPL	H	H	H	H
4,4	H	H	H	H	H	H	H	H	H	H
5,5	DD	DD	DD	DD	DD	DD	DD	DD	H	H
6,6	H	SPL	SPL	SPL	SPL	H	H	H	H	H
7,7	SPL	SPL	SPL	SPL	SPL	SPL	H	H	H	H
8,8	SPL	SPL	SPL	SPL	SPL	SPL	SPL	SPL	H	H
9,9	SPL	SPL	SPL	SPL	SPL	S	SPL	SPL	S	S
10,10	S	S	S	S	S	S	S	S	S	S
A,A	SPL	SPL	SPL	SPL	SPL	SPL	SPL	SPL	SPL	H

H = Hit
S = Stand
DD = Double Down
SPL = Split Pair

CHAPTER FIVE

An Introduction to Card Counting

In Chapter One we learned the basics of the game—that is, player options and other fundamentals. In Chapter Four we covered Basic Strategy, which is a predetermined set of rules proven by computer simulation that represents the best possible way to play each hand. If you understand the game inside and out, and have committed every Basic Strategy decision to memory such that you can recall what to do almost instantaneously and under any circumstance, then you're probably ahead of about 99 percent of the blackjack-playing population. But that's not good enough. Because, as mentioned earlier, playing perfect Basic Strategy gets you only to about even with the house. Your bankroll will go up and down, and after some period of time you'll inevitably find yourself about even or at worst losing only a modest amount. But who wants to do that? Let's leave "being even" to the weekend warriors. We want to win in the long run. And there's no other way to do that but to keep track of the cards.

The basic principle behind counting is actually quite simple. It amounts to nothing more than changing the way you play—and even more important, the amount you bet—based on what cards have been dealt. Remember that there are only a finite number of cards (regardless of how many decks are used); so by keeping track of those played, the counter acquires knowledge of what cards remain. And, in overly simplistic terms, when more high cards than low cards remain, the players often hold the advantage. Of course, only the card counter knows when such a situation will occur, and in that lies the keys to the kingdom.

A common misconception is that the actual process of card counting becomes more difficult as the number of decks in use increases. That's not the case at all. In fact, counting down a single deck or a hypothetical shoe comprising 99 decks are essentially equally difficult. The difference lies in how frequently or infrequently the advantageous situations arise. In a single-deck game, the advantage player doesn't have to wade through deck after deck before finding a truly ripe situation on which to capitalize. Or put another way: advantage situations present themselves at a greater frequency when fewer cards are used. Thus, the number of decks in use has more to do with governing opportunity than it does with posing more or less difficulty.

Remember that the dealer is forced to abide by a predetermined set of rules. He must draw on all totals of 16 and below, and stand with 17 or more. Think about it. That's a vital part of the overall equation. In fact, it's this rule and this rule alone that, in essence, represents the foundation on which the entire process of card counting rests. When an excess of low cards has been dealt (resulting in an abundance of high cards remaining), the player is more likely to end up with a winning hand—whether that occurs by simply beating the dealer outright or because the dealer ultimately must draw additional cards and thus has a higher likelihood of busting. And, not surprisingly, the reverse applies during highly negative counts, when a lot of high cards have been dealt and a preponderance of low cards remains. Whichever the case, the proficient card counter bets more when he has the advantage, and less (or not at all) when he doesn't.

The Five Core Concepts

Many people erroneously assume that counters somehow memorize every card that's been dealt. That's simply not the case, and I'm sure there isn't a human on Earth who could remember every card dealt from a six-deck shoe, and then on top of that process the information in a way that would enable him to take advantage of it.

Instead, the entire process begins with something you already know: *Basic Strategy.* (That's a bit of good news, isn't it?) For the non-counter, Basic Strategy signifies mastering the game, since it presents the best possible way to play each hand. For the card counter, however, Basic Strategy represents just the beginning.

The second part of the process involves assigning a point value to each card (positive numbers for low cards, and negative numbers for high cards), and then keeping a cumulative total as the cards are dealt. This is called keeping a "running count." When lots of low cards are dealt, the running count rises. Conversely, when high cards are dealt, the running count drops. By the way, it's not too uncommon for the running count to fluctuate many times between positive and negative, or to stay either positive or negative for a prolonged period. And, of course, the shuffle represents "ground zero." Every time the dealer shuffles, whether you're playing single-deck blackjack or staring at an eight-deck shoe, the running count returns to zero.

The next step is to convert the running count to what's called a "true count." The true count is the running count divided by the number of decks or half decks yet to be played. A true count is needed for correct playing decisions, in that sometimes a card counter will deviate from Basic Strategy. But even more important, the true count is needed in determining how much to wager on the next hand. Think of the true count as a function applied to the running count to get a true read on how advantageous the remaining cards really are. Remember: The running count simply fluctuates up and down, with no relevance to how many cards have been dealt, or more important, to how many remain. Whereas the true count takes into account exactly that.

Step four is to deviate from Basic Strategy if necessary, under certain circumstances. As mentioned briefly in the last chapter, there are times when *deviations from Basic Strategy* are advantageous, based on the true count. Each situation (your hand versus the dealer's upcard) has a threshold, or index number, associated with it; and it becomes favorable in some cases to draw when Basic Strategy says to hit, or vice versa, depending on the content of the remaining cards.

The final step is to determine how much to bet on the next hand. "Betting strategy" is the last of the five core concepts. Obviously, with a high true count, the player has the advantage and should bet more. With low or negative counts, the casino has the advantage, and the card counter should be betting the minimum allowable, or not betting at all. And betting strategy doesn't just mean "bet a lot when you have the advantage." Correct betting strategy entails a structured approach that takes into account not only player advantage, but factors such as your overall bankroll and how much or little you want to expose it to the ups and downs of normal statistical fluctuations.

There you have it. Those are the five core concepts that comprise card counting at the professional level. And we'll be going into each one of them in greater detail shortly.

Fortune *and* Fame?

You walk into a casino and people know how good you are. *Yeah, right.* If you're looking for the bright lights of fame and notoriety, you've come to the wrong place.

Now why would I write such a thing?

I say that because I want to keep you grounded. Yes, it's a trip walking into a casino worth $2 billion knowing you can beat them at their own game. Of course it's personally gratifying to tackle something challenging whole-hog, master it, and come away with a brand-new car or ten out of twelve mortgage payments compliments of the nearest riverboat. But if you're a winner and a true master of everything it takes to card count successfully, then nobody but you and perhaps a few close friends or relatives will know how successful you really are. Because being an expert at blackjack is unlike being an expert at most other things. In other walks of life, superior authority lends itself to prominence—things like public speaking engagements or perhaps a business card with a few fancy letters following your name. But in the world of advantage black-jack, the successful counter must instead remain as anonymous as possible in order to avoid exposure that could make playing with an advantage more difficult than it already is. Sounds crazy, doesn't it? Yes, it does, but unfortunately that's the reality of the situation. And the reason why is because card counters take money directly from the casino's bottom line—and not from the pockets of fellow patrons as do, for instance, professional poker players. In poker, the casino takes a small percentage of each pot. Every poker hand played is money in the bank for the house, no matter what player actually ends up winning the hand. That's certainly not the case in blackjack. Any amount won by any player at blackjack impacts the casino's bottom line. That's why poker legends like Phil Hellmuth and Johnny Chan can sit so comfortably in front of the wide-angle lens. Casino executives aren't looking to bar those guys. In fact, the casino industry thrives on the popularity generated by the high-stakes poker crowd.

The long and short of it is this: in blackjack, the better you become, the more quickly you become (and you've heard this term before) persona non grata—if you're reckless or greedy, or not careful about maintaining your longevity. So, ultimately, it's best if nobody but you knows how good you really are. Get used to this fact very fast: card counting is a solitary art form.

"Bad Beats" Don't Just Happen to Poker Players

Poker players are always complaining about "bad beats." What's a bad beat? In poker it goes something like this: A skilled sharpie and a novice are the only ones left in a hand of $10–$20 stud. Six cards have been dealt. The pro holds two pair—aces and fours—nothing showing. The guy who shouldn't even be at this table holds a 3, 4, 6, and 7 among the six cards that are his. Three 5s have already shown. The skilled player bets. The novice, sitting at a $10–$20 thanks to yesterday's $2,000 slot hit, calls and in doing so hopes to catch the only card in the entire deck that could possibly win the hand. Can you guess what card he receives? You guessed right if you said a 5.

Slot machines aren't the only thing smelling like roses in this player's world. Our novice gets the one remaining 5 and beats the knowledgeable player by drawing to an inside straight and catching a 5 on the last card, or "on the river." That's not supposed to happen, but it does, and in the world of poker that's known as a bad beat.

Unfortunately, poker isn't the only game in which bad beats occur. Bad beats occur in blackjack too—in a different form—and I'm sorry to say there's just no way around them. The nice thing about bad beats in blackjack though, is that they sometimes lead to "good beats" later on in the deck. Let's take a look at a blackjack bad beat.

Imagine that you're nearing the end of a six-deck shoe. You've played all night and at no table has any count really gone positive enough for you to do some damage. Finally you find a table that obliges. The count goes through the ceiling, and you're dealt a pair of 8s against a dealer's 5 with a "fat-boy" (a large bet) in the betting circle. You split the 8s, and on the first 8 you're dealt a 2. You double down and receive a queen for 20. On the second 8 you draw yet another 8 and split again. You're dealt an ace for 19 and stand. On what is now the third 8 you receive a 3 for a total of 11, and double down—again. This time you get a 9. Your three hands total 20, 19, and 20, with the equivalent of five maximum bets sitting on the table in front of you. But you've noticed that the guy in the last seat has been playing erratically. Sure enough, the dealer gets to him, and with a 13 against a dealer's 5, the player inexplicably draws and busts with a 10 of hearts. The dealer next turns over her hole card, a 10, and then promptly draws a 6 for 21. That, in a nutshell, is the blackjack equivalent of a bad beat.

As an advantage player who expects to win, you're crushed. You've waited all night for a juicy shoe, and it finally came along. You put the big one out there, split to three hands, doubled down on two of them, and ended up with a 19 and two 20s. And then devastation—thanks to some guy whom you wish would go back to holding hands with a one-armed bandit.

It happens all the time. Well, maybe not all the time. But it does happen often enough, and prompts me to expound a little on a question I'm asked over and over again: Do the actions of other players affect you?

The answer to that question, believe it or not, is actually "yes" and "no" at the same time. Yes, other players can certainly affect the outcome of your hand in the short term (as illustrated above), but in the long run (and remember, as a card counter all you are really concerned with is the long run) they should have no effect on your bottom line. In other words, in the long run the bone-headed moves of other players should be beneficial as much as they are detrimental. It all evens out in the end. Trust me on that one. Your 1.5 percent advantage will yield just that—nothing more, nothing less.

Of course, that doesn't mean an in-the-bag win (there really isn't any such thing) that suddenly becomes an excruciating loss isn't devastating. It can be, and often is. Those guys in the end seat do contribute to the "ulcer factor." Because not only have you not won, but you've lost to boot. So a $500 loss under these circumstances is really a thousand-dollar swing. With a large enough bet on the table, a bad beat caused by another player straying from Basic Strategy certainly could mean the difference between a winning and losing trip. And trying to put one like that behind you is the toughest thing in the world. But you have to. There's no other choice. *You have to move on.*

You hear about it all the time: players afraid of sitting in the last seat or "third base" because it's the seat that's required to make the last "hit" or "stand" before the dealer draws his cards. And then there's the complainer in the middle seat who yells and screams at the guy on the end for drawing when he should have stood. I mentioned something above about bad beats sometimes leading to good beats. Well, here's what I mean. Someone should remind that guy with the big mouth that the blackjack he gets five hands later with the biggest bet of his life on the table *would not otherwise have occurred* had his friend in the last seat not drawn an extra card five hands earlier. Or when the dealer goes on to bust six times in a row later in the shoe, it may be entirely due to the fact that that guy on the end stood eleven hands back, instead of hitting. Get what I'm saying? It's all interrelated. In fact, it's interrelated so much it's unrelated, in a way. The lesson here is that the sequence of the cards depends on many, many variables, and not just on the actions of one player in one circumstance. If you're going to bawl people out for hitting or standing when they should've done otherwise, you should spend as much time thanking them later if a preponderance of hands work out favorably for you at some subsequent point in the shoe. Remember, when a non-counter deviates from Basic Strategy, the only player that he's really hurting, in the long run, is himself.

But you're human, and it stings like hell when you lose a fat-boy, especially because you as a card counter have put so much effort into eking out your 1.5 percent. Believe me, I know, and I'm sorry to say there's no other way but to endure the pain, unfortunately. It just comes with the territory.

Now, if you're someone who is prone to let your emotions get the better of you, or if you still don't want to take my advice about how the actions of others have no effect on you over the long run, then simply find another table when you see someone who obviously doesn't know what he's doing. Of course, in a crowded casino, that isn't always easy—but if it helps you play a better game, then by all means don't hesitate to do it.

As for me, in all the years I've been counting cards, I've been the victim of countless bad beats. Here's one I'll never forget, and what makes this one extra gut wrenching is that it involved a player trying to put one over on the casino. So keep in mind that bad beats do come in all shapes and sizes, and you never know when one is about to happen.

I Still Hurt over This One

It's late one night during the week in Northern Connecticut, and I'm playing heads up with the dealer—a good situation—with good penetration. I'm at a $25 game in the middle seat, with mid-shoe entry allowed. To this point, I've muddled through a couple of rough shoes, down about $700 or so since walking in. Overall, though, it's been a tough set of cards.

But, I'm thinking, all that may be just about ready to change. With six or so hands left in the shoe, the count suddenly starts rising. Unfortunately, that's also when another player comes along, looks at my $25 table, and then jumps into the game at first base. He buys in with something like a $10-dollar bill, two fives, and five singles, which, for starters, means the six or so hands that would've been dealt at a very high count may now amount to only four or five.

Now I don't make a habit of prejudging anyone, but I must admit that if I were *forced* to pick someone out of all the players in the casino that night whom I thought just might be capable of causing a problem—any problem—this guy would certainly have been my first choice. What do you think—irony or coincidence? I'll let you decide.

Anyway, the count continues to rise and so my bets increase accordingly. The next two hands I lose. But during those hands, from a few less-than-common moves he makes, I notice that the guy at first base appears to know Basic Strategy inside and out.

The count goes through the ceiling. I spread to two hands of $250 each. He gets a blackjack, of course. I split on one hand and double down on the other—for a total of $1,000 on the layout—and lose again. All of it. But I'm just warming up. Now comes the bad beat I'll remember for the rest of my life.

The count is still through the ceiling. But complicating matters is the fact that heat is on the way. The phones are ringing, I'm getting glares from the pit, and every suit in the place seems to be in a huddle at the podium. But it's the last hand of the shoe, the true count is through the ceiling, and I'm losing my butt. Should I head for the door or play one more hand at a very high advantage?

I spread to two hands of several hundred each, no doubt pushing the limit on what this club is going to tolerate before coming down on me in some way or other. Probably not the best thing for future play, but the moment gets the better of me, especially with the advantage I'm holding on this final hand of the shoe. It's my last hand in the joint, win or lose, no matter what happens.

He gets a 14; I get two 20s. The dealer shows a 4, and begins the process of finishing the hand by starting with my friend in the first seat.

Inexplicably, the guy at first base makes a half-hearted tap on the table, a signal for another card. Just as inexplicably the dealer, without even so much as raising an eyebrow, begins the process of giving him one. By this point, what I'm seeing has started to become slow motion to me. Often dealers who see a move blatantly contradictory to Basic Strategy will hesitate long enough to make sure the player really wants to do what he is indicating—especially if other players have fat bets on the table. But not this dealer. His left hand extracts a card from the shoe, and his right arm warms up to deliver it.

Then at the very last second—just as the dealer's hand is about to snap the card down onto the felt in front of the player—the guy waves his hand wildly back and forth—signifying that he *doesn't* want an additional card. But it's too late. The card, a jack of clubs, is already lying there on the table, staring up at the three of us.

The guy on my right jumps out of his seat, still shaking his hand back and forth just inches above the card.

"I didn't want that. I didn't want that. Look at my hand."

"But you signaled for a hit," the dealer says.

"No, I did not," says the player.

"Yes, you did," says the dealer.

"I'd never hit that hand," the player says, after several expletives. "You have a 4 showing. No one hits that hand."

"I'm sorry, but you gave me the hit sign."

By this time both the floorperson and the pit boss are hovered over the table, figuring out the best way to resolve the situation. Both find a second to evil-eye my twin-tower stacks, and the paint sitting in front of each.

Over the years I've seen disputes resolved a number of ways. I've seen a card like that burned. I've seen it offered to the next player. I've even seen pit personnel rule in favor of the player if they think it was the dealer who actually made the mistake. But on this one, a resolution isn't anywhere in sight. I wonder why. Is it possible that the pit boss has come to the same conclusion about this guy that I had come to just several minutes earlier? Is the fact that they are in the process of identifying me as a card counter going to play a role in how they would decide to proceed?

Finally, the pit boss gets on the phone and requests that the surveillance team—the guys in the back room watching a wall of video monitors—reviews the tape and come to a conclusion. *Great.* If the surveillance guys weren't on to me already, they're on to me now.

Something like fifteen minutes goes by as my bets and I sit there under the lights. But it gives me enough time to think more about this character's scam. Basically, his ploy involved trying to take advantage of the obvious. Timing is the critical element, and the combination of a weak hit signal followed by an adamant stand signal was to be the sequence no matter what card ended up face up on the table. For if the card turns out to be a small card and his hand greatly improves as a result, even if his hand is still shaking back and forth, the card won't and can't be taken away. Both he and the casino would just have to live with the consequence of his "mistake." On the other hand, if the card was a bust card, which in this case it was, his argument then becomes somewhat logical: that no one in his right mind would actually take a hit on 14 against a dealer's 4 (which at a $25 table doesn't happen much). Not to mention the fact that his hand is still shaking back and forth not more than two inches above the table, indicating no desire for additional cards.

The podium phone rings and the verdict from "upstairs" is that the hit sign was made—which is correct. The hit-then-stand gesture had obviously been an attempt to scam the casino. The dealer collects the man's $25 chip and then moves on to me. The floorperson and the pit boss hang around. My bets are likely the biggest action in the place at this hour of the morning.

With two 20s I stand, of course. The dealer flips over a 10 for 14, and then snaps out a 7 for 21.

I'm stunned. What should have been a dealer bust had incredulously turned into a dealer 21, against two 20s no less, with hundreds of dollars on the table. Had I won I might have walked out about even. Instead, in a matter of minutes or just a few quick hands I'd lost several thousand dollars—with the icing on the cake being a bad beat caused by a dishonest individual trying to scam the casino.

It's tough to lose the big ones under normal circumstances. But to lose one like this? Believe me when I say that bad beats come in all shapes and sizes, and don't just happen to poker players.

Thinking Long-Term

This is probably a harder concept to embrace than it first appears to be, because there's a tendency to get so wrapped up in the present that all else falls out of perspective. For instance, let's say you're up a chunk after some extended period of time, but you're in Vegas or the Caribbean for a few days and in the process of getting creamed. The tendency is to focus so much on the trip at hand—that you're down let's say $8,000 since landing on this godforsaken island—that you forget about the total plus/minus. Which is really all that matters. Sure, $8,000 may be 30 percent of a larger chunk, and represents a sizable decrease in the profit pile. But losing streaks occur—it comes with the territory. In this case, the more quickly you can focus on the fact that you're still up $17,000 since forming the bank, the better.

As you know by now, card counting isn't structured such that it allows a player to win a huge amount of money at one sitting. With that said, I'm not referring to team play or the actions of a single big player having a monster session at the tables. What I mean is that blackjack is not like roulette, for instance, where winning straight up on a number yields odds of 35:1, and where several straight-up hits can result in a huge pile of chips in comparison to what you might have started with. Instead blackjack is a mechanism that allows the proficient player to slowly extract a profit from the game over an extended period.

And that is exactly what the casinos are doing to the normal player, multiplied by the number of normal players under the roof at any given time. The only difference is that as a single player you have only one interface, whereas the casino might have thirty blackjack tables operating simultaneously, some of which might be winning while others are losing. That's why the casino isn't overly concerned with one or two tables experiencing a large negative fluctuation. Management knows that two other tables elsewhere in the building are probably experiencing a large positive fluctuation.

Thus, with so many tables operating at one time, the casino gets into the "long run" much sooner than any individual player can, and the long run has a nice way of smoothing out severe positive or negative fluctuations. For the casino, a balance is struck sooner rather than later—barring the appearance of any lucky whales—and the house comes away with a nice little profit week in and week out. You, however, operating as a solitary card counter, will have good days and bad days, good weeks and bad weeks, good months and bad months, and occasionally even good years and bad years dependent in part on how many total hours you play. Thus, the longer long-term perspective you can adopt, the better.

A One-Level or a Multi-Level?

Among the pros there is much debate as to whether it's more beneficial to learn a one-level point count or a multi-level point count, considering the latter is more complex and as a result more difficult to master. The tradeoff is that the higher-level point counts yield a slightly higher percent advantage. And considering just how difficult it is to win consistently, I'm not sure it's wise to forgo *any* opportunity to increase your edge, even if it comes at somewhat of a price. Arguments exist on both sides, with the leading proponents for level ones citing that since counters using level threes are prone to make far more mistakes than those using a simpler method, their expectations are lower. Another argument is that level-three players can't sustain for an extended period, or are unable to address the other necessary aspects of counting (the nontechnical components) while performing all of the calculations characteristic of a multi-level system. The users of level-three point counts claim that more money is put into action using a higher-level count, and thus the total expectation is higher. Or that the difference in difficulty isn't all *that* much, and if you're going to invest the time and effort in learning to count cards, it might as well be for all the marbles—especially if you plan to play for an extended period.

I'm on the fence. I use a level three only because I like the fact that it's one of the most powerful methods out there. I learned it years ago, and know it inside and out. My opinion is that the entire process of extracting money from a casino is hard enough as it is. You might as well get all the help you can get. But with that said, I tend to be a perfectionist. I work very, very hard to ensure that I'm performing all calculations with the utmost accuracy. Remember, the leading argument for not learning a multi-level point count is that the counter is much more prone to make mistakes, and thus ends up playing at even a lower expectation than a counter using a simpler system but performing it flawlessly.

Card-counting systems come in essentially three forms: level one point counts assign values of -1, 0, and 1 to the various cards comprising a standard deck. Level two point counts can assign values of -2, -1, 0, 1, and 2. And level three point counts assign values from -3 to +3. But what's the difference where it matters most—in dollars and cents? Each card-counting method also has a corresponding efficiency relating to its effectiveness versus the computer for both playing decisions and betting decisions. The higher-level point counts generally yield higher efficiencies than the simpler point counts, and that results in a higher percent advantage. But, as mentioned earlier, that comes at a price. The increase in percent advantage comes from the fact that the multi-level systems provide a more precise snapshot of what has occurred. For example, a level three point count might assign a +3 to only a 5, which is the most unfavorable card for the player. Whereas a level one might assign a +1 to a 5 as well as a +1 to several other low cards—so as not to distinguish between more-favorable and less-favorable low cards when an abundance of one or the other has been dealt. This can sometimes result in unrealized potential going unnoticed. Multi-level point counts may also involve keeping separate track of aces, in that aces are such valuable cards to the player. In a word, the multi-level point counts are simply a little more precise.

When a newcomer once asked legendary blackjack expert Stanford Wong what system she should learn, Stanford replied by writing that "it doesn't much matter what system you learn, as long as what you learn compares high cards to low cards." Stanford further goes on to imply that time is better spent debating how to implement any such system live rather than mulling over the nuances of one system as compared to another. In other words, there are many responsible methods to choose from. And more than one will get you to where you want to go.

My suggestion is to be honest with yourself. Assess your personality—strong points and weak points. If you're a driven perfectionist who happens to be good in multitasking, then my suggestion is to learn a level three point count. You won't be content knowing more advantage can be obtained and you're not getting it. Another reason for learning an advanced point count might be that you're a serious player already—one who plays frequently and plans on doing so for many years to come. Why have the ability, end up playing a million hands over the next twenty-five years, and not play at the highest level possible? On the other hand—and this is equally important—if you're serious about advancing to the next level but know you may not play with regularity, or if multitasking isn't your thing, or if you want to win but don't have to eke out every last iota of advantage to be happy; then I'd strongly urge you to consider learning a level one point count. Ultimately, of course, the choice is yours.

Chapter Six outlines a powerful one-level system, and Chapter Seven contains everything necessary for you to master a multi-level point count. Similar theory and methodology apply across both methods for some topics. Therefore, several sections contain similar information. However, each chapter is self contained, and reading both is unnecessary except for a review of what the other system entails. As far as which one is right for you, only you can answer that question. But whichever method you choose, always remember this: if winning money in the casinos were that easy, everybody would be doing it.

CHAPTER SIX

A Level-One Point Count

This chapter outlines the High-Low system, undoubtedly the most popular professional-level point count in the world today. Harvey Dubner first introduced it in the early 1960s, and over the years, blackjack luminaries like Edward Thorp, Lawrence Revere, Julian Braun, and Stanford Wong have refined it into a powerful method that combines a high playing and betting efficiency with a good deal of user friendliness. It's a level one that isn't too difficult to master, yet brings to the table an edge that meets or exceeds many other card-counting methods. But as with any point count system, the foundation for successful use of the High-Low comes only after the student has mastered Basic Strategy.

The beginning sections of this chapter delve into the basics, including card values, combinations, and how to keep a running count as the cards are being dealt. The latter sections focus on speed, and then the all-important process of converting the running count to a true count for both playing and betting purposes, which is covered in subsequent chapters.

As far as an approach to learning the material goes, you may find it most beneficial to first read through the entire chapter—to gain perspective—then return to each section individually to master the concepts presented therein. Covering the material in this way might better illustrate how each part contributes to form a comprehensive overall strategy.

The Value of Each Card

No matter how many decks are in use, as the cards are dealt history begins establishing itself. And as you know, card counting involves using history to gain a better understanding of what cards remain. That's best accomplished by assigning a point value to each card and then keeping a cumulative running total, commonly referred to as a "running count."

When the remaining cards are rich enough in 10s and aces, the player has the advantage. When the remaining cards are rich in small cards, the house has the advantage. This is largely due to several reasons, most notably that the dealer has to abide by a predetermined set of rules that forces him to draw until reaching a certain total. Other factors are that the player, unlike the dealer, gets paid at 1½:1 for blackjack, and that the player can take advantage of options like doubling down, splitting pairs, and surrender when available.

The first step in gaining an insight into what cards remain is to keep track of those cards that have already been dealt. As far as the running count is concerned, low cards like 2s and 5s have a point value of +1, whereas high cards like aces and all 10-valued cards (hereafter referred to as 10s) have a point count value of -1. So if an abundance of low cards is dealt, the running count will likely be positive—to reflect the fact that a lot of high cards remain. Conversely, when lots of high cards have been dealt, the running count should be negative—to reflect the fact that the remaining cards contain an abundance of low cards.

Table 6.1, on the next page, summarizes each card and its associated value. Study the table until you are well aware of which cards are valued at +1, which cards are neutral or have a value of zero, and which cards are valued at -1.

Table 6.1: Cards and Their Associated Values

CARD	VALUE
2, 3, 4, 5, 6	+1
7, 8, 9	0
10s, Aces	-1

Begin by taking a standard deck of cards and flipping through it, reciting the corresponding value of each card. Go through the entire deck, then shuffle and repeat the process. Study the table again if necessary, and then go through the deck a few more times. In no time at all the point count value of each card should come to you almost instantaneously.

The Running Count

The next step is to begin keeping a cumulative total. This means that instead of reciting the actual point count value of each card as shown above, you'll add or subtract as necessary to keep an overall total. In other words, if a 2, 5, king, 8, and 3 are dealt in succession, instead of reciting "+1, +1, -1, 0, and +1," you'll now recite "+1, +2, +1, +1, +2." Keep in mind that you're always adding with each new card that is dealt, so that, for instance, -1 added to a -3 equals -4, and a -1 added to a +7 equals a +6. Right from the start you should notice how your count will rise and fall depending on what cards are dealt—sometimes going positive, sometimes remaining negative, and often fluctuating between.

As you did when committing Basic Strategy to memory, spend as much time as you need practicing the running count. Repetition is key. As with so many other endeavors, the more you practice the better you'll become. Adding or subtracting only 1 (or zero) from the previous total based on the last card dealt should become almost natural after only a few hours of practice. At this stage of the game, accuracy is much more important than speed, which will develop in time.

Take a deck of cards with you wherever you go, in your shirt pocket or purse. Whenever a spare moment allows, count down a deck. Make it a game by stopping just prior to the last card and then guessing its value. If you're accurate, ending with a +1 will mean the last card is a 10 or ace. If your running count is 0, you know you're holding a 7, 8, or 9. If your count is negative, then it's definitely a low card. If you're wrong, recount the same deck without shuffling so you can isolate and correct any kind of unusual sequence that may present a particular stumbling block.

Card Combos

Any shortcut that increases speed or cuts down on the amount of processing necessary is a benefit. For that reason, grouping combinations of cards can be beneficial, even when using a method in which card values can only increase or decrease the running count by one.

Learn those combinations that sum to zero and can thus be ignored—like any high card or low card followed by the opposite. In effect, you can just skip a queen followed by a 2, or a 6 followed by an ace, or a king followed by a 5, because a +1 and a -1 cancel each other out.

As you continue to practice counting down decks, try to spot these two-card combinations when they arise—by simply gliding over them as they occur. In other words, see and recognize them for what they are, but don't waste time or energy by actually adding them together. After a few times through, you should notice an increase in speed, simply because you're no longer reciting to yourself a cumulative total after every single card.

Spend some time counting down decks in this fashion, getting more and more used to keeping a running count total by combining cards whenever practical.

The Need for Speed

In the casino world, more hands dealt means more money for the house. For that reason most dealers, especially those working from a shoe, tend to deal at a fairly rapid pace, requiring a counter to keep up with the cards or risk losing the count and thus losing any chance of knowing when an advantage over the house exists.

As far as speed is concerned, the benchmark we'll shoot for is to be able to count down a standard fifty-two-card deck in about twenty-five seconds. This is the time most proficient counters aim to either meet or exceed in order to simulate real-world conditions. By the way, counting down a deck in twenty-five seconds or less should be achieved not once or twice every so many tries, but consistently and with relative ease.

To further work on speed and accuracy, I would suggest securing as many decks of cards as possible. Make sure all are complete, and then just as you did with a single deck, begin counting down four, six, and even eight decks at a time. The reason for this is that you should become familiar with counts characteristic of multiple-deck games. You should start to see much higher positive and negative cumulative totals, along with a running count that often rises and falls with surprising volatility. This takes a little more getting used to than the relatively smaller hills and valleys characteristic of the single-deck game. You'll see what I mean as soon as you begin practicing.

Keep in mind, though, that accuracy is still more important than speed, and that the latter will come with enough repetition.

The True Count

At last we've reached the meat-and-potatoes of the entire process. Think about this for a moment: What's the difference between a running count of +26 early on in a six-deck shoe when, let's say, five decks remain, versus a running count of +26 much further along in a six-deck shoe when perhaps only about two decks remain? The most important difference is that there are a lot fewer cards to draw from when only two or so decks are remaining. Which, consequently, means the *concentration* of high cards is a lot greater. That's a very advantageous situation for the player. Think of the "true count" as a function that takes the running count and provides a more precise picture of what's really about to occur.

The true count is determined by dividing the running count by the number of decks remaining. As far as precision is concerned, estimate to the nearest half deck. For instance, in a six-deck game a running count of +24 with four decks remaining equates to a true count of +6 ($24 \div 4 = 6$), whereas a running count of +24 with only two-and-a-half decks remaining equates to a true count of a little under +10 ($24 \div 2.5 = 9.6$). So, you see, running counts convert to different true counts depending on how many decks remain.

At this point it might be worthwhile mentioning that learning the High-Low does not entail keeping a side count of aces, as is the case with many other professional level point counts. Another user-friendly facet that applies to all level one systems is that you're never adding or subtracting an amount greater than one. Which means keeping a running count is almost intuitive. Whereas for a higher-level count you actually have to add and subtract quantities other than one. But you will have to divide by numbers like 1½, 2½, 3½ and so on. That might take a little getting used to at first, but in time shouldn't pose too much difficulty as you begin getting more and more used to doing that type of division.

But how do we best determine how many cards remain? In order to do this, we use the discard tray and work our way backwards. If we're playing in a six-deck game and about two decks are sitting in the discard pile, then by process of elimination we know that about four decks remain in the shoe. Remember, as the number of decks in the discard tray gets higher, the number of decks remaining (and the number we use to divide the running count by) gets smaller. And a small number used to divide into any positive running count is a good sign, for it means we'll likely end up with an elevated true count.

But rather than go through the process of elimination each and every time we need to calculate the true count, we'll instead come to learn and use what's called a "conversion factor." In our case, the conversion factor represents the number of decks remaining based on the number of decks already sitting in the discard pile. The goal is to streamline the process such that with just a quick glance at the discard pile we're able to divide the running count by a number (the conversion factor) to arrive at the correct true count. And the only way to really become proficient at determining accurate conversion factors is to secure a good number of decks (preferably new decks or used ones in very good shape, for we're most interested in deck heights) and simulate different amounts sitting in the discard pile. Decks of cards may be available for purchase at your local drug or dollar store, or at even better prices online where gaming supplies are sold. (Decks are sometimes available for free at casino cages, upon asking.)

For an eight-deck game, you'll need about forty-six decks of cards; for a six-deck game, twenty-eight decks; for a four-deck game, fourteen decks; and for double deck, three decks. (Note: for single-deck blackjack, we employ other methods to arrive at the correct true count, covered in detail in Chapter Ten.)

Once you have the appropriate number of decks, find a place where you can set them up in piles next to one another, preferably where you can study the piles for some time and where they won't be disturbed. Divide the cards into piles that increase in half-deck increments, starting with one half-deck pile. The next pile would contain a full deck. The pile after that a deck and a half, and so on.

The six-deck player should end up with ten piles ranging in size from one pile of twenty-six cards, or a half-deck, to a pile containing 260 cards, or five full decks. The set-up for four-deck training would involve seven piles ranging in size from one pile of twenty-six cards to a final pile containing 182 cards, or three-and-a-half decks. By the way, the reason we don't bother training for any more than five decks dealt in a six-deck game, or three-and-a-half decks dealt in a four-deck game, and so on, is because modern-day blackjack is never dealt down to the last card. So, for example, in a six-deck game, you should never have to do a division based on observing five-and-a-half decks in the discard pile. (At one time blackjack had been dealt down to the last card. But your predecessors put an end to that practice long ago, unfortunately. Imagine a true count with something like eight cards remaining?)

Table 6.2 lists the various conversion factors for two-, four-, six-, and eight-deck games. Notice how the conversion factors gradually decrease, which corresponds to fewer and fewer cards remaining to be played. This has the effect of a smaller and smaller change on the running count, since dividing any one number by a smaller and smaller number results in less of a change to the original number. That's why in a multi-deck game the most advantageous situations often end up occurring just prior to the shuffle.

Table 6.2: Conversion Factors for Multiple Deck Games

NUMBER OF DECKS IN DISCARD PILE	TOTAL NUMBER OF DECKS USED			
	2 DECKS	4 DECKS	6 DECKS	8 DECKS
0.5	1.5	3.5	5.5	7.5
1	1	3	5	7
1.5	0.5	2.5	4.5	6.5
2		2	4	6
2.5		1.5	3.5	5.5
3		1	3	5
3.5		0.5	2.5	4.5
4			2	4
4.5			1.5	3.5
5			1	3
5.5				2.5
6				2
6.5				1.5

On a small index card write down the conversion factor for each half-deck pile, and place the card face up in front of that pile. Begin associating the heights of each pile with the corresponding conversion factor. The goal here is to become familiar enough with the height of each pile such that the actual number of decks present becomes meaningless—your only concern is the correct conversion factor.

Find a spare table or level surface and leave the decks set up for a while. Return to them often and study the heights of each pile and the corresponding conversion factors. Rearrange the piles and see if you can determine the correct conversion factors when the piles are not in ascending or descending order in terms of height. Work at becoming good enough to know the correct conversion factor with only a momentary glance at pile height. Remember, you're going through all this because the accuracy of your true count—aside from keeping an accurate running count—is based on how good you are at sizing up the discard pile.

At this point it might be worth mentioning that, for example, two decks in the discard pile will obviously result in different conversion factors depending on whether you're sitting at a six- or eight-deck game. So, of course, you must be cognizant of how many decks are in use—something that should and will become very obvious to you in that two, four, six, and eight-decks vary so much in size, as do their respective discard trays. After some practice one glance at the discard pile—at the cards *and the tray those cards are sitting in*—should create in your mind an association that will generate the appropriate conversion factor.

Realistically, the only two games where confusion could arise, if you're not careful, are between the six- and eight-deck game. But as a serious player, you're not likely to be wasting your time playing an eight-deck game if a six-deck game exists under the same roof, or in the same city. Unless bankroll considerations force you to play the lower-minimum eight-deck games, in which case you won't be switching back and forth anyway. And four-deck games are such unique animals that they usually exist at all tables everywhere, or not at all. In other words, the message here is that a little bit of training for the game you intend on playing, or that exists at the casino destination you're heading to, goes a long way. And the difference in conversion factors between, say, the two- and six-deck games in a locale like Las Vegas is so vastly obvious and different, that confusion between the two isn't likely to happen.

Figure 6.1, opposite, contains several illustrations showing discard

Figure 6.1: The Forever-Changing Discard Pile

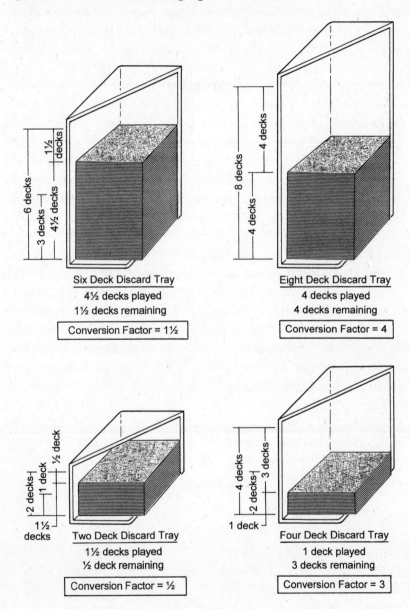

Six Deck Discard Tray
4½ decks played
1½ decks remaining

Conversion Factor = 1½

Eight Deck Discard Tray
4 decks played
4 decks remaining

Conversion Factor = 4

Two Deck Discard Tray
1½ decks played
½ deck remaining

Conversion Factor = ½

Four Deck Discard Tray
1 deck played
3 decks remaining

Conversion Factor = 3

trays, number of decks remaining as a result of the number of cards in the discard pile, and the correct conversion factors. Study these examples for a while to ensure that you thoroughly understand this process.

Summary

Well, you've made it to the end. With card values, card combinations, an accurate running count, and the ability to take the running count and convert it to a true count, you're well on your way to becoming a professional-level player. And, as if I haven't mentioned this once or twice already, I'll make the point again: practice is essential. And do know that the entire process does come together with a lot more ease once the individual components are mastered.

This chapter covered what I like to call the Core Process—that of keeping a running count and using a conversion factor to come up with a true count. As mentioned earlier, the true count is then used to make both playing and betting decisions, which are covered in Chapters Eight and Nine, respectively. Playing decisions involve deviating from Basic Strategy when it's most advantageous to do so—depending on the true count. In a similar manner, we use the true count to determine how much or little to bet on the next hand—again, depending on player advantage.

Chapter Seven outlines a level-three point count and may be skipped by the student learning the level-one system presented here.

CHAPTER SEVEN

A Level-Three Point Count

This chapter outlines one of the most powerful card-counting methods available: the Uston APC, an advanced point count developed by the late Kenneth Uston, widely regarded as one of the best blackjack players ever. Level-three systems like this one are used by some of the most advanced counters in the world. These systems aren't the easiest to learn, but then again, those looking to obtain every last iota of an advantage shouldn't be put off by the idea that mastering a higher-level point count requires a good deal of practice. By choosing to learn a level three, you're choosing to become among the card-counting elite.

The beginning sections of this chapter delve into the basics—things like card values, the running count, and recognizing card combinations are covered in detail. Later sections cover more complicated topics like true count conversions and ace adjustment.

As for an approach to learning the material, you may find it beneficial to first read through the entire chapter—to gain perspective—then return to each section individually to master the concepts presented therein. Reading over the material in this way might better illustrate how each part contributes to form a comprehensive overall strategy.

The Value of Each Card

All card-counting methods involve assigning a point value to each card and then, for starters, keeping a running track total. This section will familiarize you with each card's associated value.

Take a while to study the table below—long enough so that you can look away and still recite the corresponding value for each card. Notice how low cards like 2s and 6s have positive values, whereas high cards like 9s and all 10-valued cards (hereafter referred to as 10s) have negative values. Since tens, jacks, queens, and kings all have the same face value, it's not surprising that these cards carry the same point-value weight as well—that of -3. Disregard aces for the time being—aces are counted as zero, and are such important cards that we'll cover them in a separate section.

Table 7.1: Cards and Their Associated Values

CARD	VALUE
2	+1
3	+2
4	+2
5	+3
6	+2
7	+2
8	+1
9	-1
10	-3

Now take a deck of cards and begin flipping through it, reciting the corresponding value of each card as shown in Table 7.1. Again, skip all aces for the time being. Go through the entire deck, then shuffle and repeat the process again several more times. Continue running through the deck until you are thoroughly familiar with each card and its corresponding point value.

The Running Count

The next step is to begin keeping a cumulative total. This requires adding and subtracting the corresponding point values as the cards are dealt. In other words, if a 3, 6, and 9 are dealt, instead of simply reciting their point values ("+2, +2, -1"), you'll now recite "+2, +4, +3" to represent the cumulative total of these three cards. Keep in mind that a -3 added to a -1 equals -4, and a -3 added to a +1 equals -2.

The fact that low cards are positive and 9s and 10s are negative should make sense to you already—and that an elevated positive count, for instance, indicates that those cards already dealt have been mostly low cards.

Spend as much time as you need practicing this—learning the running count. Take a deck of cards with you wherever you go and run through it whenever the opportunity presents itself. Not surprisingly, the more you practice the more accurate you will become.

In the beginning, don't concern yourself with speed—that will come in time. Instead, get creative. Test your accuracy by stopping just prior to the last card and then predicting its value before turning it over. With the last card your running count should always return to zero, because the total of all cards both positive and negative is zero. So if your running count ends with a -3, you know that the last card must be a 5. (A 5 is the only card that when added to -3 returns the running count to zero.) If you end at zero, you know you're holding an ace. If you find yourself making mistakes, count through the same deck again, only this time at a slower pace. Going through the same deck for a second time will allow you to correct any errors or subconscious incorrect associations made due to a particularly difficult sequence.

Over time, you should notice an increase in both speed and accuracy.

Card Combos

Speaking of speed, in no time at all it should become apparent that certain combinations of cards cancel each other out, or net to numbers like -1 or +2. Counters use these combinations to their advantage, in that live conditions often dictate a "need for speed." Since there are more 10s than any other card in a standard deck, the opportunity to pair a 10 with another card presents itself repeatedly. Several of the most commonly encountered combinations involving 10s are shown in Table 7.2.

Table 7.2: Two-Card Combinations Involving 10s

COMBINATION	TOTAL
10, 5	0
10, 3	-1
10, 4	-1
10, 6	-1
10, 7	-1

Study these combinations for a moment, then run through the deck again, this time combining 10s with 3s through 7s whenever possible. This may seem awkward at first, but eventually making use of combinations in keeping the running count will become second nature.

As you might imagine, there are quite a few more. Following are some additional combinations to learn—many involving cards other than 10s.

Table 7.3: More Two-Card Combinations

COMBINATION	TOTAL
3, 4, 6, 7 with 3, 4, 6, 7	+4
2 or 8 with 9	0
10 with 9	-4
10 with 10	-6
3, 4, 6, 7 with 9	+1
2 or 8 with 2 or 8	+2
9 with 9	-2
5 with 5	+6
5 with 9	+2

And finally two three-card combinations:

Table 7.4: Three-Card Combinations

COMBINATION	TOTAL
3, 4, 6, or 7 and 2 or 8 with 10	0
Two 3s, 4s, 6s, or 7s with 10	+1

Tables 7.3 and 7.4 will require a lot more study than Table 7.2, simply because these pairings not only involve more combinations, but the combinations themselves involve so many different cards.

As for speed, let that come with time. More important at this point is recognizing and learning to make use of these combinations whenever possible, and counting down each deck as accurately as possible.

Counting Aces

The ace is such a valuable card that most advanced methods keep track of them separately, then factor in the relative abundance (or shortage) of aces using a separate, subsequent calculation. The 1½:1 paid for blackjack adds up to a lot more than most people realize. (Just as taking insurance when you're not supposed to adds up to a lot more in losses than most people realize.)

For keeping track of aces, Uston in his legendary book *Million Dollar Blackjack* recommended using various foot positions, and after experimenting with several methods I've found that to be indeed the easiest and most reliable—not to mention that the feet are almost always hidden from view. Keeping track of aces in this manner also frees up the hands to perform actions involving chips or drinks or anything else that might go into the act of appearing like "just another gambler."

Table 7.5 shows how you can keep track of up to eight aces on one foot. Read through the table and, as you do, move your feet through the various positions described.

Table 7.5: Keeping Track of Those Aces

Ace No. 1:	Toes down, heel up
Ace No. 2:	Outstep down
Ace No. 3:	Toes up, heel down
Ace No. 4:	Instep down
Ace No. 5:	Heel down, toes up and to left
Ace No. 6:	Heel down, toes up and to the right
Ace No. 7:	Toes down, heel up and to the left
Ace No. 8:	Toes down, heel up and to the right

On single- and double-deck games, aces can be counted on one foot. Multi-deck games using four or more decks will require the use of both feet, in which case I would strongly recommend that you start with the same foot every time—no matter what game you are sitting at—to avoid any possibility of confusion. On a four-deck game, you'll move to the opposite foot and simply repeat the same eight movements for aces nine through sixteen. For a six-deck game you'll start on one foot for the first eight aces, move to the second for the next eight aces, and then return to the original foot to track the remaining group of eight. And if you haven't figured it out already, an eight-deck game will require the use of both feet on two separate occasions. Again, I'd recommend always starting with the same foot, and then alternating back and forth in groups of eight. On games involving six or eight decks, the great majority of the time you'll never cycle through all twenty-four or thirty-two positions respectively, simply because no modern game is ever dealt down to the last card, and often at least an ace or two will remain in that clump of cards that ends up not being used.

Pick up a deck and again start dealing out the cards. Keep track of the running count, as usual, but now also begin to keep track of aces as they appear, moving your feet through the positions described in Table 7.5. When finished, go through the deck again, only this time start from the fifth ace position. Get used to all eight positions, then move to the other foot and continue as though counting aces nine through sixteen. It may seem unlikely at the moment, but as this process becomes more and more familiar, you'll find your feet moving almost automatically with each ace that appears.

So when do we use this information to our advantage? Well, relative ace abundance or shortage applies more to betting strategy than it does to playing strategy. So the end use of this information won't come into play until Chapter Nine. But continue practicing keeping track of those aces—because we'll need to know how many have been dealt to make ace adjustment calculations later in this chapter.

Bringing It All Together

Now it's time to bring it all together, or at least to bring together everything we've learned to this point. You know the level-three point count values for each card. You've been practicing the running count, including the use of various card combinations whenever possible. And most recently we've discussed and practiced how to keep a side count of aces.

Are we ready, then, to sit down and play for real?

No. Not even close, actually. Now it's time to work on that "need for speed" we touched on earlier. The benchmark we'll shoot for, which is one fairly common among professional card counters, is the ability to accurately count down an entire deck of cards in twenty-five seconds or fewer, while keeping a side count of aces. If the process of actually dealing out the cards slows you down, then hold the deck in your hands and simply scan through the cards in a way that offers the least resistance. In other words, don't let the mechanical process of flipping through the cards slow down that hard drive inside your head. By the way, the twenty-five-second mark is gearing you up for live casino play, where—as I'm sure you know—things happen rather quickly.

To further work on speed and accuracy, you'll need to secure as many decks of cards as possible. For this drill, four, six, or eight decks will do, but soon we'll be covering a topic in which the eight-deck player will need about forty-six decks of cards. The reason you should start practicing with multiple decks right now is that you should begin simulating counts commonly encountered in multiple-deck games. A single deck of cards just won't cut it in terms of volatility. In addition, multiple decks will also allow you to practice counting aces using both feet.

Spend as much time as necessary getting accustomed to working with this many cards. Put into practice everything we've covered to this point—making sure, of course, that you are not in any way sacrificing accuracy merely for the sake of speed. This is probably a good time to remind you that a level-three point count requires the utmost precision.

The True Count, at Last

Up until now our focus has been solely on the running count. The good news is I'd venture to guess that after many hours of practice you're probably making a lot fewer mistakes and running through those decks a whole lot faster than you were at the outset. And your feet are constantly moving as you keep accurate track of those aces, right? Yes, you certainly have a mind full. But where is this all going?

Enter the true count—the foundation on which all-important decisions are made. Consider the true count the real moneymaker—the meat-and-potatoes, if you will—of any responsible card-counting method.

The true count is what gives us the clearest picture of the content of those cards that remain. And here's why: We know that when a lot of low cards have been dealt it's to the player's advantage, because the remaining cards contain a disproportionate number of high cards. And when a lot of high cards have been dealt, the opposite is true. The remaining cards are unfavorable to the player because a lot of low-value cards remain. But *what about* those remaining cards? Let's consider for a moment the size of the pool which we are drawing from. In other words, let's pay as much attention to how many cards remain as we do to how positive or negative those remaining cards may be.

The true count can be viewed as a function that takes the running count and makes appropriate adjustments based on how many cards remain. How important is the true count? The true count is mission critical, because as you will see, a high running count early on in a multiple-deck game, or in any game for that matter, presents a very different situation than the same elevated running count with fewer cards remaining. In the latter case, a much greater concentration of high cards exists in the relatively smaller pool of cards that remains.

The true count is calculated by dividing the running count by the number of half decks remaining. For instance, a running count of +24 with four decks (eight half decks) remaining equates to a true count of +3 (24 ÷ 8 = 3), whereas a running count of +24 with two decks (four half decks) remaining equates to a true count of +6 (24 ÷ 4 = 6). So, you see, running counts convert to different true counts depending on how many half decks remain.

The next logical question is, how do we best determine how many cards remain? The answer lies in the discard tray. Remember that the discard tray holds those cards that have already been used. And, in actuality, we estimate how many half decks are sitting in the discard tray in order to then determine how many half decks remain in the shoe. For instance, if we're playing at a six-deck game and we observe four decks in the discard pile, we know that there are two decks or four half decks remaining in the shoe. Likewise, if we're playing double-deck and one deck is visible in the discard tray, then we know that only two half decks remain.

But why half decks? Why not full decks? One reason is that half decks offer more precision. Another reason is that half decks allow us to avoid having to divide an integer by some number and a half—which would be a real challenge considering how much else is going on. In any event, the only way to really practice estimating how many half decks remain is to secure a good number of decks and simulate different quantities of cards in the discard pile. Decks of cards may be available for purchase at your local drug or dollar store, or at even better prices online where gaming supplies are sold. (Decks are sometimes available for free at casino cages, upon asking.)

For an eight-deck game, you'll need about forty-six decks of cards; for a six-deck game, twenty-eight decks; for a four-deck game, fourteen decks; and for double-deck, three decks. (Note: For single-deck blackjack we use another conversion method entirely since the total number of cards is a great deal smaller. A conversion strategy for single-deck blackjack is presented in Chapter 10.)

Once you have the appropriate number of decks, find a place where you can set up piles next to one another, preferably where you can study them for some time and where they won't be disturbed. Simply divide the cards into piles that increase in half-deck increments, starting with one pile of twenty-six cards. The next pile would contain one deck, or two half decks. The next pile would contain one and a half decks, or three half decks, and so on.

The eight-deck player should end up with thirteen piles ranging in size from one half deck containing twenty-six cards to a final pile containing six and a half full decks, or 338 cards. Training for double-deck would involve three piles, a half deck pile, a full deck pile (two half decks) and a pile containing a deck and half (three half decks). By the way, the reason we don't exceed six and a half decks for an eight-deck game or three-and-a-half decks for a four-deck game, and so on, is that modern day blackjack is never dealt down to the last card. So, for example, in an eight-deck game, you'll never see or have to do a division based on observing seven and a half decks (fifteen half decks) in the discard pile.

Now for some good news: Before you get too hung up on trying to estimate half decks dealt, half decks remaining, and so on, you might be pleasantly surprised to learn that something called a *conversion factor* can make the entire process of generating the correct true count a whole lot easier. Instead of estimating how many half decks have been used and then working backwards to come up with a number by which to divide the running count, our efforts are streamlined such that a quick glance at the discard pile will automatically generate a number based on pile height, to then use in converting the running count to the true count.

Conversion factors for multiple-deck games are listed in Table 7.6. Notice that they simply decrease by one with every half deck played, or every half deck increase in the discard pile. That makes sense if you think about it, because as more cards are used, we're dividing by a smaller and smaller number, which results in less of a difference between the running count and the true count. That is why so often the most advantageous situations end up occurring just prior to the shuffle.

Table 7.6: Conversion Factors for Multiple-Deck Games

	TOTAL NUMBER OF DECKS USED			
NUMBER OF HALF-DECKS IN DISCARD PILE	**2 DECKS**	**4 DECKS**	**6 DECKS**	**8 DECKS**
1	3	7	11	15
2	2	6	10	14
3	1	5	9	13
4		4	8	12
5		3	7	11
6		2	6	10
7		1	5	9
8			4	8
9			3	7
10			2	6
11				5
12				4
13				3
14				2

Depending on which game you are training for, do the following: With a Magic Marker, write the conversion factor (from Table 7.6) for each pile on a small index card, and place the card face up in front of the appropriate pile. Then begin to associate the height of each pile with the corresponding conversion factor. The goal here is to become familiar enough with each such that the actual number of half decks present becomes meaningless—your only concern is the correct conversion factor. This, surprisingly doesn't take as long as you might imagine. Leave your exhibit set up for a while, and study it periodically. Rearrange the piles and see if you can determine the correct conversion factors when the piles are not in ascending or descending order. Over time, you'll find it easier and easier to associate the height of each stack with the number written on the index card in front of it.

At this point it might be worth mentioning that, for example, two decks in the discard pile will obviously result in different conversion factors depending on whether you're sitting at a six- or eight-deck game. So, of course, you must be cognizant of how many decks are in use—something that should and will become very obvious to you in that two, four, six, and eight-decks vary so much in size, as do their respective discard trays. After some practice one glance at the discard pile—at the cards *and the tray those cards are sitting in*—should create in your mind an association that will generate the appropriate conversion factor.

Realistically, the only two games where confusion could arise, if you're not careful, are between the six- and eight-deck game. But as a serious player, you're not likely to be wasting your time playing an eight-deck game if a six-deck game exists under the same roof, or in the same city. Unless bankroll considerations force you to play the lower-minimum eight-deck games, in which case you won't be switching back and forth anyway. And four-deck games are such unique animals that they usually exist at all tables everywhere, or not at all. In other words, the message here is that a little bit of training for the game you intend on playing, or that exists at the casino destination you're heading to, goes a long way. And the difference in conversion factors between, say, the two- and six-deck games in a locale like Las Vegas is so vastly obvious and different, that confusion between the two isn't likely to happen.

By the way, if you should happen to see the likes of eleven half decks in the discard tray of a six-deck game, consider yourself lucky to have found a table with such good penetration. Enjoy it while you can. It may be the only time in your blackjack career when at a six-deck game the running count and the true count are one and the same.

Figure 7.1, on the next page, contains several illustrations showing discard trays, number of decks remaining as a result of the number of cards in the discard pile, and the correct conversion factors. Study these examples for a while to ensure that you thoroughly understand this process.

Figure 7.1: The Forever-Changing Discard Pile

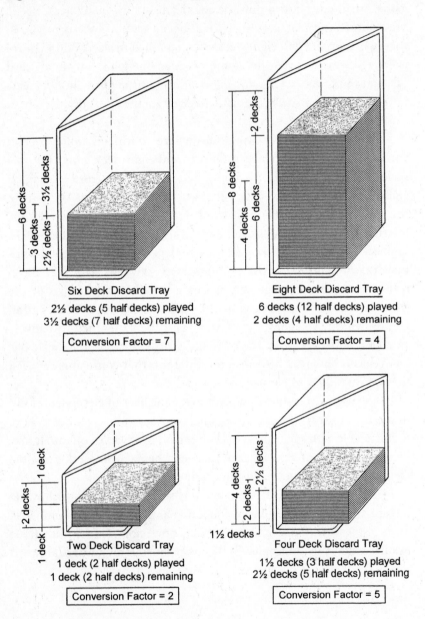

Six Deck Discard Tray
2½ decks (5 half decks) played
3½ decks (7 half decks) remaining

Conversion Factor = 7

Eight Deck Discard Tray
6 decks (12 half decks) played
2 decks (4 half decks) remaining

Conversion Factor = 4

Two Deck Discard Tray
1 deck (2 half decks) played
1 deck (2 half decks) remaining

Conversion Factor = 2

Four Deck Discard Tray
1½ decks (3 half decks) played
2½ decks (5 half decks) remaining

Conversion Factor = 5

Remember that you're going through this exercise because the true count is calculated by dividing the running count by the number of half decks remaining. And the accuracy of your true count—aside from keeping an accurate running count—is based on how good you are at sizing up the discard pile.

Ace Adjustment

This is it. The final section, where we make use of all that extra work created by keeping track of aces.

Aces are extremely important cards when it comes to betting, primarily because blackjack pays 1½:1. And calculating the proper bet size involves not only knowledge of how positive or negative the remaining cards are, but also a consideration of how many aces remain. Again, back to the discard pile. Since we know there are four aces in a standard deck, we know that, for example, after two decks have been dealt, a closer look at the cards in the discard pile should reveal on average a total of eight aces. We can apply similar thinking to four, six, eight, or any number of decks, for that matter, knowing that on average one ace should appear for every thirteen cards dealt. With that in mind, here's how we'll bring into play all that dancing around we've been doing with our feet.

(Based on foot position) when fewer than the "normal" number of aces have appeared, we say that the remaining cards are "ace rich." Similarly, when more than the average number of aces appear in the quantity of cards or decks that have been dealt to that point, we say that the remaining cards are "ace poor." For every ace we are rich, we add three to the *running count* before dividing to obtain the correct true count for betting purposes. For every ace we are poor, we subtract three from the running count before dividing to obtain the correct true count for betting purposes. Later we'll get into actual betting amounts based on this information, but for now what's important is to simply become proficient at the process that gets you to the correct true count number. Remember that this calculation (adding or subtracting to or from the running count, then dividing to obtain the true count) is done only for betting purposes—and you must return to the original running count total once the "true count for betting" calculation has been made.

Rather than explaining further at this point, let's run through an example: Two decks have been dealt at a six-deck game, and your first foot is in the seven-aces-played position (toes down, heel up and to the left). With two decks in the discard pile, the "correct" number of aces dealt to this point should be eight. Since we know that only seven aces have been dealt, we conclude that the remaining cards are one ace rich. Thus, "+3" should be added to the running count before dividing to obtain the betting true count. Another example: You're playing at a four-deck game with 1½ decks in the discard tray. The first number that should pop into your head should be six—the correct or "normal" number of aces that should have appeared to this point. Meanwhile, your feet tell you that ten aces have been dealt. What is your thought process? Ten exceeds six by four. In this case four times -3 equals -12. Thus, for placing our bet on the next hand, we subtract 12 from the running count before dividing to get our true count for betting. In time, the "normal" number of aces should become almost second nature after only a glance at the discard pile, and relating that number to your foot position will instantly determine the correct ace adjustment factor.

As with everything else, practice is key. You should already have the number of decks necessary to start running through drills. Set up various discard tray amounts, and begin cycling through the foot positions as though you were keeping track of aces. Stop at some point and glance at the first discard pile, arriving at an adjustment factor. Go through the calculation, and then move on to another foot position and repeat the processes again, this time using the second discard pile. Then do it again and again and again, each time moving to a different discard pile.

Lots to learn—I know, but nothing that the human mind can't manage with practice. What was said at the top of this chapter is probably worth repeating here. Those looking to obtain every last iota of an advantage shouldn't be put off by the idea that mastering a higher-level system requires a good deal of practice. Followed by more practice.

Summary

Is your head spinning yet? If you answered "yes" you're not alone. But at least you've made it to the end. And I guarantee that learning the entire process isn't as hard as it seems, once you become a little more familiar with each subprocess. Again, determination and practice are probably the two key ingredients needed at this point, and I'm guessing you've heard me mention the latter at least once or twice before.

In this last section let's briefly examine how all this information ties together, and the sequence in which all counts, decisions, and calculations should take place.

Take a look at the flow chart presented in Figure 7.2, on the next page. Notice how playing strategy and betting strategy involve two different procedures that feed off of the central process. Notice, too, how and where both strategies interface. Consider the running count and then the conversion to a true count as the "core process." From the core process we are then able to make more advantageous playing and betting decisions depending on where we are in the overall sequence. Playing decisions based on the true count are known as deviations from Basic Strategy, and are presented in Chapter Eight. A betting strategy dependent on the true count and other important factors, such as bankroll and the level of risk you are willing to embrace, is covered in Chapter Nine.

Figure 7.2: A Flow Chart of the Entire Process

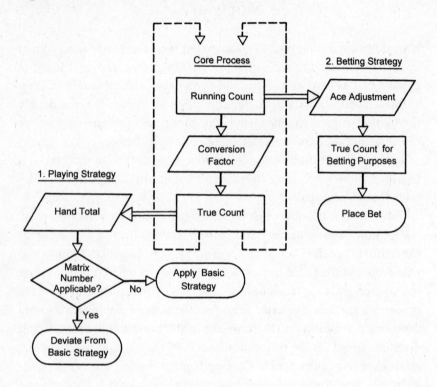

CHAPTER EIGHT

Deviations from Basic Strategy

The Tables

Remember Basic Strategy? That was the hundred and fifty or so best ways to play each hand that you committed to memory back in Chapter Four. Well, some of those situations are about to surface again. Now that we know how to calculate a true count that tells us something about content, doesn't it make sense that those original Basic Strategy decisions could probably be fine tuned a little to account for positive or negative conditions in those cards that remain? These refinements are called "deviations from Basic Strategy." And they're made based on a set of indices (or matrix numbers) relating Basic Strategy to the true count. In other words, for every Basic Strategy decision that exists, computer simulations have also figured out when the opposite action (e.g., hitting instead of standing, or standing instead of hitting) becomes the more advantageous move based on the content of the remaining cards.

I used Casino Vérité®, developed by Norm Wattenberger and widely recognized as one of the leading blackjack software packages, to simulate billions of hands over several days and generate the indices found in Appendix One (for the High-Low) and Appendix Two (for the Uston APC). The numbers in each table indicate at what true count the player should deviate from Basic Strategy.

The above is best shown by example. Suppose you use the High-Low and are dealt a 12 against a dealer's 3, with a true count of +4. Basic Strategy says to hit this hand. But remember that our true count is +4. That has relevance now, especially since the matrix number corresponding to this situation happens to be +2 as shown in the hitting and standing table of Appendix One. In this case, since +4 meets or exceeds the matrix number for this situation (a player's total of 12 against a dealer's upcard of 3), the player should deviate from Basic Strategy, or "stand," as oppose to hitting. "Behind the scenes" we are standing because based on the true count, or based on the content of the remaining cards, computer simulation has proven that we are more likely to win from the result of a dealer bust, than to win from improving our hand by drawing another card.

At times the reverse logic applies, where we are improving our chances of winning a hand by hitting instead of standing. Consider a player total of 12 again, only this time you're a counter using the Uston APC and the dealer is showing a 4 instead of a 3. Now Basic Strategy says to stand. However, let's suppose that this time the true count is -2. From Appendix Two, the matrix number for a 12 against a dealer's 4 is zero, meaning that for any true count below zero (or any negative running count), the correct strategy is to hit instead of stand. We hit this 12 against a dealer's 4 for essentially the same reason that we stood in the previous example. We improve our chances of winning the hand by drawing another card rather than by standing—even if that means, in this case, risking the chance of busting.

But does this mean there are another 200 or so matrix numbers to commit to memory?

Not exactly. In 1986, renowned blackjack expert and author Don Schlesinger published a groundbreaking article in *Blackjack Forum* that forever changed the quantity of matrix numbers applicable to multiple-deck games. Don's research revealed that of all the numbers comprising a typical numbers matrix (about 150–200 numbers), the amount of gain realized from the vast majority of these deviations contributes very little to the overall gain offered by the entire matrix. In simpler terms, Don proved that only a select few of these deviations are actually worth memorizing. The "Illustrious 18" and the "Fab 4" (as Don himself dubbed them) are those deviations either likely to occur with some degree of regularity (due to true counts that are reached with some degree of regularity), or that have realistic monetary significance due to the amount of money wagered on those hands during which they apply (positive true counts where the player is wagering a large amount, as opposed to negative counts where the player is wagering the minimum allowable).

Tables 8.1 and 8.2 show the hands on which these departures from Basic Strategy should be made, along with what index number the true count must be less than, equal to, or exceed in order to make these departures applicable. Table 8.1 shows the "Illustrious 18" and the "Fab 4" for users of the High-Low and Table 8.2 shows the same twenty-two deviations applicable to the Uston Advanced Point Count. The numbers in each table are slightly different because the point value weights for cards in each system are different.

The deviations from Basic Strategy shown in the tables that follow should be memorized, just as Basic Strategy decisions were committed to memory back in Chapter Four.

Table 8.1: High-Low Deviations from Basic Strategy

Insurance

Take insurance if the true count is +3 or higher

Hitting/Standing

16 versus 10—Stand with zero or any positive (running) count
16 versus 9—Stand if the true count is +5 or higher
15 versus 10—Stand if the true count is +4 or higher
13 versus 2—Hit with any negative (running) count
13 versus 3—Hit if the true count is less than -1
12 versus 2—Stand if the true count is +4 or higher
12 versus 3—Stand if the true count is +2 or higher
12 versus 4—Hit with any negative (running) count
12 versus 5—Hit if the true count is less than -1
12 versus 6—Hit with any negative (running) count

Doubling Down

11 versus Ace—Double down if the true count is +1 or higher
10 versus Ace—Double down if the true count is +4 or higher
10 versus 10—Double down if the true count is +4 or higher
9 versus 7—Double down if the true count is +4 or higher
9 versus 2—Double down if the true count is +1 or higher

Splitting Pairs

10, 10 versus 6—Split if the true count is +5 or higher
10, 10 versus 5—Split if the true count is +5 or higher

Surrender

15 versus Ace—Surrender if the true count is +1 or higher
15 versus 10—Surrender with zero or any positive (running) count
15 versus 9—Surrender if the true count is +2 or higher
14 versus 10—Surrender if the true count is +3 or higher

As you gain more and more experience, it should become apparent rather quickly that insurance, 16 versus 10, and 15 versus 10 (hitting/standing) are by far the most important deviations. You'll be amazed at how much value is offered by sometimes deviating on 16 versus 10 and 15 versus 10, or taking insurance at the appropriate times. I can't even begin to imagine how many thousands I've saved, for example, in situations involving two large bets prompted by a high true count—only to be confronted by a dealer's ace.

By the way, the situation just described will occur more often to the card-counter than to the normal player, because the lack of aces seen as a matter of course often prompts a larger-than-normal bet. So your exposure to dealer blackjacks in these situations also increases.

Generally, you'll find deviations from Basic Strategy will involve standing more often when the true count is positive, and hitting more often when the true count is negative. This makes sense since high cards are more likely to be dealt when the count is positive—and low cards when the count is negative.

Table 8.2: Uston APC Deviations from Basic Strategy

Insurance

Take insurance if the true count is +3 or higher

Hitting/Standing

16 versus 10—Stand with zero or any positive (running) count
16 versus 9—Stand if the true count is +6 or higher
15 versus 10—Stand if the true count is +4 or higher
13 versus 2—Hit with any negative (running) count
13 versus 3—Hit if the true count is less than -1
12 versus 2—Stand if the true count is +4 or higher
12 versus 3—Stand if the true count is +2 or higher
12 versus 4—Hit with any negative (running) count
12 versus 5—Hit if the true count is less than -1
12 versus 6—Hit with any negative (running) count

Doubling Down

11 versus Ace—Double down if the true count is +1 or higher
10 versus Ace—Double down if the true count is +5 or higher
10 versus 10—Double down if the true count is +5 or higher
9 versus 7—Double down if the true count is +5 or higher
9 versus 2—Double down if the true count is +1 or higher

Splitting Pairs

10, 10 versus 6—Split if the true count is +6 or higher
10, 10 versus 5—Split if the true count is +6 or higher

Surrender

15 versus Ace—Surrender if the true count is +2 or higher
15 versus 10—Surrender with zero or any positive (running) count
15 versus 9—Surrender if the true count is +3 or higher
14 versus 10—Surrender if the true count is +3 or higher

As you learn these numbers, keep in mind that what you're memorizing is a number that the true count is ultimately compared against—to determine if deviating from Basic Strategy is advantageous. This, by nature, means that—just as with Basic Strategy—deviations will sometimes not work out to your advantage. Or, for example, a certain deviation may be beneficial only fifty-two out of every 100 times, with Basic Strategy being the better move forty-eight out of 100 times. But deviating in this case will account for two more wins (and two fewer losses), so deviating represents an advantageous move to make each and every time the situation arises.

Deviations to Reconsider, and Those to Handle with Care

Unfortunately, playing in a certain way can (will) mark you as an advantage player, which is something the card counter needs to avoid under all circumstances. Making some deviations to Basic Strategy has "card counter" written all over it. For that reason, a trade-off between "benefit now" (in a play-of-the-hand sense) and "benefit later" (in a longevity sense) has to be considered and weighed accordingly. Let's take a few of what arguably are the more controversial or attention-grabbing deviations and examine them in more detail.

Splitting 10s

Although it is absolutely to your advantage to split 10s if the true count meets or exceeds the numbers specified in the tables, I would highly recommend always ignoring this deviation and settling for 20. Splitting 10s simply draws too much heat from the pit—heat extremely detrimental to your longevity as a card counter.

Ironically, splitting 10s is widely recognized as one of the most foolish moves a player can make. Of course, under the right circumstance, that isn't so. But 99.9 percent of the blackjack-playing population doesn't know that, believing it's unadulterated suicide each and every time. And from the casino's perspective, if you're not an idiot, then you must know what you're doing. So splitting 10s essentially comes down to this: card counter or fool? And believe me, once they're watching you, it won't take them long to figure out you're not the latter. So forget about splitting 10s. It's simply not worth the risk.

The only possible way for this move to be viewed as normal (or typical of your style of play) is for you to split 10s each and every time, which brings us right back again to the idea of blackjack suicide. So, you see, there's really no way to successfully implement this deviation—which is sad, because the opportunity to do so with an advantage does arise from time to time, especially with larger amounts on the table.

Deviations Involving 12

Another interesting group of deviations is 12s against a dealer's 5 or 6. To the general blackjack-playing population, this is a no-brainer—an obvious stand without even a second thought. But then you come along, and after playing "smart blackjack" for a shoe and a half, suddenly decide to hit a stiff with the dealer showing a 6 up. What gives?

Sometimes this deviation draws unnecessary attention as well. More often than not, however, you should have a minimum-unit bet out on the table because the deviation occurs only with a negative true count. Nevertheless, it's not what others are expecting from a solid player like you. And if you draw the card that would have otherwise made the dealer bust, it might be prudent to have some silly premonition-based excuse ready to roll.

Drawing on 12 against 5 or 6 is one move where you should assess the situation beforehand, if possible. Are you being watched by the floorperson? Will the other players start complaining (and attract the pit) if you deviate and the dealer's total doesn't work out to everyone's benefit? With a minimum bet on the table, is doing the opposite of Basic Strategy in any way jeopardizing longevity? I'm not saying *not* to deviate in this case—just that at certain times it might be beneficial to consider the potential for long-term negative consequences.

Standing on 15 or 16 against a Dealer's 10

A player who deviates by standing on a 15 or 16 versus a dealer's 10 may come across to the pit like a person reluctant to draw a card and bust, which is somewhat common among less-experienced players. To give that impression would be a good thing. However, if you're viewed as knowledgeable to begin with, and then suddenly stop drawing on 15s and 16s with coincidentally a maximum bet on the table, then you may want to think twice about how long you plan to stay at that table, or in that casino. The message here is that *something* has to give. *These deviations are far too important not to exercise, so the only alternative may be to limit the number of times they're made under one roof.*

Surrender

Surrender is an option that is either overdone by a player who doesn't know better, or is never done because the normal player either isn't educated as to the correct time to take advantage of this option, or isn't aware that it's even offered. And then there are the card counters, who know precisely when to air out not only the four Basic Strategy surrenders, but the surrenders that are actually deviations from Basic.

Deviations involving surrender, in terms of heat or visibility, fall somewhere between splitting 10s and drawing on a Hard 12 against a 5 or 6. Surrendering is definitely a noteworthy move, and will be especially interesting to casino personnel if the more unusual surrenders (e.g., those representing deviations from Basic Strategy) always seem to occur only with larger-than-normal bets on the table. Obviously, these surrenders represent more "handle with care" deviations. The message here is to certainly exercise these moves if able to do so, but do so with your antennae up and roving. Two shoes of big-bet-making-surrenders (like 14 versus 10 or 15 versus 9) that end up with lots of take-backs might call for moving on to another house before the dealer can say "checks play."

Closing Remarks

Deviating from Basic Strategy will increase earnings, which makes the whole effort worth its while. Just use this tactic with caution, knowing that a deviation is sometimes one of the telltale factors that can identify you as an advantage player. That said, there's nothing sweeter than a total of 15 with a maximum bet on the table that turns into a dealer bust—especially when the dealer's jack-draw should've been yours.

For those games where the dealer draws on Soft 17, using the indices presented in this chapter (and/or those that appear in Appendix Two and Appendix Three) will result in a small sacrifice in overall expectation, but certainly not enough to recommend learning a new set of numbers. Those indices might contain a few decisions where the correct number is slightly different—perhaps one integer more or less. But remember that you're only comparing the true count to the appropriate index number. That means only a minute percentage of the time (when the true count happens to fall between both numbers) would the resulting action based on a table derived specifically for "dealer hits Soft 17" suggest the opposite action.

Deviations from Basic Strategy are valuable, but proper bet variation as outlined in the next chapter is of even greater significance—that and finding a good game with favorable rules and good penetration.

CHAPTER NINE

Betting Strategy

Becoming a proficient card counter involves a lot more than simply learning to count cards and then just sitting down at a table and playing without some kind of larger financial plan. Betting amounts, bankroll considerations, and risk of ruin must be carefully considered. All are closely related, and come together in this chapter under one very important title: Betting Strategy.

This chapter is the true dollars-and-cents part of the process, and in many ways is one of the most interesting aspects of advantage blackjack play. Betting according to the true count requires adherence to predetermined betting levels that go up with an increase in advantage and drop as your advantage declines. But betting levels have to be chosen carefully, with the two most important considerations being overall bankroll versus hourly expectation. Unfortunately, these components are more than just distantly related. The more conservative you are with one, the more you will have to give up with the other. For example, a tight approach with regard to overall ruin avoidance will result in a somewhat compromised hourly rate. On the other hand, choose an elevated rate of return and you're sure to be looking at a higher probability of losing your entire bankroll. Finding an acceptable balance is the key, and depends to a large extent on your personal philosophies regarding time, money, and risk management.

Element of Ruin

Let's start with an analysis of ruin. Your element of ruin is the likelihood expressed in percent of losing your entire bankroll, given your advantage over the house and the size of your bets. For starters consider two players, Kristen and Susan, sitting at a blackjack table, each playing with the same positive expectation (1.5 percent) and each with a bankroll of $10,000. Kristen bets an average of $100 per hand, while Susan bets an average of $10 per hand. Who is more likely to make a healthy chunk of change in the course of a few hours? Which player is at a higher risk of losing her entire bankroll?

Though an overly simplistic example, its obvious answers are that Kristen is more likely to do both. A positive run of cards will result in a much larger win for Kristen, but with a negative run of cards Kristen will find herself heading west on I-15 a lot sooner than Susan will. And although Susan stands to win less with a favorable run of cards, she also will lose less if the run of cards happens to be unfavorable. Although both players are playing at the same game and with the same positive expectation, the price Kristen pays for the potential of winning much more money is a much higher likelihood of ruin.

Most card counters favor a pretty low chance of losing their entire bankroll, and let risk of ruin act as the driving force when determining betting strategy, rather than earnings potential alone. Five percent is a popular element of ruin percentage, and is what I use when putting together a bank and determining bet size. A 5 percent risk of ruin means you have a 5 percent chance of losing your entire bank. In terms of dollars and cents, that means you'll turn a bankroll like $10,000 into some other total on average nineteen out of twenty times, and once during that span of time you'll expect to kiss ten grand goodbye.

Player Advantage

In Chapter Eight we learned how to strengthen our playing strategy by deviating from Basic Strategy, based on the true count. Now it's time to determine a correct betting strategy—once again dependent on the true count. Keep in mind that betting strategy is even more important than playing strategy, especially for multiple-deck games.

With every point increase in the true count, the player's advantage increases on average by about 0.5 percent. (This is the case for many, but not all card counting methods.) The actual percent varies because the number of decks remaining at any given point in time is a variable. Nevertheless, the rate of increase grows ever so slightly as the true count elevates. Since players are at somewhat of a disadvantage following the shuffle (due to rules and number of decks in use), it's not until the true count reaches a little higher than +1 that with most systems, we begin playing about even with the house. At a true 3, the card counter has about a 1.0 percent advantage. At a true 5, it's almost 2 percent. At a true 7, it's about 3 percent—a greater advantage than even the casino has over players at the single-zero roulette wheel. At a true 9, it's a whopping 4 percent, and so on.

What does a 1.0 percent advantage mean with a true count of +3? For one thing, it means you're playing at a positive expectation that very hand, which means a hypothetical collective tabulation of all the bets you ever make at that advantage level should equal about 101 percent of the total amount wagered.

Figure 9.1 illustrates the relationship between player advantage/disadvantage and the true count. Notice how player advantage increases at a slightly greater rate as the true count gets increasingly positive.

Figure 9.1: True Count Versus Player Advantage/Disadvantage

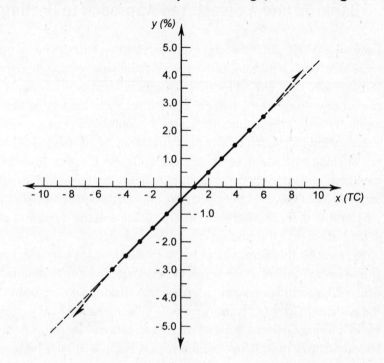

So, you see, at the core of the entire process is the simple principle of betting more when we have the advantage, like at a true count of +3 or more, and less or the minimum allowable when we don't. That's because we're more likely to win a hand as our advantage over the house increases, so our wagers increase accordingly to get the largest "bang for our buck." But even at highly elevated true counts, we can't bet too much because it's essential to always stay within an acceptable element of ruin percentage. So we walk a fine line—and size our bets accordingly. With an adequate bankroll and a structured betting scheme, we'll bet more when we have an advantage and less or the minimum allowable when we don't—and all the while embrace only a 5 percent chance of going belly-up.

Bankroll and a Structured Approach to Betting

Following are six tables that show different betting schemes based on in-creasingly larger bankrolls, starting with $2,000 and escalating right up through $100,000. The tables all show wagers based on true counts that correspond to about a 5 percent element of ruin. Each table shows a range of positive true counts, the amount in dollars you can wager while staying within a 5 percent element of ruin, and the corresponding num-ber of chips (red, green, black, or purple) in which to bet. Rather than memorize a betting scheme or attempt to figure out how much to bet af-ter every hand based on the last true count calculation, we simply find a relationship that exists between the true count and the *number* of chips to bet, rather than the amount (in dollars and cents).

Remember: think units as much as possible. $1,375 isn't $1,375 until you've cashed out and gone home, or better yet after you've doubled the bank and are sitting on some tropical beach soaking up the sunshine. In the trenches, $1,375 is 275 units if you're playing nickels and 55 units if you're playing quarters. With all there is to concentrate on while at the tables, this way of looking at money most easily facilitates betting the correct amount.

$2,000 Bank

This bankroll essentially represents the minimum amount needed to launch a structured attack on the game. With a bank of this size, we're limited to $5 minimum tables, with our true count betting sized to nickel chips.

Table 9.1 outlines a betting scheme. Our first bet with a True 3 should equal about $8. To keep things simple, we can round that up to $10, which equals two $5 chips. Notice that the "number of chips" column generally equals a number one less than the corresponding true count. Therefore, for this bankroll and unit size, we bet the true count minus one, in nickels.

Modus Operandi: "Bet the true count minus one, in red."

Table 9.1: $2,000 Bankroll

TRUE COUNT	AMOUNT	NO. OF CHIPS
3	8	2
4	13	3
5	18	4
6	26	5
7	31	6
8	36	7
9	44	9
10	53	10
11	57	11
12	63	12

On negative counts and trues below +3, bet the minimum allowable, which would be $5 per hand. That may pose somewhat of a problem in areas where casinos don't always offer $5 tables, in which case, you may be forced to play during less-popular hours like late morning or early afternoon.

$5,000 Bank

With a bank of this size we're still playing with nickels, but unlike with the previous bank we're able to play at $10 tables, which gives us a little more flexibility.

Table 9.2, on the next page, outlines our betting scheme. The "number of chips" column for this-size bank is a little more difficult to summarize than the tidy relationship found for many of the other bankrolls. However, do notice that the betting amount (not the "number of chips" column) for this particular scheme can be loosely tied to the true count times 10, at least the first five bets. Thus for a true 3, we bet $30; a true 4,

$40; a true 5, $50; and so on up to true 7, at which we wager $70. Then at a true count of +8 and above, we can summarize the relationship by citing that the amount to bet roughly approximates half the true count—only now in green chips, or quarters. Though this scheme is a little more complicated than most, it remains of utmost importance that we never compromise our 5 percent risk of ruin by over betting. This is accomplished by siding on the conservative, which we do for the majority of true counts listed in the table.

Modus Operandi: "Bet the true count times 10 up to +7,
or bet $30 with a true 3, $40 with a true 4, and so on.
Then bet half the true in green, at counts of +8 and above,
rounding down to side on the conservative."

Table 9.2: $5,000 Bankroll

TRUE COUNT	AMOUNT	NO. OF CHIPS
3	20	
4	33	
5	45	
6	67	
7	77	
8	91	4
9	111	4
10	132	5
11	143	5
12	156	6

On negative counts bet the minimum allowable. On positive counts below a true 3, fluctuate between the table minimum and perhaps one unit greater (to avoid flatlining the table minimum).

$10,000 Bank

With this bankroll we're playing at the quarter level. Thus, in Table 9.3, below, the "number of chips" column pertains to green from beginning to end.

Playing $25 per hand guarantees us a game in every casino. Notice that the number of quarters generally equals a number one fewer than the corresponding true count. Therefore, we always bet the true count minus one, in quarters. This scheme is virtually identical to the one presented above for a bankroll of $2,000, only now our base bet is $25 per hand instead of $5.

Modus Operandi: "Bet the true count minus one, in green."

Table 9.3: $10,000 Bankroll

TRUE COUNT	AMOUNT	NO. OF CHIPS
3	40	2
4	60	2
5	90	3
6	125	5
7	160	6
8	190	7
9	210	8
10	260	10
11	300	12
12	325	13

On negative counts bet the minimum allowable, which would be $25. A $50 minimum table should be avoided in that $50 represents the same amount we would bet with a True 3. On lesser positive counts, a once-in-a-while wager of two units may be made for cover purposes, if necessary.

$20,000 Bank

At this level, our base bet should still be in green. But as with the $5,000 bankroll, the upper bets will have to involve a higher-denomination chip in order to avoid building a mini Stratosphere right on the table layout. The "number of chips" column pertains to black, except for the first two levels. This level of play and up will require a good cover act, because you *will* be heavily scrutinized.

Bet the true count in green for +3 and +4. Then notice, as shown in Table 9.4, that the "number of chips" relationship can be expressed in many instances as the true count divided by two. For simplicity, you can round down for all odd-numbered true counts to bet only with black, or in the instance of higher odd-numbered trues like +9, you can add two greens to "half the true in black" for a more exacting total of $450.

Modus Operandi: "Bet the true count in green for +3 and +4.
Then bet half the true in black, rounding down or
adding a few greens when desirable."

Table 9.4: $20,000 Bankroll

TRUE COUNT	AMOUNT	NO. OF CHIPS
3	83	
4	133	
5	182	2
6	267	3
7	338	3
8	364	4
9	444	5
10	526	5
11	571	6
12	625	6

As should always be the case, on negative counts bet the minimum allowable. For cover purposes, fluctuate some on positive trues below +3.

$40,000 Bank

With a $40,000 bank, our minimum bet is $200 or more per hand when we have the advantage. Since this is four times a $10,000 bank, the progression will be somewhat similar to that shown in Table 9.3, only this time in black. It almost goes without saying that this level of play will require a tremendous amount of cover.

Table 9.5 illustrates that the "number of chips" column roughly lags along at one less than the true count. Thus, we use what by now should be a familiar correlation.

Modus Operandi: "Bet the true count minus one, in black."

Table 9.5: $40,000 Bankroll

TRUE COUNT	AMOUNT	NO. OF CHIPS
3	166	2
4	267	3
5	364	4
6	533	5
7	615	6
8	727	7
9	889	9
10	1053	10
11	1143	12
12	1250	13

On negative counts bet the minimum allowable, which would be $100 per hand at a $100 minimum table. Remember, doing whatever necessary to appear like just another player is of utmost importance if playing to a bank of this size.

$100,000 Bank

With this bank, we can wager $500 or more per hand when we've got an advantage, and still remain within a 5 percent element of ruin by following the scale outlined in Table 9.6. This betting level will require the ultimate level of cover, and even then you will likely not remain under the radar indefinitely.

The "number of chips" column in Table 9.6 shows the number of purple chips that may be bet corresponding to the normal range of true counts. The correlation is one we've used before: bet half the true count, rounding down where necessary to remain conservative.

Modus Operandi: "Bet the true count divided by two in purple, rounding down where necessary or adding a few black when desirable."

Table 9.6: $100,000 Bankroll

TRUE COUNT	AMOUNT	NO. OF CHIPS
3	417	1
4	667	1
5	909	2
6	1333	3
7	1538	3
8	1818	4
9	2222	4
10	2632	5
11	2857	6
12	3125	7

On negative counts and those positive trues below 3, get down as low as possible by betting black. As usual, do whatever is necessary to appear like just another big player in town for a few days to throw around a boatload of money.

Generally, the $2,000 and $5,000 bankrolls apply to nickel bettors, the $10,000 and $20,000 banks to those of you playing at the quarter level, the $40,000 bank to the black-chip player, and the $100,000 bank for the counter playing at the $500 level.

In many cases we've rounded down in an effort to side on the conservative—a good practice because the negative swings, when they occur, can be brutal. And there's really no other way to thwart the ravaging effects of a negative swing than to go into it holding your chips close to the vest. It's absolutely possible to learn an advanced count and play at a proficient level—only to lose in the end because your capital wasn't sufficient, or you over-bet your bankroll and fell victim to a negative statistical fluctuation. Over-betting and/or being under capitalized is perhaps the number one reason for failure among rookie card counters. Thus the importance of a correct betting strategy, which means siding on the conservative whenever possible.

As a final note, take your minimum bets seriously. And by that I mean pay close attention to the amount of time you flatline the table minimum. This especially applies following an elevated true count when the opportunity to bet substantial amounts has come and gone. The last thing you want to do is end a shoe at $600 per hand and then flatline one green for the next half hour. "Normal players" with bankrolls that can support putting out $600 on one hand simply don't spend the entire next shoe flatlining the table minimum. Cover betting will be discussed in a lot more detail in Chapter 13, and is a vital element of player camouflage, especially for those betting quarters and up.

Great Expectations

How fun is this—a section dedicated to figuring out how much money you stand to make?

To calculate our earnings expectation per hour, we use the following three parameters. Keep in mind that this is a mathematical equation, which, for our purposes, represents a theoretical result. Our real-world results will vary from what is calculated here thanks to what mathematicians call the *standard deviation*.

The parameters:

- Our percent advantage over the house

- The number of hands per hour over which this advantage applies

- Our average bet per hand

Let's summarize each to make sure we're on the same page, because in some cases there's a tendency to overestimate, which will do nothing but leave you wondering why you're not making as much as the mathematics says you should be.

1. Percent Advantage: Expect to achieve about a 1.5 percent advantage over the house, give or take a little, depending on which method you use. In reality, some cover moves such as not splitting 10s when advantageous, or an unfavorable rule variation, or poor penetration, will cost the player some expected value. Though some experts claim an advantage as high as 2 percent can be achieved over the long run, we'll err on the side of conservatism here, and go with 1.5 percent.

2. Number of hands per hour: Casinos are crowded these days, which means tables are usually full of players. As would be expected, that decreases the number of hands per hour dealt. And during those times when casinos are traditionally empty (like 4:00 A.M. on a Wednesday morning in January), gone are the days of several dealers standing around waiting for you to open a new game, or perhaps dealing to only one other player. That scenario doesn't go well with management trying to

throttle a work force more efficiently. That's unfortunate, because with fewer players you're guaranteed more hands per hour. And with a positive expectation, more hands per hour means more money earned.

Figure 100 hands per hour as an average, taking into consideration both swing shift on a Saturday night at a bustling casino like Mohegan Sun, and graveyard early on a Wednesday morning at some casino in Wendover. Let's also assume that as your experience grows, you'll become less and less willing to involve yourself in games dealt at an unprofitably slow pace.

3. Average bet per hand: For the purposes of this calculation, our average bet per hand can be estimated as roughly twice your minimum bet. In other words, playing nickels at a $5 minimum table will result in a $10 average bet per hand. With a $10 minimum bet, figure $20. At a $25 minimum table, figure $50—and so on up the ladder. This takes into account the preponderance of minimum bets made when counts are negative or only slightly positive, and the proportionately less frequent but much larger wagers made with increasingly higher true counts.

To figure our hourly expectation, we simply multiply the three variables listed above. Let's consider a few hourly expectations, just to make sure you get the idea.

A $5 player betting an average of $10 per hand at 100 hands per hour with a positive expectation of 1.5 percent would be expected to make $15 per hour ($10 \times 100 \times 0.015 = 15$).

A $25 player betting an average of $50 per hand at 100 hands per hour with a positive expectation of 1.5 percent would be expected to make $75 per hour ($50 \times 100 \times 0.015 = 75$).

A $100 player betting an average of $200 per hand at 100 hands per hour with a positive expectation of 1.5 percent would be expected to make $300 per hour (200 × 100 × 0.015 = 300).

I'll let you figure out the hourly rate for someone playing purple. Let the product of that equation serve as inspiration.

As with converting the running count to a true count, earnings expectation amounts to a function. Multiply percent advantage by hands per hour by average bet and the product is what you should expect to make per hour over the long run. Or multiply that answer by the number of hours you've played and you can get a ballpark figure as to how much you should be winning. Keep in mind that these three parameters are closely related. Increase your bet spread but slow down the number of hands per hour, and you haven't done much to increase your bottom line. Likewise, find a dealer who deals at the speed of light—but then make all kinds of mistakes—and again nothing has been accomplished. In fact, you've probably lowered your bottom line. As Don Schlesinger advises in *Blackjack Attack,* the product of the above functions is all that matters if evaluating a game from a financial perspective. Let's see what Don means, by doing one last series of calculations—at the quarter level—to illustrate just how much the product can change based on a whole different set of inputs.

Scenario: You're sitting at a table in a casino in downtown Reno, after jumping in and out of various houses along Virginia Street all night long. It's not late for a Saturday night by most people's standards, but you've been playing for hours already. Your head is spinning, but you're just now coming back from what was a difficult day at the tables . . .

Did I just make a mistake? Am I getting tired? [Translation: The 1.5% advantage has dropped to 1.3%, and in fact has been at that level for quite some time.] And I'm playing on a Saturday night at a full table? How did that happen? [Translation: One hundred hands per hour? Never in a million years. Try sixty.] And did you notice the phone ringing at the podium after that last series of large bets I *won at the end of the last shoe? Could they suspect I'm a counter? It might make sense to make one or two big bets right off the top of this next shoe, just to lessen the suspicion some. [Translation: the 1.3 percent advantage drops further, to 1.25 percent.] I know it's mathematically not a profitable move, but I'd better start trying to throw them off, otherwise my playing days may be in jeopardy. Or maybe I shouldn't max out at $325 per hand with a True 12? Maybe I should back down to $250? [Translation: My average bet now is down to $45 per hand.]*

What does our hourly rate equation look like for this scenario?

A $25 player betting an average of $45 per hand at sixty hands per hour with a positive expectation of 1.25 percent would be expected to make $34 per hour. ($45 \times 60 \times 0.0125 = 34$)

Quite a difference from what we figured earlier, isn't it?

Optimal Betting and Other Approaches

Some pros hedge against losing their entire bank by recalculating a betting scheme if they find themselves down some percentage of their original bank. In other words, a betting scheme that corresponds to a 5 percent risk of ruin with a $5,000 bank may be recalculated and as a result downsized if, let's say, the counter finds he is down $2,500 at some point in time. The obvious benefit of hedging is that you've further lowered your risk of ruin to well below that of 5 percent.

But, not surprisingly, nothing in life is free, and hedging in this manner is no exception. What results? Two interesting by-products: The first is that the recalculated bet sizes will be smaller than the original bets sized to the $5,000 bank. Thus the player must win, in effect, twice as much going forward (twice the rate, not twice as much in dollars) in order to get back to even. The second is that dropping $2,500 from a starting point of $5,000 will occur at a much higher frequency than will losing the whole $5,000, because the path to profit will sometimes dip to a level below -$2,500 but remain greater than -$5,000 before recovering and eventually going positive. The 5 percent element of ruin here means that you'll lose $5,000 5 percent of the time, which means you'll lose some amount less than $5,000 some greater percentage of the time.

Taking this concept even further, a form of "continuous" hedging is betting according to what's called the *Kelly Criterion*. Kelly betting is a method of placing bets in direct proportion to your advantage over the house, based on your bankroll size at the time the bet is being placed. Thus, Kelly betting ensures in theory that you can never tap out, because bets will rise and fall in proportion to what funds are available. But Kelly betting surprisingly (or not so surprisingly, if one thinks about it for a moment) ends up producing huge bankroll fluctuations—too great, in fact, for it to be taken seriously. Kelly betting is extremely volatile. Yes, it certainly accelerates the upward swings, but coming down is like falling out of the sky without a parachute. Without going into it in further detail, precise Kelly betting can't be used precisely in real-world play anyway—for a number of reasons such as table minimum and maximums and often having to place at least a minimum bet when the casino has the advantage. That violates the Kelly Criterion altogether.

I'm not the biggest proponent of refinancing in this manner. I like the idea of starting with a bank and sticking to the predetermined true count betting levels—and accepting the original element of ruin percentage. Hedging seems to imply that "there's no tomorrow," or that losing a bank "just cannot happen."

But many pros still use this principle, and a viable form of it is to employ some fraction of "full" Kelly betting, such as one-half or one-quarter and include a reduction for variance. In other words, when structuring a betting scheme, a full Kelly bet with a 2 percent advantage would mean betting 2 percent of three-quarters of your bankroll. For a $10,000 bankroll, that equates to $150. Betting one-half Kelly, however, would change that to a $75 bet, and betting one-quarter Kelly reduces it even further, to a $37.50 bet. Right away though, another problem becomes apparent involving this betting spread as it relates to a table minimum. The above assumes a $10,000 bank, and we're already down to a

$37.50 bet with a 2 percent advantage if betting one-quarter Kelly. What would be the bet corresponding to a 1 percent edge with only a $2,000 bank using one-quarter Kelly? Or better yet, what would the corresponding *minimum* bet have to be when playing with no advantage or with a disadvantage, such as with a negative count? Thus, fractional Kelly presents some problems for limited bankrolls. But even with minimal funds, you have to start somewhere. *And if a 5 percent risk of ruin as presented earlier represents too great of a risk for you to embrace, then I would suggest moving up to a structured approach that incorporates a one-half Kelly betting scale, and recalculating after incremental swings in your bankroll.* How often you do so is up to you, but at a minimum do so with every 10 percent change, especially for a *decreasing* bankroll.

Ultimately, optimal betting ensures bets are made in proportion to your advantage over the house, and is the most precise method of proper bet sizing. Optimal betting also ensures that you're getting the most "bang for your buck," for the money you are laying on the table, more so even than the spreads shown in Tables 9.1 to 9.6. Once you are familiar with betting in accordance with the true count, and have found a betting level and bankroll size suitable to you, the most precise and optimally correct calculation of bets sized to those parameters can be generated using one of the reputable brands of blackjack software.

Another tactic that many professional-level players employ is to make their largest bet no greater than about 1% of their entire bankroll. This will also help to reduce the chance of tapping out, since it creates somewhat of a "low ceiling." Thus, with a $5,000 bank and 1% maximum bet rule, $50 represents your top bet. Your scale would then be more conservative on the high end than the scale shown in Table 9.2, for instance, where the maximum bet reaches $150 in those instances when the true count does skyrocket. This "limitation" might allow you to put out a maximum bet at a lower true count, which would build back a little in terms of hourly rate. But doing that would also create a little more statistical fluctuation—since more money is being put into action at lower true counts having a lower percent advantage over the house. This approach forces your bankroll to be pretty sizable when compared to your betting level, and for that reason can embrace a more aggressive betting scale. Some pros believe an aggressive spread like 15 or 20 to 1 is necessary to beat many multiple-deck games, since the player must play through many hands between highly advantageous situations.

Table 9.7 illustrates small minimum bets for two *relatively* large bankrolls, with a spread of 20 to 1. Betting in this fashion, the player is really minimizing the amount of money he is putting on the table during those times when the count is zero or negative, and "airing it out" when he has an advantage. This is accomplished while still betting at about the one-half Kelly level. For the $10,000 bank, getting down to that kind of minimum will require play at $5 tables, which introduces a whole host of other concerns, primarily fewer hands per hour at very crowded tables—if tables at that minimum are even offered to begin with. The $25 minimum level would require a bankroll of about $50,000. This is essentially taking a little more than Table 9.5 to a $25 game and capping your maximum at $500 to avoid a spread that would cause the overhead cameras to start smoking. Needless to say, betting like this will require a very good cover act, and *expect lots of fluctuation.*

Table 9.7: Aggressive Betting Spreads with Larger Bankrolls and Lower Minimums

TRUE COUNT	BANKROLL	
	$10,000	$50,000
0 or negative	$5	$25
1	$10	$50
2	$20	$100
3	$40	$200
4	$70	$350
5 or higher	$100	$500

The Mind Game

What are your long-term goals? How much should you win before acknowledging some formal end to a group of sessions and perhaps a beginning of a new bank? There really aren't any hard and fast rules, but generally doubling one's bank is acknowledged as a successful plateau of sorts. Turning $2,000 into $4,000 or $5,000 into $10,000 might be as good a time as any to take a break and savor a job well done.

No, you shouldn't expect to bring $2,000 to Biloxi and come home with $50,000 four days later. It just doesn't work that way, and if you've inhaled the content of this chapter, you'll understand why. You're just not going to be betting the kind of amounts with a $2,000 bankroll that will allow for a $50,000 win. But that doesn't mean you can't double your bank over some period of time, or double several banks over some longer period of time, and eventually work your way to a level of play in which 50 grand eventually becomes a realistic expectation.

So what about the money? As strange as this may seem, you might want to stop thinking of your bankroll as money as soon as you've committed to an amount. As mentioned earlier, one way to do this is to think in terms of units—until you've either doubled your investment or tapped out. You're up 63 units, not $315. You see, our goal is for the *process* of winning to become the meaningful part, with the money either won or lost (hopefully won) being an important end result only after you've removed yourself from that process. If your starting bank is $10,000, and after finding yourself up $4,000 all you can think about is that Jet Ski you want to buy, then you may not be ready for the ups and downs that are common to a 1.5 percent advantage. After only a few more hours of play, that Jet Ski could become a boogie board. Or worse yet, a life preserver. Try not to think in terms of the goods and services any winnings might buy until you've decided to take a break or end a particular group of sessions organized under some pre-allotted bankroll.

Considering the flip side for a moment: An old adage is to "gamble" only amounts that you can afford to lose. Even though we're really not gambling in the true sense of the word—because we have the advantage—this still remains a practical bit of advice. Don't scrape together some bank that, if you lose, will have a negative financial impact on food, shelter, or any other of life's recognized essentials. Remember that one in twenty means just what it means: line up twenty proficient card counters all with the same ability and betting strategy and one of them should lose his entire bankroll. What if that somebody is you? Can you handle it financially?

How about emotionally? Let's consider the emotional side of losing by returning again to the big picture of you and your first bankroll versus a 5 percent risk of ruin. Put another way, doubling nineteen out of twenty bankrolls means one of those bankrolls isn't coming back. What if it's the first one? What kind of emotion would that trigger? Would losing $5,000 at a blackjack table devastate you? If you lost your first bank, would it destroy you emotionally, or could you get back in the ring and carry on? This might be something to think about, and to consider with great care before the dealer fans that first buy-in across the table layout.

Trip Bankroll

How much should you take along on any individual trip? There's really no right or wrong answer here, assuming you view all play under one bankroll as essentially continuous. Of course, it goes without saying that you should never find yourself in a position where the count goes through the ceiling and you're without the proper funds to make the appropriate bets. An example of that is to sit down at a quarter game with only $500 to your name. After ten hands and a short run of bad cards, you're down to $200—and then the count skyrockets. Now what? Bet $200. You lose. Now what? You walk away from a true 9—the likes of which you haven't seen in almost six hours—unable to take advantage of what could have been a profitable run of cards. Instead, you're stuck $500, plus the amount you were down prior.

So the real question ends up being, how much should I take on any particular trip so that I don't end up sitting around the pool, or watching football on the lounge television, or turning around and driving home thirty-five minutes after arriving? In a sense, then, how much bankroll is needed for an individual trip is more about preserving peace-of-mind than it is about making a hardcore financial decision.

With that said, if you live in, let's say, Naperville, Illinois, and you're playing in either Elgin, Joliet, or Aurora, then tapping out and having to go home early probably isn't the worst thing in the world that could happen. You jump in your car and you're home within the hour. But you don't want to live in Naperville and tap out after only thirty-five minutes on the first day of a four-day, three-night stay in a cabin on the beautiful shores of Lake Tahoe.

For a one-day trip to the casinos, I'd recommend taking no less than 40 percent of your entire bankroll. Those of you averse to the possibility of sitting around the pool or jumping back into your car in short order might want to take half of your entire bankroll. That may seem like a lot, but remember that the negative statistical fluctuations for this game are large—larger than you can probably imagine—even after reading Chapter Fifteen. For an extended trip of a few days, or even a week, 75 percent or more of your total bankroll wouldn't be a bad business decision.

In summary, "trip ruin" probability with lesser funds available is nothing more than its own betting and banking structure, at some other risk of ruin. And risk of ruin isn't a linear function, meaning it can increase or decrease based on both available funding and number of hours played, aside from player advantage.

Session Requirements

This is merely expanding our discussion on trip bankroll to even a greater degree. Only there's no right answer as to how much money to buy in with or to have available for a particular session. The only thing that matters is placing the correctly sized bet based on the true count.

With that said, let the effort to blend in with the crowd as much as possible also be a deciding factor. Don't buy in with $2,000 at the lone $25 table in a small casino on Fremont Street in downtown Las Vegas. Try $300, buying in again in increments if necessary as time goes on. And, of course, do this only so many times. The flip side in terms of where almost any buy-in amount isn't likely to raise an eyebrow, would be a posh Strip hotel with "black action" in all directions. For the latter, virtually any reasonable buy-in amount works. If you want to blend in with the crowd, which isn't a bad idea from the perspective of trying to remain as anonymous as possible, then simply buy in for what you see other players buying in for at the table minimum at which you intend to play. Common amounts are $100 if playing nickels, $300 to $500 for quarters, and a thousand or two at a $100 table.

Ultimately, let the drive to appear like just another gambler be the deciding factor whenever considering how your betting or buying-in appears to the house. If you're down a chunk, only rebuy mid-shoe if you have the advantage on the next hand. Otherwise, switching tables or even casinos might have some value from both mental and longevity perspectives.

CHAPTER TEN

Single-Deck Blackjack

Over the course of time, single-deck blackjack has become a much less-popular form of the game. Years ago, however, it was as mainstream as the multi-deckers you see today, and at one time afforded card counters very attractive opportunities. That's not to say the single decks of today can't be beaten. It's just that the successful player of this game may have to spend some time scouting out the most attractive playing conditions.

This chapter makes several assumptions. It assumes you have already learned and mastered the multiple-deck game. It assumes you're able to keep a running count and make true count conversions without mistakes. For those of you using a level-three point count, it assumes you've mastered keeping a side count of aces and the ability to adjust the running count for betting purposes. In short, this chapter assumes that you're proficient at all aspects of multiple-deck play, and that learning single-deck is simply adding to your already extensive knowledge of the game.

Single-Deck Blackjack . . . What Is It and Where Is It?

Single-deck blackjack is so much more of a finesse game than its multiple-deck counterpart. With so many fewer cards, you'll notice greater precision and a greater ability to predict what will happen. What does that mean? It means that when you expect a 10 to be dealt, oftentimes it is. Or when you hit on 15 or 16 with a high negative count, you rarely bust. In short, you'll notice a feel you haven't felt before, mainly because the deck has much less opportunity to stray from its balanced end, or final count of zero.

But that also means positive true counts don't stay positive for long. Whereas shoe games may stay positive for an extended period, don't blink at a single-deck game—you might miss a golden opportunity. Another interesting fact is that deviations from Basic Strategy are more important at single-deck than they are at multiple-deck, where the importance of betting far outweighs the importance of correct play modification.

Imagine yourself as a player dealing with only fifty-two cards. Imagine knowing the remaining cards are extremely ace rich and spreading to four hands of $500 apiece. (An ace dealt to a player on any hand gives that player a huge advantage.) That's the kind of game that used to exist years ago. Not surprisingly, it didn't take long for casinos to become wise, which resulted in more players getting barred, a more difficult game to beat, and eventually even a decrease in the number of single-deck games available. And know those that do remain—even to this day—are watched very closely. And I mean *very* closely.

As hard as this may seem to imagine, at one time single-deck games could be found almost everywhere. Now, many of the more modern casinos don't even offer the game. If you're outside a joint that was around when the Rat Pack played Vegas, then you've got a halfway decent chance of finding a single-deck game inside. If, on the other hand, you're standing in front of a 50 percent to-scale replica of the Eiffel Tower or a one-time Mötley Crüe motorcycle, then all bets are off. As for other destinations, it's hit-and-miss nowadays, with a lot more of the latter. Nevada is fast becoming the only place to really find single-deck with some kind of consistency. Atlantic City seems like it hasn't even heard of the game, and riverboats and Indian reservations aren't known to showcase it either. In a word, it spells headaches for casino management. Not only does it attract the card counters, but you've also got to find and train people to deal and supervise it.

The irony to all of this is that the single-deck game *is* making a comeback of sorts—in a way (surprise, surprise) that's a lot less attractive to the serious player. Single-deck games that offer 6:5 for blackjack are now springing up everywhere, including places like Las Vegas and Atlantic City, to name only a couple. Why is this happening? Why is this game morphing into a more difficult game to beat right before our eyes? The problem is twofold. Number one: *supply and demand.* Casino gambling is at an all-time high right now in terms of popularity. If you don't believe me, take a stroll down the Las Vegas Strip or visit the casino nearest you on a Saturday night and I think you'll quickly agree. Casino gambling is so in vogue right now that I think the casinos know they can offer just about any type of game and *somebody* will play it. Number two: *a large portion of the blackjack-playing population simply doesn't care.* They'll play it no matter what the rules are, or what blackjack pays. The new breed of "player" doesn't take the game that seriously, or quite often doesn't realize the severity of any particular rule change. In short, the casinos are getting away with murder. Someone please tell these players that blackjack has been paid at 1½:1 since the days of Wild Bill Hickok— with that ½:1 adding up to a lot more than most people think.

So the message here is learn and play single-deck with a discriminating eye. Learn it to become an overall expert, and exploit those games that are, in fact, beatable. But make sure the rules are favorable and understand that you'll be heavily scrutinized. If you're not getting 1½:1 for blackjack, don't play it. If your "act" isn't as good as it can be, don't play. If they're not dealing to a satisfactory depth, don't play it. Get the idea? Make sure all the parameters are satisfactory before getting involved. And then when you do get into the ring know that, in essence, you're lying faceup and naked on the stage of a binocular microscope.

Penetration, Penetration, Penetration

It seems we can't get away from this idea of good penetration—even for single-deck. And, strangely enough, good penetration for the single-deck game relates to how many players are seated at the table.

For starters, casinos are forced to work within two somewhat opposing parameters. First, dealers aren't allowed to deal down to the last card, for under those conditions counters like you and I could probably play for about a year and then retire for the rest of our lives. On the flip side, casinos also don't like shuffling after every hand—even on single-deck—because in the casino business, time means money. And the more time spent shuffling, the less time available for revenue generation. So casinos are forced to strike a balance, and that balance often ends up being a single-deck game "dealt down" to somewhere between the halfway and three-quarter point, or between what amounts to twenty-six and thirty-nine cards. The more conservative houses will err towards the halfway point, while the more liberal casinos might deal out as many as forty or so cards.

But how does this relate to the number of players at the table? Well, since the dealer is working with only fifty-two cards, the number of players at a table usually dictates how many rounds are dealt. More players use up more cards per round. Which, in turn, dictates how many cards, on average, are dealt between shuffles. Add a player to an existing game and often the result is one fewer round dealt. Add two players and even fewer rounds can be expected. Of course, those players use additional cards, but unfortunately the tradeoff isn't linear. With more and more players at a single-deck game, the dealer has to be more careful about dealing too deeply into the deck, and will often shuffle rather than deal an extra hand to avoid either running out of cards or exposing the casino to a highly beatable game. In a nutshell, a single-deck game dealt down only to the halfway point, or 50 percent, should be viewed as unacceptable and avoided altogether, while a game dealt down to 60 percent of a deck or better may be viewed as playable.

In the next section, let's examine how to figure out what percentage of the deck is being used, just by noting the number of players at the table and how many rounds are dealt between shuffles. From this criterion we can determine which single-deck games might be worth playing and which aren't worth a second look.

Avoided or Exploited

The magic number representing on average how many cards are used per player per hand is 2.7. And that's the number we can use to determine whether or not a game is worth playing, based on the number of players present and the number of rounds dealt. Ultimately, our goal is to figure out what percentage of the deck is being used.

Take a look at Table 10.1, which shows the number of cards dealt on average at a single-deck game for all possible combinations of players and rounds, based on 2.7 cards dealt per player, per hand.

Table 10.1 Single-Deck Penetration

NUMBER OF PLAYERS	NUMBER OF ROUNDS								
	1	2	3	4	5	6	7	8	9
1	5.4	10.8	16.2	21.6	27	**32.4**	37.8	43.2	48.6
2	8.1	16.2	24.3	**32.4**	40.5	48.6	N/A	N/A	N/A
3	10.8	21.6	**32.4**	43.2	N/A	N/A	N/A	N/A	N/A
4	13.5	27	**40.5**	N/A	N/A	N/A	N/A	N/A	N/A
5	16.2	**32.4**	48.6	N/A	N/A	N/A	N/A	N/A	N/A
6	18.9	**37.8**	N/A	N/A	N/A	N/A	N/A	N/A	N/A
7	21.6	**43.2**	N/A	N/A	N/A	N/A	N/A	N/A	N/A

Note the numbers in bold, which represent acceptable penetration levels. It shouldn't be surprising that most entries with numerical values appear to the left of the highlighted numbers, and represent number-of-players/number-of-rounds combinations that should be avoided.

Also note that in a few cases, such as, for example, when playing heads up against the dealer or with only one other player at the table, more than one numerical entry appears to the right of the highlighted number. Some of these entries represent unrealistic penetration levels, and won't likely be found at modern-day casinos, even though in some cases enough cards remain to deal additional hands.

Let's examine the percentages. In many cases, 32.4 cards represents about 62 percent. For six and seven players, 37.8 and 43.2 equates to 73 percent and 83 percent respectively. For four players at a table, 40.5 cards translates to about 78 percent. Are all of these penetration levels likely to be found everywhere? No, unfortunately. But decent or even good penetration can be found with a little bit of persistence. The real problem is that all of the penetration percentages for one round fewer than those highlighted in Table 10.1 are unacceptable—such as, for instance, two rounds dealt to four players, or 27 cards—which equates to about 52 percent. Even worse would be only two rounds dealt to three players, or a penetration level equal to only about 42 percent.

In summary, the number of cards and even the penetration percentages are not something worth memorizing—only the acceptable number of rounds dealt given the number of players at the table, as shown in Table 10.2. Evaluating the acceptable number of rounds per number of players should be the next step for single-deck "pre-game analysis," after rules are assessed and found to be satisfactory.

Table 10.2: Acceptable Number of Rounds per Number of Players

NUMBER OF PLAYERS	NUMBER OF ROUNDS
1	6
2	4
3	3
4	3
5	2
6	2
7	2

As for what represents the best game among those that are playable? As always, heads up against the dealer or with only one other player presents the best money-making opportunity (with all else being equal), simply because the number of hands per hour is so much higher than for the equivalent amount of time spent at a single-deck table with several players. But be careful. Don't settle for an inferior game just because you're able to play more hands per hour. Keep in mind that playing a bad game quickly in no way turns it into a good one.

Single-Deck True Count Conversion

Just as we did for multiple-deck, we'll convert the running count to a true count for both betting and playing purposes. The level three players will also factor in ace adjustments as necessary, covered later in a separate section.

Since we are dealing with so many fewer cards in single deck, we divide by what fraction of a complete deck remains, or if using a multilevel point count, how many half decks remain. Wait a minute. Dividing by fractions? How cumbersome is that? Not to worry. Let's make things a lot easier by determining our fractions beforehand based on 2.7 cards per player per hand—and changing those pesky divisions to much more user-friendly multiplications. I'm not sure about you, but I much prefer the latter.

Let's run through an example, first without the prep work and then with our fractions already predetermined.

> The First Way: You're a level one player and your running count is +4. You *estimate* that about ⅔ of the deck remains, requiring that you divide +4 by ⅔. Dividing any number by ⅔ is the same as multiplying that same number by ³/₂s, so you do the multiplication because it's conceptually easier and come up with a true count of +6.

The second method requires that you memorize a bunch of conversion factors and then keep track of the number of rounds dealt, acknowledging how many players are seated at the table. For example, you're playing heads up against the dealer and it's the third round of play since the shuffle. The conversion factor, from a table of predetermined conversion factors that you've already memorized, is 1.5.

> The Second Way: You're a level one user playing heads-up, and your running count is +4 in the third round. You multiply +4 by 1.5 to end up with a true count of +6.

As you can see, both methods get you to the same product. The first method requires you to be quick on your feet when it comes to dividing or multiplying, the second that you simply keep track of how many rounds have been dealt and apply some preliminary memorization. If you'd rather do the prep work up front, then you'll find the following tables useful. Unfortunately, different numbers of players result in different conversion factors because the total number of cards dealt per round changes with each additional player. By the way, an added benefit of doing the prep work is that conversion factors also eliminate the need to continuously guesstimate what percentage of the deck remains. And if you're wondering about any adverse effects from using a constant 2.7 cards per player per hand, realize that the alternative is an estimation of how many cards remain in the form of a fraction and then performing a function on that number. We live in a world of approximations. Deviating from Basic Strategy involves only comparing the true count to another number—not matching it exactly. And for our betting strategy, we did quite a lot of rounding to determine betting levels against a 5 percent element of ruin. So exactness is relative—and using 2.7 cards per player per hand is more than exact enough for the process of determining how far into the deck we are at any given moment.

Tables 10.3 through 10.9 list the conversion factors for heads-up play right up through a full table of seven players for both the level one and level three point counts presented in this book. In several instances, conversion factors have been rounded to make each group easier to memorize. Don't be overwhelmed, for it isn't as much memorization as it seems. First and foremost, you're learning the conversion factors for either a level one or level three, but not both. Secondly, look for patterns or logical sequences or similarities. For example, conversion factors for the heads up level three game start at 0.6 and graduate by a tenth with each hand dealt, from the first hand right up through the fifth. The last two rounds are 1.3 and 2. Conversion factors for "two players level one" contain almost all 2s and 5s: 1.2, 1.5, 2.0, 2.5, and 4.5. Another easy one is the six player level three: 0.8 and 1.8. Look for any way that makes the sequence of numbers easier to memorize, and use it.

Table 10.3: Single-Deck Conversion Factors—Heads Up Play

NO. OF ROUNDS	LEVEL 1 PC	LEVEL 3 PC
1	1.1	0.6
2	1.3	0.7
3	1.5	0.8
4	1.7	0.9
5	2	1
6	2.5	1.3
7	3.5	2

Table 10.4: Single-Deck Conversion Factors—Two Players

NO. OF ROUNDS	LEVEL 1 PC	LEVEL 3 PC
1	1.2	0.6
2	1.5	0.7
3	2	1
4	2.5	1.3
5	4.5	2.3

Table 10.5: Single-Deck Conversion Factors—Three Players

NO. OF ROUNDS	LEVEL 1 PC	LEVEL 3 PC
1	1.3	0.6
2	1.7	0.9
3	2.7	1.3
4	6	3

Table 10.6: Single-Deck Conversion Factors—Four Players

NO. OF ROUNDS	LEVEL 1 PC	LEVEL 3 PC
1	1.3	0.7
2	2	1
3	4.5	2.3

Table 10.7: Single-Deck Conversion Factors—Five Players

NO. OF ROUNDS	LEVEL 1 PC	LEVEL 3 PC
1	1.5	0.7
2	2.7	1.3

Table 10.8: Single-Deck Conversion Factors—Six Players

NO. OF ROUNDS	LEVEL 1 PC	LEVEL 3 PC
1	1.5	0.8
2	3.7	1.8

Table 10.9: Single-Deck Conversion Factors—Seven Players		
NO. OF ROUNDS	LEVEL 1 PC	LEVEL 3 PC
1	1.7	0.9
2	6	3

My recommendation would be that if you do plan to explore the single-deck arena, first learn only the conversion factors for heads-up play and play involving one other player. In that case, the number of conversion factor progressions needing memorization initially becomes only two: Table 10.3 and Table 10.4. Then, if you find that a casino near you offers a beatable game, go back and learn the additional conversion factors presented in Tables 10.5 through 10.9. But remember that hands per hour is an important part of the expectation equation—especially at single-deck where shuffling occurs at a higher frequency.

Ace Adjustment (for Level Three Players)

Note: This section is for those using the level-three point count presented earlier. For those of you using a level one, please proceed to the following section entitled "Single-Deck Betting Levels."

Just as you did for the multiple-deck game, single-deck ace adjustment involves increasing or decreasing the running count accordingly—depending on the abundance or lack of aces in the remaining cards. In single-deck, obviously, we're only dealing with four, so things should be a little easier. You certainly won't be tap dancing as much as you were for the six-deck game.

Four movements—the first four as outlined in Chapter Seven:

Ace No. 1:   Toes down, heel up
Ace No. 2:   Outstep down
Ace No. 3:   Toes up, heel down
Ace No. 4:   Instep down

That's all there is to it. As for relating the number of "normal" aces to the number of cards dealt, we begin by determining how many aces, or fractions of aces, should appear on average with each hand dealt. This, of course, takes into account that there are four aces in a standard fifty-two-card deck—or that one ace should be dealt on average every thirteen cards—and also on our now-familiar knowledge that on average 2.7 cards are dealt per player per hand.

Take a look again at Table 10.1 (p. 141), specifically noting the total of twenty-seven that appears in the fifth column of the first row, corresponding to the fifth round during heads-up play against the dealer. This total happens to be only one card more than twenty-six, which represents exactly one half of a deck—the quantity of cards over which, on average, two aces should appear. Since it takes five rounds to deal out twenty-seven cards, we simply divide two by five to determine the "normal" number of aces per round for heads-up play against the dealer—in this case 0.4. We can do the same for any number of players. For four players, interestingly, 13.5 cards are dealt per round. Thus, the average number of aces that should appear after one round of play is one. If no aces are dealt, the remaining cards are one ace rich, and just as we did for multiple-deck, we add +3 to the running count before converting to obtain our true count for betting purposes. If, on the other hand, two aces are dealt in round one of this same game, then we know the remaining cards are one ace poor, and thus -3 is added to the running count before converting. The process is similar to the one we learned for multiple-deck except that, for single-deck, we keep track of how many rounds are dealt while knowing the normal number of aces that should appear per round. The difference between that product and how many aces have actually appeared is what we apply to (multiply by) our familiar ace adjustment factor of 3, in order to determine how much we should add to the running count before dividing to obtain our true count for betting.

Following is Table 10.10, opposite, which lists the "normal" number of aces that should appear each round, based on the number of players at the table. Use this as your starting point, as it already takes into account how many cards, on average, are dealt per hand.

Table 10.10: Average Number of Aces per Round	
NUMBER OF PLAYERS	**AVERAGE ACES**
1	0.4
2	0.6
3	0.8
4	1
6	1.5
7	1.7

Single-Deck Betting Levels

As mentioned earlier, if you choose to play single-deck, you'll be playing in a fishbowl. You will be scrutinized. So your act has to be a good one—correction, has to be a great one.

What can be done to decrease the amount of scrutiny? Well, we have to keep track of the cards—that's the very essence of what we're doing. Really, the only alternative is to scale down the betting some, perhaps spreading from one to four units or, at a maximum, one to six units and no more.

A decent spread is obviously still a necessity, to uphold the fundamental logic of betting more when you have the advantage and less or not at all when you don't. But we can't put out the big spreads achievable in multiple-deck games—like 12:1, 14:1, or more. It's just impossible to suddenly put that much money out onto the table and get away with it for any length of time. In fact, spread like that on single-deck and you'll be escorted to the door more quickly than you can say the words, "positive expectation."

So use the true count in the same way you would for multiple-deck, only top out at four to six units depending on circumstances such as scrutiny from pit personnel, length of time you expect to be at the table, etc. Hopefully, this will keep you below enemy radar or at a minimum buy you enough time to do some damage and move on.

Deviations for Single-Deck

I've mentioned a few times earlier how single-deck blackjack is more of a finesse game than its multiple-deck counterparts. For that reason, deviations from Basic Strategy play a somewhat more significant role. The tables below highlight a few more deviations that the single-deck player might want to add to those presented in Chapter Eight.

As we all know by now, single-deck blackjack is a unique animal. First and foremost, the game has to be offered. Second, the rules that apply shouldn't negate too much of the achievable advantage. A third point, worthy of mentioning yet again, is how closely single-deck blackjack is scrutinized. And last, but certainly not least—although not related to single-deck only but definitely applicable—the earnings potential for many variations to Basic Strategy is negligible, specifically those with very high thresholds or those that apply when betting the table minimum. For all of the above reasons, I minimized the following data in a number of ways. For example, indices for pair splitting were not considered because in some casinos doubling after splitting is allowed, while in others it isn't. That would mean having to learn two sets of numbers—for pair splitting alone—to be completely accurate in all cases. Another example is omitting some soft doubles—more specifically, those pertaining to doubling on Soft 20. Think about it for a moment: would we really want to double a Soft 20 at a single-deck game while under scrutiny? Probably not—unless your idea of a good time is getting backed off or barred. Mine isn't, so I'll pass on those as well.

A final consideration I made before presenting the data in Tables 10.11 and 10.12 (pages 152–53), is whether to present indices for single-deck or for multiple-deck. Now, you're probably asking yourself why I would ponder that in a chapter devoted specifically to single-deck. The answer lies with again considering all those parameters that must be reached for us to sit down at a single-deck game to begin with. What are we getting for our effort, and what is lost if, for example, we apply multiple-deck indices to the single-deck game? Keep in mind that if we learn the multiple-deck indices, *what we're gaining is the ability to apply these additional indices always*—no matter what game we are sitting at. As for what is lost if playing a single-deck game with multiple-deck numbers: not very much. Don't forget, the only time any specific index number would be incorrect are those few instances when the true count would fall precisely between the two.

In consideration of the above, let's go with the multiple-deck indices. Go ahead and apply these numbers to both single- and multiple-deck games. And don't lose any sleep over the slight loss in expectation—especially if you log enough time at multiple-deck games using these extra indices.

In honor of Don Schlesinger's truly landmark discovery of the "Illustrious 18," let's call these additional variations the *"Industrious 18,"* for those hard-working counters among us who want to expand their range of index numbers. Those playing single-deck games are now armed with a few more variations to apply. Meanwhile, those of you who learn these numbers but end up playing only multiple-deck not only glean a little bit more advantage, but can now sit down at a single-deck game if the opportunity ever presents itself.

These numbers again come from the tables located in Appendix One and Appendix Two, which are the result of several billion hands of simulations.

Table 10.11: The Industrious 18 for Level-One Players

Hitting/Standing

A7 versus Ace—Hit if the true count is less than +1

Hard Doubling Down

11 versus 10—Hit (don't double) if the true count is less than -4
10 versus 9—Hit (don't double) if the true count is less than -1
9 versus 5—Hit (don't double) if the true count is less than -4
9 versus 4—Hit (don't double) if the true count is less than -2
9 versus 3—Hit (don't double) with any negative (running) count
8 versus 4—Double down if the true count is +7 or higher

Soft Doubling Down

A8 versus 3—Double down if the true count is +6 or higher
A8 versus 4—Double down if the true count is +3 or higher
A8 versus 5—Double down if the true count is +2 or higher
A7 versus 2—Double down if the true count is +1 or higher
A7 versus 3—Hit (don't double) if the true count is less than -2
A5 versus 3—Double down if the true count is +5 or higher
A5 versus 4—Hit (don't double) if the true count is less than -2
A4 versus 4—Hit (don't double) with any negative (running) count
A3 versus 5—Hit (don't double) if the true count is less than -1
A2 versus 5—Hit (don't double) with any negative (running) count
A2 versus 6—Hit (don't double) if the true count is less than -1

Table 10.12: The Industrious 18 for Level-Three Players

Hitting/Standing

A7 versus Ace—Hit if the true count is less than +1

Hard Doubling Down

11 versus 10—Hit (don't double) if the true count is less than -4
10 versus 9—Hit (don't double) if the true count is less than -1

9 versus 5—Hit (don't double) if the true count is less than -5
9 versus 4—Hit (don't double) if the true count is less than -2
9 versus 3—Hit (don't double) with any negative (running) count
8 versus 4—Double down if the true count is +7 or higher

Soft Doubling Down

A8 versus 3—Double down if the true count is +6 or higher
A8 versus 4—Double down if the true count is +4 or higher
A8 versus 5—Double down if the true count is +2 or higher
A7 versus 2—Double down if the true count is +1 or higher
A7 versus 3—Hit (don't double) if the true count is less than -1
A5 versus 3—Double down if the true count is +4 or higher
A5 versus 4—Hit (don't double) if the true count is less than -1
A4 versus 4—Hit (don't double) with any negative (running) count
A3 versus 5—Hit (don't double) if the true count is less than -2
A2 versus 5—Hit (don't double) with any negative (running) count
A2 versus 6—Hit (don't double) if the true count is less than -2

Preferential Shuffling

Preferential shuffling is the practice of shuffling early during positive decks and dealing deeper or putting off the shuffle during negative decks. Sometimes this occurs without the dealer's even realizing it, as an excess of high or low cards clumped together at any point in the deck may tend to promote this "naturally." For example, if the count goes highly positive it means an excess of low cards has been dealt. But because a lot of low cards have been dealt, the dealer is probably a little farther along in the deck than usual—since a lot of low cards are typically involved in hands during which many players draw additional cards. Conversely, a lot of high cards at the beginning of a deck result in a highly negative true count—but a lot of pat hands—which means that the dealer probably has more cards remaining in his hand than he normally would at any given point during the deal. Thankfully, the negative effects of natural preferential shuffling are neither large nor continuous.

The real detriment lies with those dealers who actively look to preferentially shuffle by keeping track of the cards themselves, or by simply observing a preponderance of either high or low cards and then dealing an extra round or shuffling early, depending on which is more beneficial to the house. Obviously, this occurs only in those casinos that do not use a cut card to determine when a shuffle is warranted. In any event, beating a preferential shuffler is like trying to swim against a rip tide: it can't be done. The unknowing player, unfortunately, ends up being dealt more hands under highly negative conditions and fewer hands when he has a relatively significant advantage.

On single-deck games the astute card counter should always remain watchful for preferential shuffling. Falling victim to this practice is extremely detrimental to the bottom line, and should be avoided at all costs.

Card Eating

This technique is a finesse move that works especially well at single-deck games, and accomplishes three glowing positives simultaneously. It's best illustrated by example.

Let's say the count goes through the ceiling initially, then nose-dives into the negative. You had been out on the table with $200 a hand, and there's no way you now want to drop to a minimum bet of one $25 chip, especially with a suit now watching your every move. Spread to two hands of $50 each. That accomplishes the following, in this kind of situation. It drastically decreases the amount wagered, yet has the appearance that the amount is still significant, as it involves two hands instead of just one. Playing two hands of $50 each also has a lower risk of ruin percentage than $100 placed on one hand. And finally, and perhaps most important, two hands moves the dealer towards the shuffle point more quickly—which is always a good thing if you find yourself wallowing in the wasteland of a negative deck, wishing for the shuffle. Once in a while, a second hand might even cause the dealer to shuffle, in which case you have just invoked a player-benefiting preferential shuffle. Imagine that?

Closing Thoughts

By now it should be pretty obvious that the single-deck game is a pretty unusual animal—a finesse game requiring a different mental approach and some special handling. As with multi-deck players, the serious single-deck player is a counter who has trained specifically for the game.

Something we haven't touched on yet, but which is worthy of a mention before ending, is that single-deck is almost always dealt face down, so you'll have to count those cards in a way that, at first, will likely seem awkward or unusual—especially if you're used to only multiple-deck games. The only cards visible at first will be your own—after you pick them up—and the dealer's up card. Additional player cards coming as the result of player hits are dealt face up, and can be counted immediately. But remember to count each player's hole cards as well, which will be visible either when the player busts or at the end of the hand when his cards are spread out faceup on the table layout. Do note that a player's hole cards will end up on the table as the two cards closest to the dealer. You'll see what I mean when you observe single deck being dealt.

CHAPTER ELEVEN

Blackjack Team Play

A group of card counters with covert signals working together under-cover—who dreams this stuff up? It sounds crazy, doesn't it? Like a bunch of mad scientists plotting something loony?

Enter blackjack team play: an exciting and profitable approach that involves working together with others to substantially increase profits. In a nutshell, the members of a team either combine bankrolls and play independently or work together and employ methods that allow for dramatic betting spreads—often undetected by the casino. The end results are profits many times over what the solitary counter might expect to make over the same period of time.

Some of the more prolific blackjack teams of the past (and present) include those organized by Kenny Uston and Thomas Hyland, and the recently famous 1990s team from the Massachusetts Institute of Technology (MIT). Kenny's teams of the seventies and eighties won millions. Tommy Hyland's teams are huge and operate successfully all over the world—even to this day. The MIT team has been chronicled in Ben Mezrich's 2002 *New York Times* bestseller, *Bringing Down the House,* eventually to be released as a full-length feature film. The MIT team and a few others had a complete management structure that included outside investors, aggressive recruiting, and extensive training for all team members.

Advantages and Disadvantages

Team play has several advantages over grinding it out as a solo counter. One methodology, known as the Big Player approach, allows for a large betting spread under highly favorable situations while simultaneously disguising the fact that a card counting operation is ongoing. Another methodology involving a joint bank among all the members of a team allows a group of counters to get into the "long run" more quickly—the long run being that magical span of time somewhere beyond the hills and valleys of the short term. A combined bankroll will also produce a smaller risk of ruin—or allow larger bets—which in turn will yield a higher hourly rate. On a social level, a pleasant result of successful team play is the camaraderie that should develop among team members. It's almost inevitable, especially among a group of people with the same interests all using their heads to "beat the system."

Team play also has its disadvantages—organizational challenges leading the way in terms of possible problem areas. Varying degrees of competency, motivation, dedication, and other differences are all examples of hurdles that sometimes must be overcome. Unfortunately, even dishonesty enters the picture once in a while. And enough can't be said for maintaining good morale—essential for a group working together in an arena where the highs are high and the lows are, at times, nothing short of exasperating.

But a well-managed and dedicated team has tremendous potential—as long as its members are unified and have the highest regard for team longevity.

The Big Player Approach

A well-armed blackjack team might consist of four or five card counters, also known as spotters, and a counter designated as the team's Big Player. All enter the same casino at different times—avoiding interaction of any kind. The spotters proceed to position themselves at various tables in relative proximity—perhaps within the same pit or even spread out over two or three pits in close proximity. The spotters then begin either back counting a table by standing behind it and keeping track of the cards, or actually playing for nominal amounts, only for the sole purpose of signaling in the Big Player when the count indicates a significant player advantage. Signals, naturally, are nothing more than normal movements that anyone might make, and are used to convey the count (and number of aces, if applicable) to the Big Player, who then enters the game betting amounts closer to the higher end of a structured betting spread.

To anyone watching—including casino personnel—the betting levels of the big player start as large and continue as large, substantiating the idea that this player simply bets at those levels all the time. And since the big player obviously wasn't present for some previous part of the shoe, casino personnel couldn't come to suspect him or her as an advantage player. All the while the spotter either moves on to another table or continues to play at the same table, betting the minimum allowable or keeping bets low enough to avoid any kind of scrutiny. When the count drops off, the Big Player simply leaves the game, again looking for a signal from another spotter that his or her table has gone highly positive.

The end result is getting more money "into action" on highly positive counts, when the players have the advantage. And this is accomplished without any individual spotter's having to "spread" significantly—as would be necessary if working alone.

Team Signals

Signals are the lifeblood of the entire process, and can be any kind of motion or movement that logistically can be interpreted by another team member. The one requirement, of course, is that all signals are discreet enough to give and receive in full view of casino personnel—and won't look like gestures trying to convey some type of information.

Essentially, two types of signals are necessary. The first type would be a group used to convey information not in any way related to the count. Let's call these "communication" signals. Wanting to end a session, calling a Big Player into a game, or even signaling a bathroom break are all necessary bits of information that at some point need conveying. Otherwise, one teammate won't know for certain what the other teammate is doing—which might lead to a missed opportunity or some other situation better avoided.

The second type of communication necessary is a signal used to convey either the running count or the true count, depending on what level system is being used. We'll call these "count" signals. Teams opting to use a multi-level point count will require a lot more signals because the *running count* and the number of aces played are both bits of information needing representation—so that a true count for betting purposes may be calculated by the Big Player before reverting back to the running count. Whereas, for those teams using a one-level count without a side-count of aces, the spotter can simply determine the true count and convey *that* directly to the Big Player. Once in the game, the Big Player can simply work backwards by multiplying the true count by the number of decks remaining (or the correct conversion factor as illustrated in Chapter Six) to determine the running count for subsequent hands.

Since communication signals are used to transfer information to a receiver who may not be within earshot, these signals must be of the silent variety. Count signals, on the other hand, can be either silent or audible for level-one teams—depending on team preference—and for practical reasons should be silent for level-three teams due to the number of signals possible. Audible signals used by level-one teams should be those that would pass for nothing more than a player making small talk or thinking out loud in a noisy casino.

Communication Signals

These can be of any kind, as long as discretion is maintained. In a few instances some may be developed that might suggest, just by nature, the desired bit of information being communicated. For instance, I've often used rubbing my eyes as a way to signify the desire to "call it an evening."

It's natural, especially late at night, and it's also something people do when they're tired. Of course, you must be careful not to rub your eyes at just the wrong moment. The last thing you want to do is have a spotter start to get up from a table just as the true count goes through the nearest bubble.

The table that follows lists common bits of information often needing transfer between members of a blackjack team in full operation. Included is a translation and sample movement or motion that could serve as the signal. Remember that the signals shown below are examples. Feel free to use them—but realize it might serve your team better to develop some that aren't already published in a book outlining blackjack team methods.

Table 11.1: Communication Signals

COMMUNICATION:	TRANSLATION:	SIGNAL:
"Negative shoe . . . no need to hang around here."	A counter might want to let a Big Player know that he would be better served hanging around another spotter.	Tilt of head to one side
"The cards are getting warm . . . you might want to stick around."	Unless another spotter is calling you into a game, stay here.	Rubbing nose
"Big Player needed."	Get over here fast. The count just went through the ceiling.	Rubbing back of neck
"Come on in!"	This is what we've been waiting for. Let's make some money.	Rubbing chin
"I'm taking a break."	I'm going to the bathroom, or for food, or getting off my bottom because it hurts.	Stretching
"I'm getting heat."	I've noticed casino personnel taking special notice of me.	Rubbing right forehead
"You're getting heat."	I've noticed casino personnel taking special notice of you.	Rubbing left forehead

COMMUNICATION:	TRANSLATION:	SIGNAL:
"Abort due to heat."	From the spotter to the Big Player: Don't come in due to heat. From the Big Player to the spotter: I'm not coming in due to heat.	Moving hands through hair
"Abort for any other reason."	No translation necessary.	Both hands in pockets
"Leave the casino quickly. Go to pre-arranged meeting place."	Abandon ship, immediately.	Hands on hips
"What's the count?"	No translation necessary, and hopefully asked only by a Big Player to a spotter.	Scratching ear
"Understood."	I understood the previous signal.	Visible exhale
"Change tables."	Move to another table, farther away from this floorperson, or to a less-crowded table.	Arms folded
"Let's call it a session."	I'm tired, or we've won or lost enough, or we've worn out our welcome.	Rubbing eyes

Count Signals

Because advantage blackjack play entails having a predetermined betting strategy, the Big Player can place his first bet after being called into a game based on the call-in signal alone—without even knowing the count. That's because the "come on in" signal is made only when a certain count threshold is reached, and should involve a specific amount. Certainly all communication signals are important, but communicating the count from spotter to Big Player is where the money train begins and ends. Typically, a spotter would call in a Big Player and soon after communicate the count, followed by the number of aces, if applicable. A specific sequence of signals should be established ahead of time (and practiced) to avoid any chances of miscommunication.

Let's begin with methods of communicating the count for a level-one system, followed by what really is the only viable method of signaling for teams using a multiple-level point count.

Level-One Point Count

A spotter for a level-one team can convert the running count to the true count and convey that information right to a Big Player entering the game. This way, the Big Player is already armed with what information might be needed for deviations from Basic Strategy. But remember that the Big Player must reverse the process and convert the true count back to the running count if he or she is to be involved in the next hand.

The signal indicating the true count can either be a silent, subtle movement or an audible cue in the form of a key word said as part of a longer sentence. It really depends only on which method team members feel most comfortable with.

Audible signals can include the use of a mnemonic to help in remembering which signal stands for what count number. For example, since many people consider "7" a lucky number, a verbal cue that the true count is +7 might be any statement with the word "luck" or "lucky" in it.

- "Another slot jackpot? How do people get so lucky?"

- "I'd rather be lucky than good any day of the week."

- "With my luck, it's not happening any time soon."

Any of the above would work, all of which are comments commonly heard in a casino. Mnemonics may be used for all positive true counts. Cats supposedly have how many lives? Aren't there five gold rings in the Christmas song, "The Twelve Days of Christmas"? Why not use "ring" or "rings" for a True 5, and "cat" or "cats" for a True 9?

The trick with using audibles, of course, is to sound natural—as though you're thinking out loud or simply making small talk with the dealer or other players at the table. Thankfully, small talk at a table is common, and it's highly unlikely you'll have to use the same audible twice in a row during the same sitting. And even if that does happen on occasion, rest assured that no one is really paying that close attention. The MIT teams used audible signals, which is now known by most informed casino bosses. So be extra careful if your team decides to do the same.

Another benefit of using audible signals—in addition to being able to use mnemonics as a helpful aid in remembering what signals stand for what count number—is the fact that the eye in the sky can't relate a specific motion of one player to the arrival and large betting of another, if surveillance tapes are later analyzed.

Go ahead and come up with ten or so mnemonic words that could be used as true-count indicators for counts ranging from +1 to +10, and create a list. If you're naturally reserved, or think you or your teammates might sound foolish making utterances similar to the examples given above, then perhaps silent communication might work better for you. The last thing you need is to have to repeat something verbally that sounded awkward the first time—because the Big Player didn't hear you. In that case, feel free to devise a group of nonaudible signals similar to those presented in the next section.

Level-Three Point Count

In that the level-three point count includes a side count of aces, teams using this method will require the spotter to convey both the running count (instead of the true count) and the number of aces played. The Big Player will then convert this information to the true count for betting purposes. Conveying only the true count to the Big Player won't work since the true count for betting entails including the relative abundance or shortage of remaining aces. Ace adjustment also eliminates the possibility of reversing the process to calculate the correct running count for future hands, as a Big Player can do for teams using a level-one point count.

Since the running count can vary so widely, a great number of signals are necessary. To facilitate the conveyance of this information in live play, we go back to elementary-school math by acknowledging the existence of both the "ones place" and "tens place" for every two-digit number. For example, the number "26" contains a "6" in the "ones place," and a "2" in the "tens place." Considering that running counts occasionally reach up into the fifties (mostly at multiple-deck games using six or eight decks), six different signals are needed for each group of ten. For the ones place, a separate group of nine movements or positions is needed to signify the numbers 1 to 9.

Let's use our hands, since each has five fingers. For starters, let's agree that when the palm of the left hand is facing down, the five fingers starting with the thumb will represent 1 through 5. When the palm of the left hand is facing up or sideways (or not facing down), the first four fingers starting with the thumb will represent 6 through 9. And we'll let each finger on the right hand represent a span of ten numbers, starting with the thumb signifying from 10 through 19, the pointer 20 through 29, the middle finger 30 through 39, the ring finger 40 through 49, and the pinkie 50 through 59. To convey the count, simply touch the appropriate finger on the left hand using the appropriate finger on the right hand. The only exceptions are for running counts of +1 through +9, and counts of exactly 10, 20, 30, 40, and 50. For running counts of +1 through +9, we'll leave out the right hand altogether. A subtle twitch or casual movement of the thumb with the left palm facing down would signify +1. A subtle movement of the index finger while facing down would indicate +2, and so on. Get the idea? With the palm of the left hand facing up or to the side, a subtle movement of the index finger would indicate a running count of +7. Now for +10, +20, +30, +40, and +50: For a running count of +10, the right thumb touches the middle of the left palm. For a running count of +20, the right index finger touches the middle of the left palm. For a running count of +30, the middle finger of the right hand touches the palm of the left, and so on for running counts of exactly +40 and +50.

Table 11.2, opposite, contains a large sampling of signals for running counts between 0 and +60. Note that the thumb signifies 1s and 6s, the left index finger 2s and 7s, and so on—the fingers that most people likely would use if counting with their hands.

Table 11.2: Count Signals

COUNT	SIGNAL
1	Left palm down, slight movement of thumb
2	Left palm down, slight movement of index
3	Left palm down, slight movement of middle
4	Left palm down, slight movement of ring
5	Left palm down, slight movement of pinkie
6	Left palm up, slight movement of thumb
7	Left palm up, slight movement of index
8	Left palm up, slight movement of middle
9	Left palm up, slight movement of ring
10	Right thumb in left palm
11	Left palm down, right thumb touching left thumb
12	Left palm down, right thumb touching left index
13	Left palm down, right thumb touching left middle
14	Left palm down, right thumb touching left ring
15	Left palm down, right thumb touching left pinkie
16	Left palm up, right thumb touching left thumb
17	Left palm up, right thumb touching left index
18	Left palm up, right thumb touching left middle
19	Left palm up, right thumb touching left ring
20	Right index in left palm
22	Left palm down, right index touching left index
27	Left palm up, right index touching left index
31	Left palm down, right middle touching left thumb
36	Left palm up, right middle touching left thumb
40	Right ring in left palm
48	Left palm up, right ring touching left middle
54	Left palm down, right pinkie touching left ring
59	Left palm up, right pinkie touching left ring

A nice aspect of this particular set of signals is that the arms and hands can be in just about any position—as long as the position is natural and the hands are in full view of the Big Player at the proper moment. Realize that we're not making a specific movement—rather, we're posing in a specific way, at least with our hands. That allows a running count of +19 one time to be conveyed by picking with the right thumb at the nail on the ring finger of the left hand while it's facing up. The next time the right thumb might interlock with the left ring finger (with the left palm facing up) while both hands are seemingly at rest on the table or in a spotter's lap. After practicing these signals, you'll see that a "bridge" or "union" can be made in several ways, including many that wouldn't seem unusual to an onlooker. Of course, though many positions appear quite normal, there's obviously a right way and a wrong way to go about this process. Remember that casual is key. A pose that resembles someone practicing yoga would obviously not be a good signal to use in the middle of a casino. Practice in front of a mirror if necessary, and, of course, extensively with other team members.

For aces, develop your own set of signals. Those that you have a hand in developing may be easier to learn and remember than those suggested in a text. If you're coming up empty, one method might entail touching a certain place on the body, and then moving up or down from there for a greater number of aces dealt. Another method used by some teams when spotters are actually playing is to simply employ a stack of chips on the table so that the total value of the chips in the stack signifies the number of aces dealt. Of course, that requires the spotter to maintain both certain types and numbers of chips—such as red nickels or white dollars. If you do decide to employ this method, aside from your needing to avoid the overly obvious movement of adding a single chip to a stack of white dollars every time an ace is dealt, here's a word of caution: don't have a stack of white chips on the table at a $25 game for seemingly no purpose. Common sense would say that after a while it looks mighty suspicious, especially if you're always adding or subtracting chips from it. Again, being discreet is key. And remember that ceiling-level cameras are always rolling. Taking a chip from one stack and adding it to another might be very apparent to someone reviewing surveillance tapes.

A nice aspect of the count signals shown in Table 11.2 is that in many instances a succession of movements isn't necessary to convey both the count and the number of aces played. For example, let's say that the signal for twelve aces played is left hand below the chin. With a running count of +32 and twelve aces played, the spotter can accomplish transmitting both signals with one pose: palm down, middle finger of right hand touching index finger of left, while both hands are under the chin. Perhaps the spotter has leaned forward and has both elbows resting on the edge of the table? A little bit of improvisation may be necessary at times. The trick is to do whatever seems natural.

As a final note, consider changing signals periodically—in the same way many computer networks require password changes every so often. It's just a security precaution that may be worthwhile if your team operates for an extended period. And practice. Just as with the many other facets of advantage play, for a team to work together like a well-oiled machine requires a good deal of practice.

The Call-In Threshold

So when does all this covert communication take place? Most of it occurs as a Big Player is being called into a game. Some communication signals may be sent and received at other times, but count signals are communicated only when necessary, or when a Big Player requests such information. Generally, a 1 percent advantage may be used as a suitable threshold, which, as we all know by now, generally corresponds to a true count of +3. The amount of the Big Player's first bet should be dependent on team bankroll and the team's agreed-upon risk of ruin percentage. As mentioned earlier, the Big Player need not know any count initially—but should know the "true" or have the ability to calculate it by the time it becomes necessary to play his or her hand.

Playing Together While Playing Apart

Another team approach involves playing together in one sense while playing apart in another. This is a lot less complicated than Big Player team play, in that interaction among team members is virtually nonexistent—except in one small but very important way: behind the scenes, several counters share a joint bankroll.

Sharing a bankroll allows each counter to make larger bets. In fact, each counter can play as if the entire bankroll were his, assuming each counter upholds the same risk of ruin percentage and plays with the same level of proficiency. A third counter of equal ability contributing the same amount to the joint bank would allow all three to again increase their betting levels while maintaining the same risk of ruin—and substantially increase earnings potential. And the total amount won doesn't just equal three times the original counter's expectation—it's three times *each* counter's original expectation, or the number of players on the team squared times any solo counter's expectation.

Teams using this approach don't even have to play at the same time, or in the same casino. In fact, team members using this approach should avoid playing in the same casino for several reasons—the most obvious being that it doubles team exposure. It also shrinks the available playing field. For example, casinos that offer eight-deck games on the main casino floor sometimes offer a few six-deckers with elevated minimums in the baccarat pit. Having one team player at one table in the bac pit may leave only one or two tables available for a second. The logistics of a situation like this should be avoided.

Team meetings are necessary and fun, to share experiences and information on beatable and not-so-beatable games, or to comment on where heat is rampant and where it isn't. But probably the most important reason to meet, especially early on after the formation of a new team or bank, is to review group finances. A team just beginning that encounters a rocky start might want to adjust betting levels some if that option was agreed upon at bank formation. Of course, the only way such a decision could be made would be if a meeting were called to share up-to-date results among team members.

An excellent benefit of team play, mentioned earlier but worth expanding on a little more at this point, is that several counters playing at the same time get into the "long run" a lot more quickly than any individual counter playing on his or her own. In other words, the results begin to look a lot more like the mathematics a lot sooner, which helps to smooth out those inevitable negative swings. In a similar way but on a larger scale, the casino is a living, breathing example of being virtually immune to adverse statistical fluctuation. Multiple games operating at the same time all contribute to a shared bottom line. For instance, if a player hits a particular roulette table for a lot of money, it's likely that the table would show a loss for the day in question. But the combined result of all the roulette tables in the casino that day would likely still produce a positive bottom line.

In the end, the effect of an advantage applying continuously should ultimately prevail, thanks largely to what mathematicians call the Law of Large Numbers, which very much applies for a team of card counters all playing at a positive expectation. In everyday language, that means the losses posted by one or even two team members would likely be offset by the team's combined results. Even a counter suffering through a severe negative swing gets a break. Playing alone, the poor unfortunate might have thrown in the towel. But instead he can revel in the success of the group as a whole and perhaps, more important, live to play another day.

Why Some Teams Fail

There is a whole host of reasons as to why some teams fare so much better than others, or why some teams fail altogether. Staffing, compensation, training, funding, scheduling, and even negative forces such as casino heat and the consequences of that heat are just some of the many issues confronting successful blackjack team operation. In many ways, running a successful team is very much like running a successful business. Only the strong survive and prosper for an extended period.

And, just as they are in many forms of business, people are a blackjack team's most important asset. But as we all know, people aren't the same—even those who share a common interest. Different people obviously have different personalities, talent levels, stamina, etc. And what fills one person's cup often does not fill another's. So, as if winning consistently in a casino wasn't tough enough already, enter a wide variety of human factors that must be dealt with or addressed to allow for a team's greatest asset to function at its highest level.

Let's look at some of the most common reasons that some blackjack teams fail, or where problem areas are likely to occur:

INADEQUATE PLAYER COMPENSATION Does the team bankroll consist of equal contributions from all members? If so, winnings are likely to be split evenly. However, what if certain members of the team have invested more than others, and thus have more at stake? Take this a step further by considering a team in which some percentage of the bankroll has been provided by an investor or group of investors—people likely never to see the inside of a casino. Then how are the dividends awarded?

A common split is 50 percent for investors, 50 percent for team members, with the 50 percent team split based on each member's total time spent contributing to the effort.

But what if one team member is responsible for generating a large percentage of the win? Or what happens if one team member contributes very little to the overall win? Is each member entitled to the same amount?

Generally, my feeling (and I'm not alone in this belief among many of those who have organized profitable blackjack teams) is that to penalize a team member for enduring the inevitable negative swings we all must wade through is somewhat unfair. What may be done, however, is to further break down the percentage owed to players, perhaps awarding 35 percent or 40 percent based on hours logged with 10 percent or 15 percent based on contribution to the win. The secondary split also acts as somewhat of an incentive—helping to maintain each player's desire to contribute to overall team profitability.

In the end, the best approach is, not surprisingly, to be as fair as possible. Provide a large enough percentage to those in the trenches to make their efforts worthwhile. By playing at the highest level possible, respect those who are putting up good money to make the whole endeavor possible. And investors—remember that nothing happens without the players.

Can anyone say, "Labor and Industrial relations"?

DISHONESTY FROM WITHIN Let's face it. We're dealing with large amounts of cash. Thankfully, most players realize that better gains can be had by remaining a teammate in good standing than by pocketing some portion of a win and possibly jeopardizing involvement with a successful enterprise.

Open polygraph testing is an option, and has been employed by several teams down through the years. A policy of being able to test anyone on the team at any time certainly acts as a deterrent to anyone inclined to be dishonest. A better situation would be a team of people so tightly knit that complete trust exists among all team members. Unfortunately, though, that can't always be, especially when the recruiting process involves selection based on interest, ability, etc. In the end, a certain amount of trust must be given to all team members—there's simply no other way. This reality elevates the importance of being highly selective during recruitment, whenever possible.

In summary, address this topic head-on by agreeing to a plan during team formation. Obtain a polygraph or use of one if necessary. For those inclined to cheat or steal: don't do it. Is jeopardizing a longer-term reward really worth the short-term gain? Take pride in playing on a profitable team, and enjoy the camaraderie. Make lifelong friends—not enemies.

TEAM MEMBER'S BEING "MADE," AND SUBSEQUENTLY BACKED OFF OR BARRED
Up until now we've discussed internal conflicts. Now let's talk about an

external one, and what to expect in advance to minimize the possibility of its happening.

In today's world, casinos actually compete for customers. One way to do this is to offer give-backs or "comps" to those players who wager a lot or play quite regularly. To do this, the casinos like to offer almost everyone a player-rating card to be handed in prior to playing at any table. Casino personnel then estimate the amount of money bet on each hand or spin of the wheel, and the total time over which the rating applies, to establish what's called a player's "action." Not surprisingly, the greater the action, the larger the comp. The problem for us counters is that everyone naturally likes to receive complimentary goods or services. Therefore, to deny a rating and thus "pass" on any complimentary rooms, foods, beverages, or other freebies is looked upon as odd—very odd. In fact, you're either a criminal with a few skeletons in the closet, or a card counter. So not being rated often translates into more scrutiny than does just getting a card to begin with and taking what each house wants to give you. The catch, of course (and there's always a catch, isn't there?), is that to obtain a player-rating card you must give a name, address, and date of birth.

Big players and spotters alike: *expect to be asked to get rated if playing*—which means you will have to provide that personal information, or somehow provide an alternate identity. Just make sure everyone on the team doesn't give addresses that are all from the same geographic area—especially if your team is using the Big Player approach. Consider this for a moment: if you were a shift manager at a casino in Gulfport, Mississippi, what would you think if on some Wednesday morning five guys playing blackjack—all appearing not to know one another—produce only Nevada drivers' licenses? Conventioneers, you say, who all happen to be from the card-counting capital of the world? Guess again.

In summary, have an identity ready to go. Expect to get rated, and get rated if the request is made. For Big Player teams: don't all come from the same place. For Joint Bank teams: no two counters should be playing the same casino at the same time. If you're "made" as part of what is labeled a blackjack team operation, you'll most likely be barred. For a Big Player team, that should mean the end of play for all team members in that casino for some time. For Joint Bank teams, other team members should be able to continue playing there, albeit with a heightened sense of alertness towards heat that might in any way relate. Once in a while it might be helpful to put yourself in the shoes of casino management, and to take a good, hard look at what you and your teammates look like from the other side.

BURNOUT Yep, this happens too. Just as with any other endeavor, too much of anything—even a good thing—can lead to such problems as burnout and exhaustion or loss of interest.

We all need a break from the blinking lights. Work hard and play hard as a team, but definitely take breaks—and I mean extended ones. Encourage each member to get enough rest, eat right, and exercise when going at full force. And remind everyone from time to time that high-stakes blackjack can be a roller-coaster ride of emotional highs and lows.

In Closing

Team play can be lots of fun—and profitable too. But with so much time and money at stake, there's no room for failure or to take lightly any role or responsibility bestowed on you by your fellow teammates. The highest standards should be maintained and to do that team members should be tested to ensure that they are battle ready. Tests should include, but may not be limited to, Basic Strategy decisions, running-count accuracy, true-count conversion accuracy, deviations from Basic Strategy, and proper bet sizing. As well, signaling should be practiced and tested until the process becomes virtually automatic.

Given so many different aspects of successful team operation, it may be wise to develop a set of rules or guidelines that team members can refer to at any time—guidelines that cover in writing everything from compensation percentages to individual record keeping to the most efficient use of time.

Your fellow teammates are counting on you and your 110 percent commitment to excellence. Don't disappoint them.

CHAPTER TWELVE

Casino Countermeasures

Introduction

This is where the fun begins. After you've learned and are proficient at the mechanics of card counting, this chapter and the one following become the two most important in the entire book. Because the best card counter in the world can't make a dime if there aren't any casinos left for him or her to play in.

Consider the irony here. The casinos offer a game to the masses. You study the game and become good enough to beat it consistently, using only your head. You join a select few who represent only the tiniest fraction of the blackjack-playing population. But that doesn't matter to the casinos. The fact that you can beat the game consistently makes you an individual to prevent from playing, whether that means barring you, backing you off, or instituting any one of several countermeasures available within the law. It's so absurd it's comical. But the casinos are where the cards are dealt, and where the money is. So not only must you maintain the highest level of technical proficiency, but you must also learn how to fly beneath enemy radar. It's one of the reasons I didn't put my picture on the back cover of this book.

Let's take a look at things from the casinos' perspective, to see why such actions are taken against someone playing at only a 1.5 percent advantage.

Their Perspective

"Hey, it's my game and you're in my house," says a certain mid-Strip casino in close proximity to the Flamingo Hilton. "I can do whatever I want."

Sounds a bit childlike, but that's essentially what's going on. And how a state law or casino control commission responds will vary by locale. Different jurisdictions have different policies. And casinos themselves have different levels of tolerance. For example, my two-year-old son would probably have a good chance of being barred from the casino I'm alluding to above—and he's just learning to count (as in 1-2-3 and so on). Relating to card-counter tolerance, this particular casino's reputation borders on the ridiculous—a fact well known throughout the card-counting community.

The above is an extreme example, and, obviously, a bit of an exaggeration. Generally, the bigger casinos will have a little more tolerance than the smaller ones. But that's strictly a generalization. Tolerance for card counters involves betting levels as much as it does one casino management team being more or less paranoid than another. Bottom line: as a card counter you're simply *not welcome*—period. If discovered you'll be dealt with, and how you're dealt with may or may not depend on stakes, how long you've been playing, or whether you're sitting in a sawdust joint or beside marble columns and beneath an ornate ceiling.

Our Perspective

Talk to any proficient card counter and he'll tell you that even with a 1.5 percent advantage winning isn't easy. Only a dreamer would say, "Hey J-Buk, let's hop a puddle-jumper over to the Bahamas this weekend and make 50 grand."

Card counting just isn't structured like that. Okay, playing for large enough stakes, you can make 50 grand in a weekend. But playing with an

edge is really only worth what the mathematics of your expectation
equations says it's worth. Remember that 1.5 percent isn't a huge advantage. The profits come, but only in due time. In fact, one of the biggest
gripes card counters have is when casino personnel assume we simply sit
down at a table and in little time walk away with half of the chip rack. An
informed floorperson knows that doesn't happen every time. And, in
fact, many not-so-good counters out there are probably playing at well
below 1.5 percent.

So what's the problem, if we're not pulling $50,000 out at whim? Are
we a threat to any casino's bottom line?

No. Unless a grind joint is being hit really hard, only a bona fide whale
is a threat to any casino's bottom line, and that threat exists only over the
short run of time. But barrings and back offs and heat still occur, and often it makes little difference whether you're winning or losing. As alluded to earlier, it all boils down to whether or not you're viewed as an
advantage player. Let's take a look at several reasons why casinos put up
such resistance:

- The casino is a business just like any other. Let's face it, compe-
  tition is steep and upkeep is expensive. It costs lots of money to
  build hotels with suites the size of small cities, give out free
  drinks all night long, and maintain a workforce right down to
  the guy whose duties include imprinting the hotel's logo in the
  sand of every ashtray. A well-run business tries to address or
  eliminate all inefficiencies, no matter what size. Imagine a
  house in the dead of winter. Advantage players are like open
  windows in that house—windows open perhaps only a crack,
  but nevertheless open. Another example: why do most companies turn off the warehouse lights when the warehouse isn't
  operating?

- Card counters take up space. In a casino, a blackjack table is
  worth so many dollars per square foot. And a seat at that blackjack table is worth "x" dollars an hour when filled, with "x"

being dependent on a number of variables ranging from player skill to average bet size. To the casino, a card counter playing at a positive expectation represents a reverse cash flow. In fact, it's a situation similar to the swing experienced when you lose a hand you normally should have won. Instead of winning $450, you lose $450, resulting in a $900 swing. If a seat is worth $69 per hour to the casino, and you're making $63 per hour, then the total swing for the casino is actually $132 per hour—a bit higher than just your take-away amount.

- Word gets around, and coming down hard on any and all advantage players prevents a casino from becoming known as "easy."

"J.J. mentioned the Galapagos Island Casino is dealing its four-deck game down to under half a deck."

"Really? I'll be in that part of the world next Tuesday. I was planning to hit Easter Island's casino, but since penetration in the Galapagos is so good I'll go there instead. And I think Kaitlyn is planning a trip next month. I'll mention it to her as well."

From the casino's perspective, call it the gnat syndrome: one becomes two becomes four becomes eight and so on. One gnat isn't bad, but when is there ever only one?

Note, too, that information like penetration levels is meaningless to non-counters. The casinos aren't getting extra market share from normal losing players, only an increase in visitation from card counters.

- Heat comes down because you become the focus of management's attention. Let's face it—standing in a pit for eight hours a day watching a bunch of blackjack tables can get a little monotonous. Things move right along night after night after night, without much to distinguish one eight-hour shift from another. Then along comes this college kid whom you discover can actually beat you. All of a sudden you have the ability to directly impact the well-being of your casino. So, of course, you take action.

- Situations become personal confrontations. I've experienced all kinds of heat in my career, from civilized back offs to uncivilized barrings to procedural changes that were made with an undertone of hostility. In the instances when I've encountered uncivilized treatment, it was obvious that the parties involved had it out for me simply because I was an advantage player applying a skill with which I had become proficient. It seemed to become somewhat of a personal confrontation—my playing in their pit, or on their turf, and beating them. I suppose it's just the sadder side of human nature for some people to become antagonistic towards others who are good at something cerebral, or who stand to gain from their ability. If card counters must be barred, backed off, or treated unlike everyone else, then why not make it strictly an unemotional business decision, and leave the antagonism out of it?

- Resistance exists because it's allowed to exist. After all, what industry provides the number one source of income to the state of Nevada? With that said, why should the State limit what casinos can and cannot do while staying within the law? I don't believe it's really any more complicated than that.

So the game of cat and mouse goes on. But with the challenge of beating casino blackjack growing more and more difficult, it becomes imperative not to let heat become yet another obstacle that stands in the way of becoming a successful card counter. Make no mistake about it—being identified as an advantage player is a detriment. The goal should be to become so good in your "act" that you can play with a positive expectation right under their noses, for at least *some* length of time without their ever knowing.

Being identified as a card counter means you're failing to fly beneath enemy radar. The times I've been barred in the past represent severe inadequacies in my approach to the game. Thankfully, it's been some years now since that last happened, and it probably had as much to do with my underestimating the consequences as it did with my being young and perhaps a little naive. Which brings us to the final point of this section.

If you're a newbie, it's probably a little difficult to read a section like this and really embrace it—without having ever actually experienced getting barred, backed off, or having to abide by a specific change in rules applicable only to you. I think too many beginners just assume that they'll never come up against countermeasures like the ones they read about in books like this. To that I say, if you become a serious player and spend enough time in the trenches, you will experience casino countermeasures sooner or later—no matter how good your act may be. It's simply impossible to play with any kind of regularity and not encounter them.

The Cat-and-Mouse Game

How does someone get identified as a card counter? Basically, it all starts and ends with bet variation. Of course, if you study every card as if your life depended on it, or your lips move faintly to the sound of +1, +2, etc., expect to eventually get read the riot act. But assuming you don't make those types of cataclysmic blunders, it all comes back to the size of your bets and how they differ from one another. Which means, at least from our perspective, it all boils down to a cat-and-mouse game—or to the art of engineering the largest bet spread possible without standing out in a crowd. If you bet the table minimum, except on the last hand of the shoe when out goes the table maximum, you're going to do more than just raise a few eyebrows. You may not immediately be pegged as a counter, but the red flag has been raised. Which means you'll probably be watched a whole lot closer than you were previously—either by several pairs of human eyes, or worse yet, by a bunch of electronic ones.

Knowing you're under surveillance is a lot better than not knowing you're under surveillance. Unfortunately, being observed, in many instances, is something you won't know about until only after it's too late. What's more, someone in the surveillance room may be counting down the game as well, and watching how nicely your bets now correlate with the rise and fall of the count. Now your spread to two hands of $400 each will have somebody somewhere nodding his head with assurance that you're someone better off back out on Las Vegas Boulevard.

But wait. The casino manager suddenly shows up in the blackjack pit you're playing in. Then the pit boss comes over, folds his arms, and stands about twelve inches off of the dealer's right shoulder. All of this is going on while a mini-conference is being held back at the podium—with at least one boss in the group giving you the hairy eyeball. By this point, hopefully you know that somewhere along the way your act wasn't as good as it should've been—or that you've overstayed your welcome. The next movement made is by the dealer, who steps aside so that the pit boss can either read you the Trespass Act, back you off, or give the dealer instruction to invoke any one of several other countermeasures we'll talk about next.

Wanted: Dead or Alive

Congratulations. You've just sat through your first barring, back off, or procedural change instituted just because you're an expert at the game. Now, may it never happen again.

When a player is identified as a card counter, the first step is for management to decide what course of action, if any, to take. More often than not what they decide depends on the laws governing the state or the grounds on which the casino is located. That's why, for example, in Las Vegas a card counter can be barred from play whereas in Atlantic City he can't. But that's not to say a casino remains defenseless in those locales where barring a person from play isn't allowed. When casinos can't bar or back off an advantage player, they resort to any one of several rule or procedural changes that negate the counter's advantage over the house—thereby accomplishing essentially the same thing as legally removing him or her from the premises.

Countermeasures imposed against advantage players come in several forms. Let's examine each one in detail, so you'll know exactly what you're up against or what to expect in the event you're identified as a card counter. Let's start with the most severe.

Being Barred

If this is allowed by the authority having jurisdiction, it means that you are no longer allowed on the premises, and must leave at once. Picking up where we left off above, the dealer will step aside and the floorperson or pit boss will read you a legal statement that essentially advises, "you are no longer welcome in this casino." Behind the scenes what is really going on is that the casino you are sitting in has decided to exercise its rights as a private club (which it is) and by doing so is able to pick and choose its members. The statement you'll hear will further advise that "if you refuse to leave or return to the premises after being barred, you may be arrested for trespassing."

If you're sitting at a blackjack table, this means picking up your chips and proceeding immediately to the cashier's cage, where your chips will be converted to cash, and then leaving through the nearest door possible. The whole time you'll be escorted (like a criminal) by several members of the casino's security force.

Trespassing? You've got to be kidding me, right?

Wrong, unfortunately.

You're not being barred because you're too good of a card player. (Well, you are, but that's not the official ruling.) You're being barred because the casino becomes a private club that all of sudden no longer wants your action. That's some really fancy footwork relating to the law, isn't it? But, unfortunately, that's the reality of the situation if you're playing in a state like Nevada, for instance, where the casino industry and the government hold hands in the night.

Being Backed Off

This is an interesting one, and provides for a little bit of comedy just in so far as what it means. When you're backed off, the casino will advise that you are no longer welcome to play blackjack, but you *can* (and, in fact, are welcome to) stay and play any other game offered by the casino. "If you continue to play blackjack, you will be asked to leave, and if you then refuse or return to the premises at some later time, you will be arrested for trespassing."

In other words, play any of our other games where obtaining an advantage is impossible, but don't play blackjack.

If you weren't smiling over the "private club" ruse, I'm sure you're smiling now.

Rule or Procedural Changes

This is an interesting one, too, because this is what happens in a jurisdiction in which barring or backing off an advantage player isn't allowed by law.

As mentioned earlier, several rule or procedural changes can be made that essentially eliminate the possibility of obtaining an advantage over the house. The pit boss or floor person will come over to the table and instruct the dealer to do one or more of the following:

1. Place the cut card in the middle of a freshly shuffled pack of cards, forcing a reshuffle after dealing out only about half of the shoe. (In some cases the cut card is placed only a deck or two from the front—even more absurd.) Since such a limited number of cards is dealt before a re-shuffle becomes necessary, the likelihood of a positive true count high enough to invoke a large bet becomes virtually nonexistent. If there are a lot of players at the table, the cut card, at worst, will likely be placed in the middle rather than towards the front, with the hope that the other players won't notice, and therefore won't complain about short deals or a dealer seemingly always shuffling. But a six-deck shoe in which three decks are cut off reduces penetra-

tion so much that a proficient counter will likely leave the game in search of greener pastures.

Once, many years ago, a pit boss came over to a table I was playing at (with one other player) and instructed the dealer to shuffle *after every hand*. This wouldn't have been memorable except that I was playing a four-deck shoe. I sat there for a short time just to absorb the absurdity of it all: Shuffle four decks of cards. Decks extended for player cut. Cards placed in shoe. Shoe made ready to deal. First card burned. Deal one hand. Pay off or take wagers. Remove cards from shoe. Locate cut card and distribute. Place all cards in discard tray and then shuffle all over again.

I hung around for two complete cycles, then left the casino and the city.

2. Specify a maximum bet—one that allows no vertical spread. For example, at a $25 table, the floorperson might tell the dealer that the person sitting in seat number two is not allowed to bet over $75, even though all other players at the table are still able to wager up to the table's posted maximum. With a spread of only 3 : 1, winning in the long run becomes impossible, as the limitations imposed will in effect eliminate any opportunity to make significant profits when the time is right.

3. Limit the advantage player to one betting spot. Often counters will spread to two hands for reasons we'll talk about in Chapter Fourteen. To institute this restriction, the floorperson might instruct the dealer that "the person sitting at third base is only allowed to play one hand." This countermeasure is often made in conjunction with other limitations, such as capping a player's maximum to much less than what the table maximum allows other players to wager.

If any of the above ever happens to you, including being backed off or barred, expect some unusual reactions from other players at the table. So

you wanna be Rain Man, you say? Well, unfortunately, for those 3.3 minutes that any or all of this takes to go down, you are. It's not every day
that the normal casino-goer gets his game stopped in the middle of the
shoe so that the casino can escort another player to the door—a fellow
player who from his perspective has done nothing wrong.

One more relevant point: countermeasures vary in terms of how
detrimental a specific incident may become. A worst-case scenario is for
your picture to be faxed or sent to other casinos in the same city, with a
warning that you're an advantage player currently "in town." When that
happens, your face might end up in a stack of papers on that podium
you see in the middle of every blackjack pit.

The shuffle-after-one-hand incident mentioned above occurred because I had been barred from another casino earlier that day—and the
barring casino had sent my picture all over town. In other instances
you might be barred or backed off in one casino and remain totally
anonymous in another. The advice here is that anything can happen,
and that nothing is off limits. I've heard of more than one counter
catcher following a card counter to another casino, where the catcher
then informed management about the existence of an advantage
player in the house. I've been followed to the parking garage—which
actually was kind of creepy—in an attempt, I believe, to obtain my li-
cense plate number. Luckily, I realized I was being followed and doubled back in a long hallway leading to the garage elevators—only to
confront the counter catcher hiding behind a building column. (This
sounds ridiculous, but it's true.) He didn't have much to say, but the
awkwardness of the situation seemed to squelch any further advance
on his part.

Needless to say I didn't return to that house for years. But eventually I
did, and can even get a game dealt to me there today, on certain shifts.
Which brings to mind an interesting note to close this section on.
And that is: no matter how bad any casino countermeasure turns out to
be, time—as it always seems to—really does become the great equalizer,
given the turnover rate prevalent in today's casino industry. Of course,
that's not always the case, especially if you've made a really lasting im-

pression. But more often than not, if you handle a barring correctly and let enough water pass under the bridge, after a good amount of time it may be possible to play again under that very same roof. And the odds of that happening increase dramatically if you limit yourself to playing on another shift, or if the members of the barring team are no longer employed by that casino.

The Griffin Agency

No chapter on barring or casino countermeasures would be complete without a mention of Griffin Investigations, Inc., of Las Vegas, Nevada. This is an agency contracted by many casinos to aid in identifying, thwarting, and catching thieves, casino cheats, and—as sad as this sounds—card counters. Watch any current television show highlighting the surveillance technology of a modern-day casino and there's a better than average chance you'll hear the name or see an agent from this company working in conjunction with some casino's security force.

Years ago, the agency developed the infamous Griffin "mug book" containing the names, pictures, and associates of undesirables, including card counters, that are considered threats to casino operations. Many of the photos and mug shots on file of card counters are pictures taken by the client casino's own video surveillance system, and shared with the Griffin agency. Today's version of the book is electronic. One television documentary showed a live video surveillance feed from an Australian casino to the car of one of Griffin's most famous agents, whereupon the individual under surveillance was compared to everyone in an existing electronic database. A match resulted in the agent's revealing all information on file about the player to the client casino, which then allowed casino personnel to decide on what action would be most appropriate.

Thus, if you're a card counter and you're in the Griffin database, your risk of being barred, backed off, or experiencing any kind of countermeasure is a lot more likely than it would be for a counter who has managed to stay out of it. A listing of those casinos that subscribe to Griffin can be found in Stanford Wong's *Current Blackjack News.*

Facial Recognition Software

With advances in technology occurring every day and surveillance systems becoming more and more intricate, turning up the volume in the war against advantage players seems inevitable. Leading the way at present is the use of facial recognition software (FRS) to identify those people the casinos deem as undesirable, for whatever reason. And of course, card counters continue to end up in this category.

The technology includes reading facial characteristics that no two people share, such as the exact distance from one pupil to another. Biometrics information is read from a picture taken by a casino's surveillance system, and run against a database of previously identified "undesirables." Casinos using FRS are then able to thwart advantage players quickly and effectively—or at least those who have been previously barred, backed-off, or identified. Of course, not all casinos are equipped with this technology and glitches are common, but as time goes on, expect both the numbers of casinos with FR capability to grow and the technology itself to become more and more sophisticated.

If You Get Barred, Backed Off, or Are the Reason for a Rule or Procedural Change

So what do you do if the worst happens? If you're sitting at a blackjack table and the pit boss comes over and reads you the riot act?

The best thing to do is leave the casino, immediately. If you're being 86'd, you'll first get an escort by casino security to the cashier's cage to cash in your chips, followed by an escort to the nearest doorway. Say as little as possible, or say nothing at all other than that you have a desire to leave. Don't resist—there's no gain to be had by remaining in a casino that's barring you from play, backing you off, or changing procedures so much that it no longer offers a game worth playing.

Going back a few years, barrings and back offs would involve hustling a card counter off into a back room and then detaining that person for some time against his or her will. Interrogations sometimes included verbal abuse, and some even became physical confrontations before the counter was then ejected from the premises. These incidents truly upheld the "wild" in Wild West, and thankfully were more prevalent in the days before major corporations owned Las Vegas. Nowadays, with lawsuits as popular as they are, most major corporations have too much to lose to endorse or encourage the physical harassment of advantage players. But how any particular member of any given corporation, such as a security guard, for instance, handles himself in a heated situation depends on his character. Keep in mind, too, that not all Nevada casinos are owned by Fortune 500 companies. There are many around today that in the not-too-distant past have been slapped with six-figure lawsuits from card counters seeking compensation for damages suffered as a result of harassment.

The key is showing your desire to leave once you've been read the Trespass Act. Even today, casino personnel might still try to get you into a back room for interrogation, along with requesting identification and holding a picture-taking session. If you are actually being "backroomed" against your will, ask that the police be called. Then ask if you're being arrested. If you're not being arrested, say, "I'm leaving. Do you plan on holding me against my will?"

The long and short of it is that you should avoid being "backroomed" at all costs. In Nevada and in many other jurisdictions, if you're barred for any reason other than misconduct, *you must be asked to leave the premises before being detained.* That's your ticket—take it and leave as fast as possible. You neither have to show ID nor pose for a picture against your will. It's only if you refuse to leave, for whatever reason, that they then can back-room you and detain you for the authorities. Or if you've committed a felony on the premises—which you haven't because card counting doesn't qualify as one. If you're forced against your will into a back room to either show identification or to undergo a picture-taking session, it's probably time to consult an attorney. That's definitely a lawsuit, and could end up being your most profitable blackjack session to date.

Keep in mind that how you react to a circumstance might also play a role in how damaging or not a particular incident becomes. If you cause a scene, which some counters are prone to do, you're creating a not-so-pleasant, lasting memory in the minds of casino personnel, which might not be all that beneficial twenty-four months down the line. I can say that I've managed to again get a game in virtually all of the casinos where I've been 86'd over the years, thanks in large part to a quiet exit and the passage of time. Always think, "Will my actions or words have any adverse impact on the possibility of being able to play and win again here in this casino, sometime in the future?" If the answer to that question is "yes," then another choice of words or an alternative course of action is likely the better choice.

The best policy is to remain calm and cool. The reason is that, after all, you are sitting in their house, playing at their tables, and winning from them in the long run. And they do have the law on their side. So a polite answer to any questions asked, along with a hasty exit, is without a doubt the most productive course of action.

On Attorneys and Lawsuits

Card counters have been successful in bringing charges against casinos for wrongdoing, usually relating to being barred, harassed, or having had to undergo something against their will. Rulings have gone both ways. And settlements obviously can vary greatly depending on the lawsuit and what each party has to gain or lose.

The process relating to filing a lawsuit, getting your day in court, and ultimately getting compensated, not surprisingly, can be a long and arduous one. If you do decide to step into this arena, make sure your case in solid and you have the time and the patience to follow through where necessary. As far as legal counsel, several attorneys are available who have expertise in this area of the law. Most are located in Nevada, and can be found on the Internet or through local telephone directories.

CHAPTER THIRTEEN

Longevity

Longevity in the world of card counting means the ability to keep playing as an advantage player without being backed off, barred, or encountering a rule or procedural change that compromises your advantage. A card counter who becomes known in more and more casinos may be jeopardizing his or her longevity as an advantage player. And, as mentioned in Chapter Twelve, the best counter in the world can't make a dime if he or she isn't allowed to play.

In this chapter we'll discuss methods that will help to prevent this from actually happening. What's interesting is that after mastering the mechanics of the process, to increase overall expectation one must either play more often, play with a larger betting spread, or play only in more favorable games—all of which tend to generate heat and thus the potential to adversely affect longevity.

Consider *camouflage* as anything used in an attempt to extend longevity. Camouflage can be a change in your physical appearance or persona, or even something done at the table in a playing or betting sense that makes you appear like just another player. The entire package you present to the world, or more specifically to casino personnel, defines what in the card counting world is known as your "act."

You've got to have an act. It sounds ridiculous, but it's true. You can't just sit there counting down the cards like a computer, or winning and losing big hands with no kind of emotional attachment. Does that mean you have to be the life of the casino? No, of course not. But consider some type of reaction as mandatory—especially if you're playing for quarters and up. Not surprisingly, the higher the action, the more involved and convincing your act needs to be.

Personal Camouflage

This is all about you—what you're wearing, the words you say, how you carry yourself, etc., as you might appear to a casino supervisor trying to determine whether or not you're an advantage player. Does your betting and playing style or how you carry yourself fit the person you appear to be? It should. But it doesn't always. For example, a quiet young male in jeans and sneakers playing $25 to $400 a hand who admits to being an engineering student at the nearest technical school is going to get scrutinized pretty carefully. Any experienced casino boss would peg a kid like this as a card counter in less than half a shoe. Now, put the young man in designer clothing with an expensive gold necklace and maybe have him mention that his father owns half of all the auto dealerships in South Florida, and all of a sudden $100 to $1,200 a hand makes sense. Get it? You want to always fit the money you're "throwing around."

Identity

This is an interesting one. You expect to win and in fact end up doing so, which allows you to graduate to a higher level than, let's say, a normal player who loses over time. So the dissimilarity that arises between who you are and the level of your play in many ways becomes inevitable. Thus, not keeping pace by not changing who you appear to be, or not adopting an identity that "fits," will undoubtedly lead to a lot more scrutiny.

How far should one go to change "who you appear to be"? That's entirely up to you, and ultimately will be dictated by the stakes you play and your level of success. For black action and up it might be in your best interest to have a completely new identity ready to go, especially if you want to sound natural when the casino host comes over and starts chatting with you. This would, of course, require some preparation. For example, if you're suddenly in the electronics industry as the owner of a small but very successful company that does classified work for the government, it would be prudent to know something about electronics.

Be selective in choosing an identity if the one you really own doesn't fit the level of your play—but know that identity well enough to be able to talk intelligently about subject matter relating to it. Casino bosses are human beings too. Conversation can go anywhere, and it won't always be about blackjack if you're someone they'd like to retain as a customer. (Yes, it gets that ironic.)

Dress

I suppose someone could be dirt poor and somehow scrape together blackjack capital. But after all is said and done, it doesn't hurt to look the part of a player, if at all possible. Fashionable or stylish clothing wouldn't hurt if you're betting green, black, or even purple. A smart scientist is a scientist who breaks down and buys an expensive leather jacket with some of his blackjack winnings and chalks it up as the price of doing business. A dumb scientist is a scientist who dresses in drabs and spreads from $50 to $750.

Jewelry doesn't hurt either. Even a fake Rolex isn't a bad idea if you don't want to go the full price for a watch of that quality. Isn't it an old saying that you can tell the success of a man by the shoes he is wearing?

Handling Checks

How well do you handle checks? If you're a card counter, your answer should be, "not too well."

I've been playing for so many years that I can do things with chips that make most people's jaws drop. I can shuffle checks flawlessly. I can drop the middle one of three, spin it and put it back up between the other two—using no more than three fingers. I can make a chip jump other checks or have it walk down the back of my hand. But when I'm at a table and under the lights, never would I dream of doing any of the above. There's no reason to. In fact, I constantly remind myself to be a little clumsy.

As you gain more and more experience, you're going to get better and better at handling chips. It's inevitable. The chips feel good in your hands, and your hands feel good moving them around. Resist the urge, if possible.

If you're right-handed, use your left to handle checks, or vice versa. Or even better, next time you're near a roulette wheel, watch the chip-stackers that sometimes assist the croupier in gathering piles to pay off winning bets. Watch what they do with chips between spins for things you should never do between hands or during shuffles.

Don't Worry—Be Happy

Another interesting one. You're supposed to have a good time in a casino. But because a lot of people lose, that isn't always the undercurrent of emotion that seems to be prevalent. That's where you come in. Make it hard for casino personel to dislike you. Too many people throw their hat into the ring without assessing how they'll feel after possibly losing. My Uncle Bob said it best when once he asked, during his one and only trip to Atlantic City, "How come no one is smiling?" Atlantic City aside, you need to be that one happy person he was looking for.

Engage the dealer and other casino personnel. Say something positive. Be upbeat. Even among advantage players, there's far too much war waging and not enough romancing of the stone. Ian Andersen, in his excellent and cutting-edge book *Burning the Tables in Las Vegas,* says it best when he suggests something to the effect that card counters should view casinos as customers, not entities that need to be beaten to a pulp and then kicked out of disrespect. It doesn't have to be an all-out battle, and shouldn't be, since you're already predestined to win the war.

Disguises

Disguises are always an option. These, of course, should be of the highest caliber, designed by professional Hollywood makeup artists. You want to avoid undue attention, not attract it. Those of you who aspire to play for big-time stakes may benefit from a disguise eventually. But a good disguise isn't cheap and also isn't available through most telephone directories, so you would really have to need one before I would recommend going through the trouble and cost of obtaining one. High-profile players of the past like Kenny Uston have used disguises with varying degrees of success.

Peripheral Vision

Use it, whenever possible, card-wise and people-wise.

Card-wise, peripheral vision doesn't work during the initial deal—as the dealer speeds around the table giving each player his initial two cards—but it can be used quite effectively as the dealer goes around dealing additional cards to those players who request them. Cards with paint (such as a jack, queen, or king) are in fact rather easy to spot through peripheral vision. And since all 10s have the same value, there's no need to know whether any particular card was a jack or a king. If you see the faintest hint of yellow or gold, subtract the appropriate amount from your running count. This tactic shouldn't be used on every hand—you'd go nuts if you did—but it's certainly one to keep in mind for those instances where some mileage may be gained from using it.

People-wise, use peripheral vision to monitor your surroundings. Know where pit personnel are at all times. Be aware that counter catchers might be standing behind you. If a floorperson is watching your game, or watching you with particular interest, it may be time to put some specific camouflage into action, or it may be time to simply leave the casino and save the rest of the dealer's rack for another day.

To Be Rated or Not to Be Rated?

This is a big one, and applies to all betting levels because nowadays almost everyone gets "rated." Getting rated requires that you give in a player rating card so that a supervisor can track your betting levels, time spent at the table, and ultimately whether you win or lose. Multiple entries over time then allow a casino to establish a player profile. Since almost everyone welcomes the comps that come along with being rated, to decline a rating isn't normal, and as advantage players we want to avoid *anything* that could potentially be categorized as unusual or that could bring on additional scrutiny. So be that as it may, we should obtain and submit a player-rating card whenever a rating is requested. And at the upper-limit tables, casino personnel will almost always request a rating if, in fact, you don't initiate the procedure.

The glowing positive about being rated is, of course, all the freebies that you can expect to come your way, which certainly has value. In fact, dining on the house or staying overnight free of charge enough times—when you would otherwise have paid for these goods and services—adds up to significant value.

The downside to being rated, aside from having to give a name and date of birth, is that your play is tracked, and therefore the casino has a running tabulation of your total plus/minus. If, at year's end, you're the only one among thousands of players who have logged significant table time, and for some reason you remain well in the positive, your name is going to show up in capital letters, blinking, and in italics. As we've noted time and time again, this is not something you want to happen.

There are several ways to combat this problem of standing out in a crowd ranging from quick and simple to drastic and time consuming. *Burning the Tables in Las Vegas* outlines how to legally change your identity. Various identities then allow you to play under different aliases if the process is repeated time and time again—which means it will be harder for the casinos to detect an advantage player in their customer databases. Andersen does caution, however, that methods like this one are time consuming and expensive, and certainly aren't necessary for all players at all betting levels.

One simpler method I've observed involves taking advantage of the moment. And that moment occurs all day long on the day a new casino opens. It happens time and time again: all formal procedures thrown out the window because hundreds of people want cards—and those same hundreds want to "get playing." And there's such a rush on the casino's part to issue plastic that often little or no verification procedures are followed.

Once a rating card is yours, try to blend in with the masses. Do exactly what an advantage player wouldn't do: play other games *to a limited extent* and get rated for that action. Try to make bets that are as close to even as possible. Take a game like craps, for instance. Betting the "pass" or "don't pass" with odds is playing at a small disadvantage. Chalk up the "mathematical loss" as the price for prolonging your longevity. How could you possibly be a card counter if your electronic rap sheet shows action on craps and roulette? Of course, have a game plan (a bet and a prearranged amount or span of time) that ensures wagering on these other games doesn't significantly reduce your blackjack profits.

If your mind is set on declining a rating, then at a minimum have a good reason for doing so. Say you're only going to be playing for about five minutes because you have dinner reservations, show tickets, etc. Of course, make sure that your line can stand on its own. If there's no show at the Riviera on Mondays, there's a good chance that a Circus Circus boss just might know that. After all, he's been working that part of the Strip for the last twenty-five years.

Declining a rating is easier at casinos that for you are one-shots, or those that you know you won't be visiting with any kind of regularity. Number one: you don't have the problem of having to repeat the same spiel to the same boss two weeks later. And two: you're not losing much comp value, because you won't be playing there for any significant length of time anyway. Imagine that? You can actually tell the truth: that you really aren't going to be under this roof long enough to actually make filling out a form worth your while. Even if it's not the truth, in large locales like Las Vegas where it's easy to spread yourself around, you can say something like, "I'm only in town for a night, and the last time I was here a volcano was the talk of the town. I just don't get out here often enough to make getting rated worth my while."

Or you can flat-out lie and say that you have a gambling problem, and that under no circumstance can your girlfriend or husband pull mail out of the mailbox with a casino logo as part of the return address. Can they guarantee under any and all circumstances that you won't get any marketing literature? I've had casino personnel back away from me in horror after suggesting that one. What better way to lose a customer than to be the reason his wife finds out he's gambling (again).

There's no question that declining a rating will make you stand out. Here's to hoping your camouflage is so strong that you can get away with it. If you're a smaller-stakes player it's possible. But for a larger-stakes player, I'm not sure that declining a rating every time won't eventually bring on the dogs. It should be no surprise that someone spreading from $100 to $1,200 per hand is going to get a lot more scrutiny than someone spreading from $5 to $60. Regardless, whether big stakes or small stakes, the one suggestion I have for those who must decline a rating and do so continuously is that you become a master of the hit-and-run style of play: very short sessions and then move on, without returning to that casino again for some time.

Order Alcohol

If you have a drink in your hand or in front of you on the table, you can't possibly be a serious blackjack player, can you? I'm not suggesting you actually drink a stiff one. I'm only suggesting you order one or carry one around, for the visual it provides. My drink of choice is a gin and tonic, because I can order one, take a sip, and then take it to the men's room and dump it. There I fill it back up with water and then it's bottoms-up in front of the nearest floorperson.

If you can act a little intoxicated, go for it. Add the effects of alcohol to any good act and you've probably got yourself a winner. Again, less is more and realism is key. The goal here is not to be a loud drunk, but merely another social player making the most out of his or her time in the casino. The nice thing about *acting* a little drunk is that drunks by nature are unpredictable. So whatever you utter, in a sense, qualifies.

And apologizing for "feeling no pain" should be a disclaimer for any part of the drunken act that really bombs.

Betting and Playing Camouflage

Betting and playing camouflage relates to ways an advantage player can mislead bosses into thinking you're not the advantage player you really are, by what you bet and how you play. This is accomplished by betting and playing in a way that isn't consistent with known card counting methods, at least at opportune moments or for short periods of time. Some ploys sacrifice expectation, but as long as too much isn't lost, a good misleading bet or play at just the right moment might be chalked up to the price of doing business at the world's blackjack tables. As you gain experience, it will become more and more obvious when to use a certain ploy or which one works best with your overall act. The trick here, of course, is *not* to sacrifice too much expectation. Remember that every bet you make at true counts below +1 brings with it a negative expectation.

Betting: After a Win

If you win a hand and the count drops, do not lower your bet. Do what most ordinary players do—let the initial bet ride again as you "hope" for a hot streak. Only card counters adhering to a predetermined betting scale lower their bets after a win, when enough high cards have come out to lower the true count.

Betting: After a Loss

Try to avoid increasing your bet after a loss, even if the count continues to rise. This applies more so towards the top of your betting scale. At the lower end, a slight increase can be gotten away with if it isn't too blatant. Think about it: There aren't too many people around who do this, other than players using some type of progression, or method that involves increasing your bet after a loss. And it's quickly obvious to any boss or to surveillance that you're not one of those. So what else can you be?

Betting: Off the Top

Bet more than one unit off the top a fair percentage of the time. Don't do it every time, so if studied, it doesn't appear like a mechanical foil. Do it a fair percentage of the time, and vary between two and three units so that surveillance sees more than a minimum wager following the shuffle. The negative expectation of these wagers will cost you a few dollars over the course of a year. But it's money well spent if it ends up buying you a few more maximum bets somewhere along the way.

Betting: Low-Balling

This would be dropping to a very low wager or even the table minimum during a high positive count—for perhaps a hand or two. When you're doing this, you're obviously giving up expectation. But it can throw some bosses for a loop, or at least leave them scratching their heads. Most of them know that the true count can't fluctuate that wildly after only a few cards have been dealt. The only problem with this ploy is that it's tough to gauge its success in the middle of doing it. Let's face it, the game is hard enough as it is. It takes a rigid soul to wade through the muck, hit a high positive true count, and then pass up on even one chance to put it out there. Not to mention those times when the dealer puts an ace-jack down on the table in front of you and your minimum bet. This ploy will definitely establish you as a volatile bettor, but get ready for some heartache. Again, though, call it the price of doing business if in the end it gets you a game you would otherwise not have had.

Betting: As the Biggest Fish

If at all possible, don't be the biggest bettor at the table. If you're playing quarters, for instance, this is most easily accomplished if you don't play at a nickel or dime table where most of the action amounts to red. A table with a player betting a little more than you is ideal. Going too far in the other direction would be to play at a table with another player betting very large amounts, where all eyes both human and electronic are focused on the game.

Betting: On Pocketing Chips

If you can get away with pocketing chips, then by all means do so. This appears to lower your overall win when it comes time to "color up." Essentially, we're looking for every little bit of help we can get, and if dropping a few checks into your pocket makes you appear like you've won less than you actually have, that's a positive.

But don't be spotted doing this, as it is a method employed by many advantage players. If you are spotted, you might be asked for all of your chips during color up. If that happens, suggest something to the effect that the only way you seem to be able to leave a table is if you play mental games with how accessible your chips are. Suggest a weakness in your own character. It will rarely be countered, and may be taken as a valid explanation as to why you were dropping in the first place.

Betting: Beginning Large Because You Ended Large

If you end a shoe with large bets because the count had been sky high, then start the next shoe with a bet as large or almost as large. This will hopefully cast doubt on any suspicion that you're an advantage player. If you win the hand, continue to leave it large. If you lose it, step it down considerably to match more closely where you'd normally be. Yes, leaving it large off the top will cost you a few dollars at the end of the year, but returning to the minimum and staying there for possibly an entire shoe after previously betting the ranch isn't a good idea either.

Betting: Avoid All Patterns

Don't always bet two or three off the top, then like clockwork drop back to the minimum to wait for a rise in the true count. Don't always step it up in the same fashion. Parlay whenever possible, if given the opportunity, without straying too far from your predetermined betting amount. (Recall that we mostly rounded down in our betting strategy determination, so a little difference here or there isn't going to matter much.) Hesitate once in a while as you decide how much to bet. Sometimes bet with confidence, other times with trepidation.

Betting: Spreading to Two Hands

Spreading to two hands may reduce scrutiny somewhat, as it often avoids the presence of a huge bet on one hand. But too many card counters spread to two hands only for their maximum bet. Their bets rise and rise and rise on one circle and then top off with two large bets on two separate hands.

If you're going to spread to two hands, then you must also spread to two hands at times other than when placing your maximum bet. Again, think patterns. This is definitely a pattern, and should be avoided.

Playing: Head-On or Heads-Up

Realize that anyone playing "head-on" or "heads-up" (playing one-on-one) with the dealer normally looks at all the cards being dealt—simply because all the cards dealt are only your own and the dealer's. So playing head-on by its very nature negates the need to scan the table for the purposes of keeping the running count. Playing head-on, then, in this sense inherently offers a bit of camouflage just by you being the only player at the table.

The downside, however, is that many card counters like to play head-on due to the number of hands per hour it's possible to log. Once again, a tradeoff depending on how you look at it.

Playing: "Wrong"

This *will* cost you money, and using this ploy comes down to a fine line between losing expectation while ensuring that some gain is being had by doing it in the first place. This is very similar to low-balling because it's doing the exact opposite of what you're supposed to be doing.

Some counters like to make a few stupid moves early on in an attempt to throw the bosses or surveillance off the trail when first being analyzed. "This guy can't be for real—he just stood on Soft 17." Again, its effectiveness is tough to gauge, and for that reason it's imperative to make sure that the price you are paying isn't too high.

Playing: Avoiding Some Variations

As I mentioned in Chapter Eight, I would strongly recommend that you never split 10s, and even consider not drawing on a 12 if the dealer holds a 5 or 6. These moves stand out like a red nose at a temperance meeting—and the short-term gain that may be realized from winning the hand(s) may come at a longer-term price of being identified as a card counter.

Playing: Making Use of Dealer Tallies

On shoe games in virtually all casinos, the dealer tallies up and announces the total of each player's hand as the player draws more cards. Make use of this audible while feigning disinterest in cards other than your own whenever possible. If you see or hear that a player has a total of 14, and then after asking for a card the dealer announces that the player's new total is 19, you know a 5 must have been dealt. A crafty one is a situation in which you notice another player has a total of 12. If the player draws a card and the dealer almost immediately collects the cards and the bet, you know without even looking that the last card dealt had to be a 10. Add to your running count as appropriate. Anytime you can establish lack of interest in other players' cards while still maintaining a correct count—especially in front of a boss—is a golden opportunity that should never be passed up.

Playing: Consult With Players, or Casino Personnel

At least one person at the table is likely to know some degree of Basic Strategy. If you have an opportunity to show that you seemingly *don't*, then by all means take advantage of this. I've asked a floorperson hovering over my game, "What does the book say?" countless times over the years, knowing full well "what the book says," and what I would end up doing no matter what his or her answer was. By the way, I wouldn't call a floorperson's attention to a calculated strategy variation, but if he's staring down at my game I might suggest that the reason I'm standing on my 12 against the dealer's 2 is that "I have a hunch a picture card is coming." Or, "every single time I get this hand and draw a card, I bust." Casino personnel are used to hearing oddball explanations for why gamblers play a certain way. In other words, when in Rome act like a Roman.

Call me an actor, but all of these little things add up and collectively go a long way towards leaving the door open for future visits to that same casino. After a while, the game of it becomes the game within a game at which you instinctively try to become more and more proficient.

By the way, the ability to play flawlessly and still converse with pit personnel comes with practice. Speak if you're spoken to. It will separate you from the advantage player who can't look up from the table—for even a second.

Playing: Always Insure a Blackjack

After reading Chapter Four, it should be pretty clear that insurance is a wager completely independent of what cards you have in front of you, and that taking it or not taking it is based solely on the true count and nothing else. Yet most players, when they are dealt a blackjack, take insurance if the dealer shows an ace. They're so happy to have gotten a blackjack that they hedge just to make sure they get paid for *something*— whether it's the blackjack or the insurance wager. As you should know by now, that's living for the moment and not living for the best bottom-line results. So, just to appear like one of those players, consider taking insurance on every blackjack when the opportunity presents itself. Feel free to announce while doing so what a great thing this insurance wager is—because it "guarantees" a win.

Playing: Camouflage for Black and Up

One more nod to Ian Andersen, who came up with what has to be one of the cleverest ideas for camouflage ever devised. It works off the fact that most players who deviate are doing so because they simply don't know what they're doing. It's the card counter who sometimes deviates from Basic Strategy and sometimes doesn't—based on the true count—who often finds himself under heavy scrutiny.

Ian wondered what type of reaction would occur if some deviations were made *every* time the opportunity to make them arose—rather than only when called for by the true count. Surely a player who always stood on 12 against a dealer's 3, or who always doubled down on 10, would look like a player who simply doesn't know Basic Strategy.

With help from Don Schlesinger and Stanford Wong, Ian was able to come up with this most innovative method of disguising advantage play. Don determined the cost to the player of making certain misplays and Stanford ran simulations to determine win rates based on various playing profiles that incorporated making these deviations at every opportunity.

The beauty of the deception lies in the fact that at high true counts, when large bets are being made, the deviation actually represents the correct move to make. It's only when betting lower amounts, dictated by the count, that the player is actually sacrificing expectation and playing "wrong." But the pit sees these plays being made every time—plays that don't represent correct Basic Strategy. And so more times than not the advantage player is left to play relatively heat free.

An interesting by-product of this method is being able to obtain a larger betting spread—because you're not viewed as a threat. The beauty here is that the larger betting spread can then be used to make up the cost of the camouflage. Not to mention the fact you've also bought yourself countless more hours in which to ply your trade. Pretty ingenious, isn't it?

Of course, we shouldn't all start making the same wrong moves, for then the entire charade would lose its luster. A more in-depth description of what Ian Andersen calls the "Ultimate Gambit" is outlined in *Burning the Table in Las Vegas*. As well, Don Schlesinger's *Blackjack Attack* can be used as a guide in determining what deviations to choose and which ones would best suit your style, bankroll, and psyche.

This type of camouflage comes at a price, but surprisingly not at the price one might expect. Win rates for employing some of these plays on

a consistent basis aren't much off from the win rate established by playing perfectly, and deviating only when called for. The trick is picking deviations that don't have a large negative cost—that when executed aren't
giving up a lot of expected value. But the plays you pick must be those
that come up with enough regularity to put forth the camouflage you're
trying to lay. A true balancing act, if you take a step back and look at it
all. But one well worth it if you're in need of beefing up your cover.

So who really needs this degree of camo? Certainly, if you're playing
black and up you qualify, and will stand to gain by using it. Red chippers
won't need it, and those of you playing quarters fall somewhere in the
middle. A quarter player with a good act who wears out the soles on his
best pair of walking shoes probably won't need it. But if there's only one
boat floating in the nearby river, or you've been getting a lot more heat
than you can ever recall getting in the past, this might be time to give
such camouflage some strong consideration.

Time- and Place-Related Camouflage

In this section, let's talk about what you can do to minimize exposure in
terms of physical presence. Sometimes scrutiny will arise from wearing
out your welcome, or from being a repeat visitor a few days or weeks or
months too soon, or simply because one casino is linked in some way
with another that already had the full court press on you to begin with.

Hit and Run

Obviously, this doesn't apply if you're in a locale with only one or two
casinos. But if there are more than a few in which to play, there's no reason why you need to spend too much time under any one roof. Put on
your best pair of walking shoes and keep moving. Granted, some games
are not worthy of play for whatever reason (rules, penetration, etc.), but
anywhere several games are available, there's no reason to wear out your
welcome at any one joint. I can't overemphasize the importance that you
keep moving if the locale you're in allows for it.

Different Shifts

Plan your trip, as much as possible. Again, if you're in a locale like Las Vegas, make note of where and when you play so that a second sweep through those same casinos can occur on another shift. With so many games available, it's conceivable to log many hours and not play in any one place more than once or twice.

Also, avoid playing *through* shifts, if possible, as your exposure doubles. This applies in all casinos. Day shift starts anywhere between 10:00 A.M. and noon, and ends between 6:00 P.M. and 8:00 P.M. Personnel on swing shift come in immediately following, and last until between 2:00 A.M. and 4:00 A.M. Graveyard workers then arrive, spanning the early-morning hours until 10:00 A.M. to noon. Ideally, you should be nowhere in sight when one shift ends and another one begins.

Maximum Playing Time

Limit play under one roof to a maximum of about an hour and a half—even less if your betting or playing has been especially noteworthy. You will soon see that some sessions, just by the hands you get and the bets you make, will be more telling than others. If this occurs, consider moving on even sooner.

C'Ya

Leave after making large bets near the end of a shoe, especially if you've made several large bets near the end of previous shoes. If you leave after a big ending, win or lose, it could easily pass as doing so because you've either won or lost your limit. Players come and go for this reason all the time. Leaving after several large bets at the end of a shoe also gets you off the table without having to make one or more large camouflage bets off the top of the next shoe.

Mergers and Acquisitions

Know your casinos, and which ones are affiliated. If you're identified as a card counter in one casino, then you can bet sister casinos of the one that identified you will be on high alert. Thus, you shouldn't go strolling into the Claridge ten minutes after getting capped off at Bally's Park Place. Or take the tram from Treasure Island to the Mirage after getting backed off at TI. What do the Excalibur and Mandalay Bay have in common? These days, a different name doesn't necessarily mean there's no affiliation.

In Summary

The need for a good act is paramount. I can't overemphasize how important this becomes once the mechanics of card counting have become second nature. Ultimately, you should find and use whatever works best for you. The best act is one that entails a variety of different components, and even some that you might develop specific to you or your style of play. Yes, I know—it's ludicrous to have to resort to all of this on top of everything else a card counter must accomplish. But, unfortunately, that's the reality of the situation. So start practicing your alter ego, and remember to keep moving if at all possible.

In the end, every effort should be made to come across as "just another player." That means reacting negatively to losing a big hand, and not hesitating to sometimes flaunt a big win in some simplistic way—*because that's exactly what the typical player does.* Even though I may not feel like pounding the table in disgust, or raising my arms in celebration—because I've been down both roads a million times before—I'll go through the motions as part of my act. Just for the sake of trying to appear like a player with blood running through his veins. Remember, though, that you and your act have to come across as legitimate and convincing at all times. A poor act is worse than no act at all. And often, less is more. So by all means make sure your emotions and actions are as natural as possible and let the moment dictate how much or little is needed.

CHAPTER FOURTEEN

Maximizing Profits

Soon after launching any successful business venture, the enterprising entrepreneur will look for ways to maximize profits. For the card counter, this essentially boils down to playing more hands per hour, finding games that offer more favorable rules or conditions, or implementing a larger betting spread. Call those "the big three." But accomplishing some or all of these bottom-line boosters isn't always possible, for a variety of reasons. Let's take a look at these three in closer detail, as well as some other factors that both directly and indirectly influence earnings potential.

The Big Three

Hands per Hour

In case you haven't noticed, gambling (or "gaming," as the spiffy people like to call it) is *en vogue* right now. And because of that, casinos are often crowded—sometimes with more people than the number of tables can handle. This is, no doubt, a good problem for the casinos, but a bad problem for the advantage player. Remember that hands-per-hour is a critical component of the earnings expectation equation. Double the number of hands per hour and you've doubled your expectation. Here's a comparison to keep in mind: playing heads up against the dealer should yield over two hundred hands per hour, whereas playing at a full table might amount to sixty. That kind of difference on a consistent basis will surely make itself known at the bottom of your total win/loss column.

Ideally, we should do everything possible to seek out games where we can play either heads up or at a table with only one or two other players. Unfortunately, though, this isn't always possible, mainly for the reason mentioned above. One way of trying to get around this problem is to play at off hours like early in the morning, or mid-afternoon. Casinos are so much less crowded at these times, presenting more of an opportunity to find an empty table or one with only one or two other players. And weekdays, of course, are better than weekends.

Avoiding crowded conditions will be more of a challenge for the nickel player than it will be for those playing black or green. Depending on locale, red chippers may be limited to those hours between 9:00 A.M. and 12 noon. Newbies might even prefer the slower game offered by a full table, at least for a little while. But it won't be long before you begin searching for better conditions. In fact, it won't be long before the thought of playing at a full table will probably make you cringe.

"The More You Bet, The More You Get"

This phrase sounds like one you might hear from the mouth of a carnival slickster. But in essence it truly applies to the advantage player. As one goes up the betting scale, however, it becomes harder and harder to appear like "just another gambler." As nickels become quarters, quarters become black, and black becomes purple, the bright lights you must play under become brighter and brighter and brighter. But the mathematics of a 1.5 percent advantage still applies: thus, the more you bet, the more you do, in fact, get over the longer run of time.

With that said, it would be an injustice not to again remind you that the more you bet, the larger your negative swings will be. That doesn't rhyme like the title of this section, but unfortunately it rings just as true. As alluded to often in Chapter Nine, your betting scale and your risk of ruin are closely related. Bet more to win more, but know that you'll have to increase your bankroll in some corresponding fashion. That, or embrace a larger risk-of-ruin percentage.

So how much money do you think you'll put into action over the course of a year? The answer may surprise you. A part-time counter playing quarters probably puts about a million dollars into action over a twelve-month period. A red chipper probably comes in at about $150,000. And a counter playing black could easily log upwards of $5 million in a year's time.

How is that possible? We'll tally for the green chip player since he or she represents middle ground between black and red: Let's assume you play $25 per hand. That means your average bet is around $50. Let's also assume you play 100 hands per hour, and roughly 200 hours per year. By the way, two hundred hours per year equates to one four-hour interface per week—a very likely total for the capable part-time player, and in some cases probably a little conservative.

$$\$50/\text{hand} \times 100 \text{ hands/hour} \times 200 \text{ hours/year} = \$1,000,000/\text{year}$$

Red chippers may have a problem getting in 100 hands per hour, for the reasons mentioned earlier. And so the product of this equation for the nickel player won't be proportional. Keep in mind that these are estimates for dedicated, part-time players. Double or triple these amounts to calculate what a full-time player puts into action on an annual basis.

Penetration Is Paramount

"More favorable rules and conditions" often boils down to this: penetration, penetration, penetration. And, by the way, I'm not talking in any way about what this word more commonly is used in reference to.

Certainly being able to split pairs up to four times is a favorable rule. And certainly a game where the dealer stands on Soft 17 is better than one in which he draws. But once you come to terms with these play-of-the-hand-type rules, all that remains is how deeply into the deck or decks the dealer is dealing.

Penetration is the single most important factor to advantage blackjack play, and should be at the top of your priority list every living, breathing second you are within ten feet of a blackjack table. Of course, bet spread is also of prime importance, but penetration should dictate whether or not you even play to begin with. It's also likely that finding a game with good penetration may take some time. Consider this time well spent. Don't fall into the trap of settling for what's available—you'll be spinning your wheels for no reason, especially if penetration is better somewhere else. If penetration isn't acceptable, don't even bother playing.

Following are a few finer points regarding penetration:

- Some casinos use shoes with notches that force dealers to create consistent penetration levels, whether good or bad. Often, these shoes have several different notches for several different penetration levels, any of which can be used upon direction from management.

- Some dealers can be influenced as to where the cut card is placed, especially on those tables having shoes without notches. Influenced, in this case, means using verbal persuasion or tipping as a method to gain better penetration. However, the utmost tact should be used when attempting to persuade dealers to deal more deeply into a shoe.

- Penetration levels can vary from casino to casino. Thus, if levels are borderline at one venue, keep in mind that better penetration could exist elsewhere. As well, some casinos change penetration levels from time to time. This may be an attempt to bolster profits by increasing the number of a hands per hour dealt, or an attempt at thwarting advantage players like card counters or card-counting teams.

- Penetration can vary depending on geographic locale. Some areas are known to have better penetration levels than others. This simply becomes a function of experience. I always ask friends (who know their way around casinos) to check pene-

tration levels for me when I hear that they're traveling to destinations that offer casino gambling.

- Casinos with consistently good penetration seem to be more
  proactive or aggressive in identifying, backing off, or barring
  card counters. This isn't always the case, but I have seen it
  (sensed it) time and time again.

How good is good penetration? By today's standards, Table 14.1 can be
used as somewhat of a reference guide in evaluating penetration levels
for multiple deck games. (Adequate single-deck penetration levels were
covered in Chapter 10.) Unfortunately, today's penetration levels, in general, are a little less advantageous than those of years past.

Table 14.1: Penetration Levels (in Decks Remaining)

	GOOD	FAIR	POOR
Double Deck	X < 1 deck	X = 1 deck	X >1 Deck
4 Deck	X </= 1 deck	1 deck < X </= 1.25 decks	X > 1.25 decks
6 Deck	X </= 1.25 deck	1.25 decks < X </= 1.75 decks	X > 1.75 decks
8 Deck	X </= 1.5 decks	1.5 decks < X </= 2 decks	X > 2 decks

At the end of the day, the more time dealers spend shuffling, the less
time casinos are foisting their advantage over the masses. Thankfully,
this creates natural sorts of checks and balances. A cut-card close to the
bottom attracts players like you and me, while a cut-card too far forward
means fewer hands dealt per hour. So, for the casinos, it all comes down
to a balancing act, which is all fine and good except for one thing: with
regard to penetration levels, most casinos are penny-wise and dollar-
foolish. These days, most houses have more action than they know what
to do with. Yet their fear of advantage players forces that cut card farther
and farther forward. Poor penetration levels are responsible for so much

loss in earnings—all in an effort to thwart the tiniest fraction of the blackjack-playing population. It just doesn't make sense. Over the course of a year, the revenue lost due to time wasted shuffling will without a doubt far surpass what walks out the door in the pockets of advantage players—guaranteed. Yet poor penetration levels are everywhere.

Back Counting

This approach involves keeping track of the cards from behind a table, and then entering into a game or wonging-in (named after legendary blackjack expert Stanford Wong) only when having an advantage. Just as when sitting at a table, wagers are made according to a predetermined betting scale and appropriate strategy variations are made when necessary. The big difference between back counting and a play-all approach is that you may be playing only a few select hands per shoe, and then moving on if the count suddenly goes negative. This style of play avoids any interface when the player is at a disadvantage.

The results of "The World's Greatest Blackjack Simulation," performed by Don Schlesinger and John Auston, and contained in Schlesinger's *Blackjack Attack,* clearly show how back counting for shoe games is far superior to that of the more traditional play-all approach. In many instances, win rates of between one and a half to two units per hour for play-all become win rates in excess of two units per hour using this method of play. A wonderful tactic, this back-counting approach, isn't it?

Now for the bad news—and unfortunately it relates to this recurring requirement of having to appear like just another gambler. One downside to back counting is how obvious it appears to any floorperson watching you—*and they will be watching* if you're seen for some time lingering behind a table and then jumping into the game for a hand or two before moving on. To back count successfully you must obviously keep an accurate count. So that means laying eyes on every card dealt. Then, of course, there has to be an empty spot at the table that stays empty until you're ready to occupy it. Finding an empty spot, or any playable spot, may be less likely these days with casino gambling as popular as it is. The $50 or $100 tables in the baccarat pit are an option, but how many times can one really stand around there jumping into one of only four games operating? Not to mention the fact that many bac pit blackjack tables are often "no mid-shoe entry." And back counting the packed nickel and dime tables often just isn't viable. That really leaves only those $25 tables that aren't crowded—which, given the current conditions, isn't always a reality either. So how do I back count then, with its being a rather obvious method and one not well suited for crowded conditions and casinos that don't allow mid-shoe entry?

As you can see, there are definitely hurdles to overcome for this method of play. But the method is a good one, *if the conditions and your act allow you to pull it off.* Often in a shoe game the count will go positive and stay positive, so you won't be jumping out after only a few hands. An obvious question is, "On what true count should I enter a shoe game?" That all depends on the conditions. If you like lots of advantage, then enter only with a true 3 or above. But be prepared to do some waiting around. If your threshold is lower, say +1, for instance, then you'll be wagering money at a lesser expectation, but that will ensure that you have a betting circle to put your chips in if the count suddenly goes through the ceiling.

With either approach you will stand out, to some degree. So a strict time limit should apply to how long you stand behind tables under any one roof, or how many times you jump in and then out of a game after only a few hands. As far as the crowds, I don't have much advice to offer, other than to find out when the casino you're in is typically the least crowded, and to play at that time whenever possible.

Relevant but not relating to the actual mechanics of the process: back counting requires comfortable shoes, patience, and a big heart. You'll need comfortable shoes because you'll be doing a lot of standing around and walking. You'll need a lot of patience while searching for the right opportunities—and then missing some of them after investing the time to count down half a shoe. And last but not least, you'll need a lot of heart because of how critical every hand becomes when the actual number of hands played isn't very large. Since you're only playing in select situations, the large bets you do make will have a lasting impact on your short-term results. Lose a fair share of your big bets while back counting and you're almost guaranteed to be a loser that day.

A compromise of sorts, which involves the spirit of back counting while using the play-all approach, is to start a shoe or new deal, but leave the table if the count goes negative. Staying in the game during other periods, such as when the count hovers around zero, may just have to be chalked up to the price of doing business if back counting isn't a viable option, or will mark you as an advantage player.

Let's explore this option of getting-out-when-the-count-goes-negative a little further in the following section.

Leaving Negative Shoes

"A penny saved is a penny earned." I'm many years from being a senior citizen, but believe it or not, this philosophy really applies during shoes that go negative and stay negative.

If you're playing at a four-, six-, or eight-deck game, leave the table if the running count goes double-digit negative, especially in the early part of the shoe. There's no sense in throwing money away, which is what you are doing since house advantage increases as the count becomes more and more negative. Sitting out negative shoes will make you somewhat of a table hopper, and after you've read Chapter 13 it should go without mention that care should be taken to make sure your actions aren't bringing on additional scrutiny. One method to circumvent changing tables is to ask for a "button." The dealer will place a plastic disc or spacer in your betting circle, and your seat is then held until your return. Now you can visit the restroom or take a walk away from the table right in the middle of the shoe. If you do this, you should come back at the shuffle and not before, otherwise it will appear odd that you have returned but still choose to remain out of the game. If you're playing a "no mid-shoe entry" table, then you can come back to the table at any time, for you won't be allowed to re-enter the game until the shuffle—your desired outcome to begin with.

And sometimes it's worthwhile to have a reason for leaving. The restroom is a good one. Having to check the sports book screens is another. Making a cell phone call is yet another. I wouldn't leave the same table over and over again for no apparent purpose other than to avoid a particular group of cards. Those bubbles you see in the ceiling are everywhere, and if you're under the slightest bit of a suspicion, then walking aimlessly through rows of slot machines every couple of shoes supports the logic that you're a card counter avoiding negative shoes.

Playing Multiple Hands

Playing multiple hands cuts down on fluctuation, and when done at the right times gets more money into action.

A player's chance of losing two hands of "x" amount is less than his chance of losing one hand of twice "x." However, the card counter who spreads to two hands should determine how much less each hand should be so that the total amount played on both doesn't expose him or her to playing at an elevated risk of ruin.

Stanford Wong in *Professional Blackjack* advises that the player spreading to two hands can wager 150 percent of what the player might have wagered on one. Thus, a $200 bet on one hand can become two hands of $150, totaling $300 worth of action for no additional exposure. And this additional $100 of action weighs in nicely on the expectation equation.

But there's a catch, and here's what it is. *One should only spread to two hands if doing so doesn't cut down too much the total number of rounds dealt.* Otherwise, the total action may actually end up being less. For example, three rounds of $600 (played as two hands of $300) ends up totaling less money on the table than five rounds at $400 per hand (played one at a time) before the dealer's shuffle. And the last thing we should be doing in advantageous situations is decreasing our total action.

In *Blackjack Attack,* Don Schlesinger determined that when playing heads up against the dealer, the card counter should stick to only one hand. However, add one or two other players to a game and it becomes advantageous, in terms of total action, for the counter to spread to two hands.

And a final note on spreading horizontally. Never play three or more hands. Years ago that could be done, but nowadays a move like that simply draws too much heat.

Grind Joint or Glam Palace?

You've seen them both. The grind joints are the casinos of yesteryear—left over from the days when entertainers like Frank Sinatra and Sammy Davis, Jr. had their names in lights up and down the Las Vegas Strip. The glam palaces are the modern-day wonders—complete with their own lakes, volcanoes, mountains, canals, and jungles. Aesthetics aside, let's take a look at the important differences between the grind joint and the glam palace as far as the advantage blackjack player is concerned.

The grind joints often advertise better games or better rules. The tradeoff is that these smaller casinos are known to be a lot more intolerant of professional-level players. They'll often sweat black action, as compared to a glam palace where it might take some time for heat to develop. But the glam palaces are also the houses that have rows and rows of eight-deck games, or six-deck games with such poor penetration that playing isn't worth your while.

Ultimately, it's your choice. For me, the ideal is a glam palace with good penetration that doesn't sweat my action—at least not for some time. Perhaps mixing it up—a little grind, a little glam—may be the best strategy for you.

Here's a summary that doesn't define every situation, but for the most part holds true in a general sense:

> Grind Joint: Lower minimums, sometimes better games, and less crowded. Will sweat any level of advantage player action.

Expect more scrutiny and less tolerance from older bosses who have seen it all.

Glam Palace: Higher minimums, sometimes less advantageous games for any number of reasons, and crowded. Less scrutiny up front but surveillance capabilities that rival the Pentagon's.

Maintaining Discipline

Resist the urge to play in lesser games, whether they are bad from a rules perspective or in terms of penetration. This will require you to analyze a game for a short time before simply sitting down and buying in for chips.

Let's say you drive two hours to a solitary casino on an Indian reservation in Northern California. The rules are marginal at best, and the poor penetration levels make playing an exercise in futility. Do you abstain, or are you one to play just for the sake of a little action? After all, you did drive all that distance.

Keep focused on winning—not just playing. Often, finding a good game can take up as much time as actually playing in one.

Money Management

This is somewhat of a misnomer in gambling circles. Talk to 99 out of 100 gamblers and they'll tell you about the importance of money management, and how vital it is to "quit when you're ahead."

I'm sorry to rain on this parade, but there really is no such thing as money management. You are either playing with a positive expectation or a negative one. And that alone determines whether you will win or lose in the end—and the end (or the bottom line as of your last play) is really all that should matter.

Always quitting while you are ahead is mathematically impossible. It puts a greater emphasis on the moment than on the final result achievable by the method employed. No doubt it's nice to savor a $3,600 win, but that win might put you higher on the winning graph (of percent advantage versus time) than you should be. And for that reason, the long arm of expectation will eventually bring you down to size. (We'll expand on this concept a little more in the following chapter.)

So, in fact, for an advantage player it all comes down to *time*. If you're playing with a positive expectation and you stop playing, in a sense you're actually sacrificing earnings. Likewise, a gambler playing at a negative expectation actually saves money by discontinuing to play.

Reading, Rereading, and Continuing to Learn

Don't read just this book. Read everything you can get your hands on relating to card counting and playing at the professional level. That's what experts do. Read and reread, in fact, as you will forget some of the lesser details that actually can make a difference.

As your knowledge base grows, explore other methods of increasing your advantage, such as, for example, shuffle tracking. Distinguished blackjack expert and author of *Blackbelt in Blackjack,* Arnold Snyder is a master at this fascinating technique, which tracks slugs of high cards through the shuffle. As Basic Strategy represents the foundation on which all of card counting builds, being a successful and proficient card counter is the prerequisite for becoming an accurate shuffle tracker.

Visit blackjack Web sites and interact with other advantage players online. Research and acquire reputable software to further hone your card-counting skills or test playing and betting strategies against all kinds of rules and conditions. But most of all keep reading and learning, and *re-reading*. I re-read blackjack texts all the time. Sometimes it takes two or three reads before something really sinks into this head of mine. You'll find how things you thought weren't so important, are in fact very important, and vice versa. Small bits of knowledge gained over time eventually become a wealth of information. And all that information translates into greater expectation in the trenches.

CHAPTER FIFTEEN

Negative Swings

Negative swings are brutal. So brutal that they can shake the most seasoned card counter to the core. For that reason, I'd like to devote an entire chapter to talking about them—why they occur, what you can expect when you're knee-deep in one, and the mindset needed to deal with this unfortunately inevitable part of the game.

Negative swings are brutal. Get used to reading that, because repetition is probably the only way to really drive home how ruthless these monsters are. Embrace the idea that when a severe one rears its ugly head you'll be questioning everything you've ever learned. In fact, negative swings are the single most common reason some card counters— and many good ones, at that—end up leaving the game.

In a way this chapter is meant to be more than just a discussion of how bad things can get. Call it rambling with the intent of touching on the many intangibles relating to losing that I think are so important to understand, and are so often overlooked by those just starting out. Or consider it a spiel on losing. Or even a therapy session before the crisis occurs.

Remember, winning is easy. Even a not-so-good card counter can tell you how he so proficiently took $3,000 from a highly positive shoe. Losing, however, is the end result of putting your best effort forward and coming up empty—sometimes repeatedly. The intent of this chapter isn't to scare you, but rather to look at the large-picture reality behind 1.5 percent, so that sometime later you aren't left scratching your head and thinking, "Where did I go wrong?"

Winning and Losing

For starters let's talk about winning trips and losing trips. I've kept accurate records over the years, and it seems that on average about six out of every ten trips are winners. Which, of course, means four out of every ten trips are losers. Winning 60 percent of the time is nice, but there's no way of getting around the fact that 40 percent is a pretty large percentage in and of itself. Consider 60/40 pretty characteristic of what you should expect going forward, if you're in solid form. I should mention that I don't have stop amounts—positive or negative. The only things that determine the length of time I'm at a table are heat, mental or physical fatigue, or a non-playing commitment. Remember that you're playing with some percent advantage relative to your level of skill, so stop amounts whether positive or negative won't really change anything in the long run. They won't help you win more or lose less—*unless* you're the type of person whose mental ability is adversely affected by losing. Then, perhaps, a trip stop-loss amount might not be such a bad idea.

Winning streaks and losing streaks really don't matter, unless, of course, the losing streak is so large that it takes your entire bankroll. As touched on briefly in the last chapter, streaks are simply positive and negative fluctuations of some greater end result. Yet I can't tell you how many times I've been enthusiastically confronted by someone eager to tell me he had "x" winning trips in a row, when, in fact, the only meter of relevance is the bottom line. If you're a nickel player, is there any difference between winning $150 ten sessions in a row or having one $1,500 day? The answer is "no." There's absolutely no difference. In this case, $1,500 is the only measure of success, and how it is achieved makes no difference. The cards are no different if you face them for three hours at a time over ten trips spanning a period of two months, or if you were to hypothetically play for thirty hours straight. The same logic applies to changing tables. You can't increase your win rate by leaving a table "up." *You* as the proficient card counter throw your 1.5 percent advantage into the ring every time you sit down, and the mathematics picks up at exactly the same point it left off last—win or lose. In fact, every player is continuously playing at some varying expectation (the vast majority at varying negative expectations) on every roll of the dice, spin of the wheel, or deal of the cards.

Let's suppose you're operating at a 1.5 percent advantage, you're averaging 100 hands per hour, and you're a quarter player with an average bet of $50 per hand. Your expectation, as we determined in Chapter Nine, is $75 per hour. You've also been keeping accurate records of your wins and losses, and since forming the bank you've logged about 120 hours at the tables. But the column way to the right on your Excel spreadsheet shows a total win of $11,675. What can we conclude from this?

Well, for starters you've been a little lucky. You should be ahead only about $9,000. But what does that mean, "you've been a little lucky"? It means you've been riding a minor positive swing. Yes—some good news. Positive swings do occur. In fact they occur at an ever-so-slightly greater frequency than do negative swings occur—since we have the edge. But the important words here are "ever-so-slightly." Remember that a 1.5 percent advantage is a slight one, and it's easy to lose sight of that when the cards are falling as if you've had a hand in placing them in the order that they appear.

Can you tell when a negative swing is coming? Unfortunately, you can't, because a negative swing is really nothing more than a predominance of losing sessions endured over some period of a time, although I suppose one could argue that every losing session is, in essence, its own little negative swing. Whichever the case, negative swings are inevitable and there's no getting around one. To keep reaching higher highs, as a matter of course you'll need to face these ulcer-producing wonders head-on—short ones and long ones. And there's no telling when a long one is coming. That's why proper betting levels and bankroll sizes are critical, and are tied so closely together. Aggressive betting yields higher highs and lower lows. So you'll win more when the cards are falling nicely, but lose a lot more if a negative swing decides to make an appearance. Not surprisingly, a more conservative betting approach will produce results that nestle closer to your expected outcome.

How Severe Is Severe?

The title of this section is an interesting question, and I'm not sure there's an answer for it.

One way to try to comprehend the potential severity of how bad things can get is to touch on what mathematicians call *standard deviation*. Standard deviation (s.d.) is a way to describe how far from our expected outcome we are likely to fall, given a certain set of circumstances, such as, in our case, number of hands per hour, total amount wagered, and positive expectation. Standard deviation sheds light on why we end sessions, weeks, months, or even years either above or below that period of time's expected result.

Let's take a look at standard deviation from the perspective of a flat betting Basic Strategy player logging about 100 hands-per-hour (a figure we should be striving for to ensure that we are maximizing profits in a hands-per-hour sense). This happens to be a convenient number in that one s.d. for such an hour of play amounts to roughly 10 percent of those 100 hands, or 10. (The actual percentage is 11, but we'll use 10 as a close enough approximation since we're using 100 hands for this example.) We can then multiply 10 by our unit size to calculate how far from our expected value (EV) this player can expect to end up *about two thirds of the time.*

For example: 100 hands per hour betting an average of $10 per hand results in $1,000 of action over the course of one hour. Our EV is 1.5 percent of $1,000, or $15. But we probably won't win exactly that amount. More likely, or about two-thirds of the time, we'll end up losing between $85 and winning $115. Since our unit size is $10, we multiply s.d. by unit size (10 × 10) to get 100, and then both add and subtract $100 to and from our EV, resulting in a span ranging from -$85 to $115. By the way, go out a second standard deviation and the answer is the high and low this player should expect about 95 percent of the time.

Remember that this is only for one hour's worth of play, and applies to the *flat betting* Basic Strategy player—and note the kind of swing possible. Given a range of -85 to 115, consider how likely it is to end in the negative, and how often. Graph this result, and the area on the negative side of the bell curve that results is pretty large indeed. And remember, that only accounts for his results about two-thirds of the time. The remaining one third can produce results that exceed this range in both the positive and negative directions. Also keep in mind that the above was calculated using only $10 units. Imagine the ranges possible for a card counter spreading 1 to 20 units of green, black, or purple action—over perhaps a period of a few weeks or months. The swings are huge and that most certainly includes the negative ones. There lies our problem, and a mathematical way of trying to put our hands around how severe "severe" can be.

When It Rains, It Pours (Sometimes)

Let's switch gears a little and take a look at how far out "far out" can be in less mathematical terms. The unpredictable nature of the weather always seems to get people's juices flowing, so let's examine a by-product of unusual weather. In the commercial property insurance industry, one of the perils typically covered under the normal insurance contract is flood. When it comes to offering flood coverage, carriers typically underwrite to what's called the 100-year and 500-year flood. Taking into account all the conditions that can lead to a flood event, the 100-year-flood and the 500-year-floods represent the highest water level expected in 100 and 500 years respectively. How does that relate, and why are we off on this tangent?

It means that we'd have to go back to about the 1500s, in some cases, to last see the results of a 500-year event. The 1500s! That's a long time ago. And for the 100-year flood, it means there's a chance that 75-year-old Harry Kadiddlehopper, who's been watching the rains come and go for three quarters of a century and telling everyone and his brother that the waters of '53 shut down the entire county, hasn't even seen the worst of it. The reason why we're off on this kind of tangent is to drive home the idea that "far out" can be really "far out." Or in short, what may seem like the worst of the worst may in fact be nowhere near how severe things can really get.

Winning the Little Ones, and Losing the Big Ones

How often does this happen? When you're in the throes of a negative swing, it happens all too often.

Mason Malmuth, in his excellent book *Blackjack Essays,* gives the following example, which illustrates the concept of self-weighting.

> You are playing craps and have been betting $1 on each roll of the dice. After 10,000 rolls you increase your bet to $1 million on roll number 10,001. Now how many times have you rolled the dice? Since your total results "cluster" about the last play, statistically speaking, you have not rolled the dice much more than one time.

Though losing a series of maximum bets or beefy double downs doesn't even come close to rivaling this example in terms of severity, nevertheless, it illustrates the overall effect of losing those hands that really matter.

Is there a difference between a negative swing and a losing streak? Not really, although I suppose some players might characterize a streak as losing a successive number of times, whereas a negative swing might involve winning and losing sessions, with the losing sessions outweighing the winning sessions to produce an overall downward trend. Thankfully, the compounding effects of a 1.5 percent advantage ensure that you don't go on losing indefinitely.

Following are several graphs that illustrate the kind of long-term upward "drift" you should see playing at a 1.5 percent advantage. The "x" axis shows time, while the "y" axis is used to plot total plus/minus. Since this is a chapter on losing, pay more attention to the valleys than to the peaks even though the peaks are a lot more fun to look at. Notice the downward slopes that occur between even groups of points that ultimately trend upward.

Figure 15.1: Winnings Versus Time

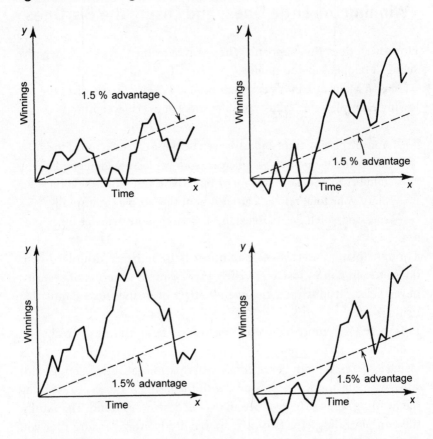

Remember, a 1.5 percent advantage isn't much, so get ready to reach a certain level, go on a losing streak, and then spend the next four months trying to get back to the total you were at originally. According to the late Peter Griffin, widely regarded for years as the game's foremost mathematician, and author of *The Theory of Blackjack*, a card counter can expect to be at some point beneath his highest winning dollar amount 98.4 percent of the time. That's a whole lot of time spent trying to get back to where you were at some point previously. The trick is to not put too much emphasis on your all time high. Spend more time looking at the general direction you're moving in.

Try to think in an "annual sense." Or even longer if you don't plan to play that frequently, because the fluctuations are so very large indeed. Thinking short-term will either fool you into thinking you have a much higher advantage than you do, or that you can't count cards at all, which is also unlikely if you're a serious student of the game.

Either during or after a severe negative swing, fight the urge to bet bigger in order to recoup. This can be disastrous, even though there might be a strong feeling somewhere along the way that you've already embraced the worst of the worst, and that further hardship is unlikely. I've had many glimmers of hope come along right in the middle of a negative swing—leading me to believe the skies were clearing, when in fact I had a lot more rain coming my way.

Savoring the Moment, Patterns, and My Personal Catastrophe

Most players find themselves with the urge to play more after losing than after winning. We want to get our money back and "recoup" after a loss. And we want to "savor" a win for some period of time without risking the possibility of losing it back. Sounds like human nature to me. The problem with this is that, as touched on earlier, the underlying mathematics picks up exactly where you left off the last time you interfaced. So savoring the win by taking a break is possible, but don't for a minute think you're avoiding something that might have otherwise occurred had you continued playing. And there's no other way to double your bank than to get right back into the ring and keep playing, no matter what happened last.

So is it better to quit a winner and then get creamed the next time you play? Or is it better to win and then give it all back, and next time not have to play with a win rate that might be significantly higher than it should be? The answer is, "six of one, a half dozen of the other." It really doesn't matter, because to repeat what is fast becoming a common theme: in the end, you'll end up wherever the mathematics says you should end up.

And patterns don't exist in terms of winning or losing. It's been said that we as humans try to find patterns in things that are random (though we have the advantage, winning or losing during our *next* session is, for all practical purposes, random). This supports why we cannot scale down in betting when we think we're on the verge of a negative swing. Who's to say when that series of losing sessions will begin? Do we really want to win less when that last session before the downturn could've been a very large positive gain? Patterns don't exist, and trying to determine when a negative swing will occur is impossible. It should also be repeated that betting heavier in anticipation of an upturn is just as fruitless. Who said you're out of your slump just because you might have had one positive session last time at the tables?

Unusual winning or losing streaks seem to be the most memorable. Or at least when true oddities occur we tend to remember them. Here's an interesting one: I play blackjack whenever possible—mostly in the United States, although elsewhere in the world as well whenever the opportunity presents itself. Over time, wins and losses are logged and the resultant plus/minus starts to approximate the theoretical result. Except at one Atlantic City casino. No matter how hard I "try," I cannot seem to win at this particular property. I win with regularity all over town, but not there. If the year were 1966 and the locale different, I long ago would have suspected that I was being cheated. But I know that's not the case. It's just some freak of probability that goes on and on and on. I've lost thousands upon thousands there, and when I win it's usually a monumental struggle and I come away with something like $75. I've examined the shuffle, the shoes, the cards, the wash—everything, looking for some sort of explanation, all to no avail. That casino is my catastrophic event—my 500-year flood spread out over years. The one thing that keeps me going back is my knowledge that sooner or later the storm has to end, whereas the superstitious gambler would have long ago stopped playing there. The lesson here again is that the negative oddities can be more severe than imaginable, whether applied to one sitting at a table or to some group of similar events that occur over a longer period of time.

Casinos Down Under

Imagine a casino experiencing a negative swing? Are you smiling yet?

It happens, but not to the multi-million-dollar glam palaces you're thinking of. And in this section I'm not talking about Australian casinos either. I'm referring to the little guys—the underground operations backed by a solitary individual or a small group of people who aren't always well versed in how volatile probability can be.

Back in the late eighties, I used to play a lot at "underground" casinos in New York City. These weren't dark and dingy basements illuminated by the dull haze of a solitary light bulb. These were "legitimate" casinos—legitimate in the sense that most offered blackjack, poker, and in some cases craps and roulette, and you could order matzo-ball soup or a meatball sandwich, depending on which venue you were in. And winners always got paid. New underground places would open and close regularly—which leads us to the moral of the story: even the "bad guys" experience negative swings.

Wait a minute. The house never loses, does it? I mean, when's the last time you've heard of a casino going belly-up? Think again. I've seen it happen many times. An underground joint would open with only two blackjack tables. Maximums varied, but were substantial enough that a full table of players betting high would mathematically require the house to have a lot of money to withstand an adverse negative fluctuation. On top of that, players at underground casinos are usually players who know what they're doing—unlike the weekend warriors that you see at regular casinos. So the house edge underground is even less.

Things would roll along smoothly for a few weeks or so, and then all of a sudden both tables would start giving away money, and the house would go down like a lead balloon. Needless to say, the doors to Casino Down Under weren't open the following evening, or the evening after that. The lesson to be learned is that entire tables often experience severe fluctuations. So bankrolling a room with a relatively small number of tables is a risky business, to say the least (and I'm referring only to the mathematical aspect). Just as with an advantage player, *time* is the only thing on a small casino's side, if both the small casino and the advantage player can get there.

Grinding It Out

Earlier we touched on the idea that what may seem like a long time to you may, in fact, not be a long time at all in the world of negative swings and probabilistic fluctuations. And so the pro must be willing to "grind it out." What does that mean? That means occasionally playing through long periods of time when no money is made at all.

Take a look at Figure 15.2. Note the two points that correspond to the same level on the y axis. What if I said the span of time between those points (on the x axis) could be 240 hours? For a player hitting the tables two nights per week for a total of four hours each night, that's thirty weeks. That's more than six months of not making a dime. Now, some period of time before or after that six-month period might have been especially lucrative, but regardless, a substitute snapshot of those particular six months could be viewed as nothing more than a flatline.

Figure 15.2: Grinding It Out

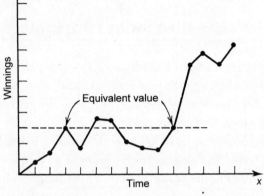

Again, as mentioned in the previous section, time is on our side. If playing properly, we always have a better chance of winning than losing. But anything can happen in the short run, so your results after forty or fifty hours are meaningful but certainly prone to be anywhere. A general rule of thumb is to consider it about 75 percent likely not to be losing around your hundredth hour of play, assuming you're averaging about 100 hands per hour at a 1.5 percent advantage. That's not bad, but 1 in 4 is certainly not a long shot.

Among the pros, between four hundred and five hundred hours is generally viewed as the threshold whereupon your likelihood of winning gets up to about the 90 percent level. That's certainly better than above, but 1 in 10 isn't that much of a long shot either. Keep in mind that some of us somewhere have to represent that 10 percent that find ourselves in the hole after four hundred and fifty hours of play. Unfortunate? Yes, but a reality that takes into account both standard deviation and small percent advantage that we're playing with. If you're still losing after one thousand hours of play (a full time player might reach this plateau in about six months), it may be time to reevaluate your ability or the games you're playing in. Perhaps you're not playing with anywhere near the advantage you thought you were.

Negative Swings Are Brutal

Remember that? It's been a while since I've reminded you. Hopefully, you've sort of embraced the idea by now, and when a bad one occurs you'll have been made aware enough to exhibit the patience necessary to weather the storm and eventually recover.

So where does that leave us? I think today's card counter needs to think long-term. And by long-term I mean at least annually or in terms of a few hundred hours at a minimum. Think four hundred to five hundred hours, and go from there. Don't put too much emphasis on prior results. And keep in mind that the most proficient of counters can still have one losing year in five.

Remember: perseverance and discipline at all times, because severe negative swings are far more brutal than words alone can describe.

CHAPTER SIXTEEN

Perspectives

On First Entering a Casino

This applies after you've been around the block a few times and have had the unpleasant experience of being on the receiving end of heat.

While at the tables it is the player who is in the spotlight—virtually, a sitting duck, to use a familiar metaphor. Surveillance, floor personnel, or anyone else that wants to observe or scrutinize your play can do so, and there's really not much you can do about it. But when you first enter a casino, it's those behind the tables who are most visible. At that point you're simply one in a crowd of hundreds milling through the room. Use this time, even before scouting the quality of a game, to look over casino personnel. This is *your* chance to scrutinize—to see who's who or who's working this shift before they have a chance to see you. There have been a number of casinos over the years in which I've gotten considerable heat on one shift, but have managed to play relatively unnoticed on other shifts, under the seemingly less-watchful eyes of a whole different set of faces.

Checking out the pit crew also allows you to see if any personnel changes have taken place. I've walked into some houses and noticed a counter catcher or floorperson who had previously backed me off at another casino—thankfully before I got into a game and gave him or her the chance to do it all again in front of a whole new cast of characters. A new face at any one casino might mean good news if it gets me a game again at the casino he or she no longer works at, or bad news if it ends my playing time at the present house—at least for the time being.

On Minimum Bets for an Extended Period

This is a tough one because you surely don't want to make larger-than-minimum bets when you don't have the advantage. But no flatline for what seems like an endless amount of time and then at the end of some shoe spread to two hands equal to ten or fifteen times your minimum bet is card-counter suicide—*even if you graduated to an upper level by only doubling your bet each time.* Newbies with regimented betting scales are prone to this kind of drastic and rapid bet variation. You might as well just wear a name tag with "card counter" written on it in bright orange letters. The bottom line is that you can't erase from an observant floorperson's mind that span of time you sat for hand after hand betting nothing more than the minimum. It was then that you made the impression of a conservative, patient player. And now you're betting the ranch? It doesn't matter how you've progressed there. You've changed too much in too short of a period. So you have to make some cover bets along the way. Which brings us full circle, especially since we don't want to be making larger bets when we don't have the advantage.

The only way not to flatline is to make some off-the-top wagers larger than your minimum. In addition, it's not a bad idea to make larger-than-minimum bets every once in a while—perhaps at neutral counts when the disadvantage is minimal. Three or four times your minimum bet with no discernible pattern, done at choice times, may gain you some "ordinary player" credit. If it buys you some longevity, it's probably well worth the price. This strategy straddles a very fine line, of course, and should be done sparingly. Betting any amount of money in excess of the minimum allowable when you are at a disadvantage is foolish, *unless* it serves some greater purpose.

The alternative is to only play for such a short period of time that any conservatism on your part can't be established in the mind of whomever is watching.

On Winning Several Large Bets at the End of a Shoe

Consider coloring up and leaving the table, and the casino, rather than having to invest again in several off-the-top cover bets at the beginning of the next shoe. This not only saves you from having to bet large without a healthy expectation, it also negates any possible heat that might arise if in the next shoe you're out on the table with peanuts. Besides, lots of gamblers leave the table after a surge of winning bets—afraid that their "luck" surely won't last. Savor the win while avoiding any possible scrutiny, and move on.

On Hanging Around Inside

Many of the newer houses now have restaurants and other attractions right off the casino floor. If you're inclined to hang around inside a casino—to eat, shop, or whatever—consider doing these activities before playing rather than afterward. You don't want to fall under heavy scrutiny at the blackjack tables, then sit with friends in a restaurant or lounge overlooking the casino floor—fifteen feet from the nearest bubble. That gives the surveillance team more time to film you, identify any of your friends or playing associates or even bar you after taking some time to review your last session at the tables.

It may sound overly cautious, but if you play often enough or for large enough amounts, any exposure above and beyond what is necessary is too much exposure.

On Too Much Play in One House

One of the greatest contributors to encountering heat, and sometimes the countermeasures imposed as a result, is too much play in one particular casino. That happens, almost always, because one house may offer rules or conditions that are so much more attractive than the rest of the pack's. Trust me on this one. I learned the hard way, when I was young and stupid and hell-bent on playing only at the best game in town at whatever cost. In the instance I'm referring to, I ended up playing one casino so long and hard that even to this day I can't get a game there, and that was many years ago. I'm not saying never play the best game available, I'm just saying be very careful not to play a game "just one more time," and then have that one more time turn out to be your last— through no choice of your own.

But doesn't it go against all logic to spend time battling a difficult game when another one is so much riper for the picking? Yes, it does, of course, but unfortunately the attempt to preserve longevity should sometimes come before the mathematics of the moment.

On When It Might Be Time for a Quick Exit

If you're aware of your surroundings (which, as a card counter, you need to be) you can almost always sense when casino personnel might be onto you as an advantage player.

If the phone on the podium rings and after answering it the supervisor makes a searching glance that ultimately ends on you, your antennae should be up and moving. If there's a huddle at the podium, during which one or two suits seem overly interested in your play, then trouble is brewing. If you notice a casino employee observing your play from behind (on the player's side of the table), then you're probably under scrutiny by the counter catcher.

Heat can come down in different ways, and the resulting action can depend on a whole host of different things, ranging from your betting level to how the casino is doing in the profit-and-loss column. Regardless, all of the above are examples of situations leading in the wrong direction, and a quick exit under such circumstances might not be a bad idea.

On Cashing Out

Don't linger at the cashier's cage. And, if at all possible, keep your head lowered when cashing out. Although there's a good chance you've already been filmed at the table (if you've been made), often it's at the cashier's cage where the best "head shots" are taken. If your pupil-to-pupil distance is going to be measured, or some other biometrics involving your face and the nearest computer, are going to be employed, here is where it's likely to happen.

If you're identified as a card counter and are cashing out a lot of chips, one cat-and-mouse tactic is to cash out at some later time—hours, shifts, or even days after you've become the latest topic of conversation.

On Returning to a "Big Win" Casino

Winning big at a particular casino and then "lying low" there is more common sense than it is anything else. If you clobber some house, try to avoid it for a while—especially if there are beatable games elsewhere. Time does wonders. You could easily get backed off if your win is still fresh in the mind of the wrong supervisor, and if you're suspected of being a counter. Whereas letting some water flow under the bridge may do wonders for preserving longevity.

On Playing Where You're Staying

Don't do it.

This is one of the cardinal rules for advantage players. You don't want to end up being ushered to the nearest doorway while your belongings are still upstairs in the very hotel casino you're no longer allowed in. Getting your bags back at that point will align any and all information that you used at check-in with the fact that you're an advantage player. Security personnel have also been known to approach identified card counters in their rooms to read them the riot act. In extreme cases, rooms have been searched, items confiscated, etc.

One way I use to combat this problem is to actually seek out and stay in hotels that have bad blackjack rules, or are known to be overzealous on barring or backing off card counters. Since you won't (or shouldn't) be playing in these joints to begin with, staying in these hotels doesn't decrease the playing field of available tables.

If you're on RFB (free room, food, and beverage) and you're logging significant time in the casino hotel you're staying in, then issues relating to your identity, covered in Chapter Thirteen, become of paramount importance.

On Winning and Losing

In some ways losing is extra hard for card counters to endure for two reasons. The first is that we actually expect to win—not because we're dreamers or over confident, but because that's what is supposed to happen. The second is that we put so much time and effort into mastering a technique that losing a chunk of change over a period of time seems extra debilitating.

I remember years ago meeting an acquaintance at a cocktail party and talking at length about the ups and downs of the game. This guy (a non-counter) had stopped playing altogether, and the explanation he gave went something like this: "The emptiness I feel after losing a figure like seven grand far outweighs the elation I get from winning the same amount." If you can identify with that statement, or if losing any amount of money would really devastate you, then you might want to reconsider this whole idea of getting into the ring to begin with. Because the losing times are inevitable, and you will at times have to "walk through hell in order to get to heaven."

On Winning Percentage

In baseball, a player has a good chance of making the Hall of Fame if his lifetime batting average is .300 or more. But a lifetime batting average of .300 means that player didn't get a hit seven out of every ten times he stepped up to the plate. That's a pretty high failure rate.

A similar situation exists in blackjack, which we'll summarize like this: A good card counter might lose four out of ten trips to a casino. A bad card counter might lose five out of ten trips. And a bad player might lose six or more trips out of ten. So the difference between a very good counter with a trip winning percentage of about .600, and a bad player with a trip winning percentage of .400, may only be two winning trips out of every ten.

Keep in mind that we're tipping the scales only slightly in our favor. That's why bad players can win and good players can lose, at the very same table or with similar cards. One big bet either way, or a few unlucky draws, can have lasting effects on our short-term results.

On Unlucky Tables or Lucky Dealers

Any talk you hear of unlucky tables or lucky dealers is nonsense. That's not to say that the cards can't come up favorable to the house in an overall sense for an extended period. They can, and do. But it's not the result of any dealer or table being lucky, unlucky, hot, cold, or any other adjective you can come up with to describe a group of outcomes that comprise a sequence of events. In fact, there's no such thing as being lucky or unlucky before an event has occurred. You're only lucky after the fact, if the results of the event are somehow favorable to you.

What does apply is that when the count is zero, negative, or slightly positive, you're at a disadvantage. As the count gets more and more negative, that disadvantage gets larger and larger. And as the disadvantage gets larger and larger, you're more and more likely to fall into that category, in hindsight, of being unlucky.

So what do I call a person who has won a multi-state lottery? I call that person "lucky."

On Tipping

Tip, but not to excess. And, of course, do so only upon winning.

Remember that the percent advantage is slight, and you're not sitting there for the fun of it like everyone else at the table. A prolonged period of over-tipping can affect your bottom line. I also don't advise tipping as you are playing, in case the session turns out to be a negative one. The last thing you want to do is make bets for the dealers all session long, and then end up leaving the table losing money. Leave that scenario for the weekend warriors who are there for nothing but a good time.

But it's also important to be fair, and if a dealer deals a good game or is a pleasant person to talk to, a tip is certainly a nice gesture. I tip after a significant win, but not to excess. Again, anything to blend in with the crowd. For longevity's sake, I want to make friends, not enemies. The loss in revenue I chalk up to the price of doing business.

Once in a great while you may be able to use tipping as a way to get better penetration. I'm referring to those instances in hand-held games when it's up to the dealer to decide when a shuffle is necessary. If you've been winning a lot of hands and the dealer keeps his or her own tokes (as is done in some Nevada casinos), then placing a bet for the dealer at just the right moment may get you another hand dealt before the shuffle. To the dealer you're running hot, and thus he may be inclined to deal one more hand if there's something in it for him. You'll see what I mean when you find yourself in that situation. It certainly can be an advantageous little move if the count is sky high, the deck is almost spent, and there's nothing more you'd rather do than get out there with a chunk *one last time* before the shuffle.

On Cheating

Many people question whether or not cheating actually occurs. Thankfully, being cheated is something you don't have to be overly concerned with—at least not at the vast majority of casinos. Years ago you might have encountered a dealer working in conjunction with the casino to cheat a high-stakes player (by dealing seconds or through false shuffling), but nowadays that's quite unlikely. For large corporations that now have involved themselves in this gaming craze, there's simply too much at stake to risk cheating one or two big spenders out of a few hundred thousand, or to have some other form of misconduct taking place on a recurring basis.

As for employees that are caught cheating—it usually involves a dealer working in collusion with another player, or perhaps a dealer working solo at trying to steal checks from the chip rack. Employee cheating is one reason for the existence of all those floor supervisors you see darting back and forth between tables. And you thought they were all there only to keep an eye on you?

If flat-out cheating is occurring, then it's probably so well orchestrated that you'll never even know it's going on to begin with. Bottom line: don't worry about it. If you must be on the lookout for something, then watch for things like preferential shuffling or unusual card-washing procedures at smaller, privately owned casinos in very remote areas.

On Continuous Shuffle Machines

These devices are used to shuffle cards *after every hand.* Many weekend warriors don't mind CSMs, but thankfully the more serious players avoid them like the plague. At the Bellagio in Las Vegas, for instance, as of this writing many tables at the lower-limit pits are lined with CSMs, whereas these machines can't be found at the higher-stakes games located closer to the cashier's cage. Needless to say, these machines nullify the concept of using the past to understand the future and represent a real detriment to the future of advantage blackjack play. So whenever the opportunity presents itself, promote the demise of these devices. Ask the average player if he ever expects to get a "hot" shoe playing at a table using a CSM. (And while you're at it you might want to also ask this same player why he patronizes 6:5 single-deck?)

On Losing and Relaxing Your Act

If you're a card counter and you're losing, you have just as much chance of getting barred, backed off, or having a procedural change affect you as does a counter who is beating the pants off the casino. If losing, newbies may be inclined to relax their act or not take the appropriate precautions if trying to recover too much too fast. Losing in no way lessens the likelihood of heat or scrutiny. Don't let your guard down. Not even for a moment. Heat sometimes has nothing to do with how you are doing at the tables—especially if it comes from a club you've played in before.

On the Emotional Side of Playing

No matter what level, playing blackjack for "money that matters" can generate lots of adrenaline. You're always looking to win—period. You want to win and win and win some more, with each session seemingly more important than the last.

Let's face it. This is a tough arena to exist in for an extended period. At a minimum you need nerves of steel, lots of heart, and a strong stomach. And you've got to be disciplined, determined, and tough emotionally. A steady and predictable upward climb is the stuff of dreams. Instead, expect to spike up and down dramatically, with an overall drift in the upward direction becoming apparent only in the long run.

In light of the above, are you the type of person who sees only that top dollar amount you reached several weeks back and nothing else? Or can you ride the roller coaster up and down, and survive the plunges?

Do you have what it takes to persevere through the tougher times?

On Keeping Accurate Records

Keep accurate records of your results, both in table and graph form. Study the results and use the data to better understand the meaning of long-term expectation, and as an aid in maintaining the integrity of your game.

Look at Figure 16.1, then use an Excel spreadsheet or create your own table the old-fashioned way. Record the day, date, shift, casino, win/loss for that session, and total plus/minus since formation of the bank, and include a large enough space along with each entry for remarks or anything of interest you may want to write down about a specific session, casino, etc.

Figure 16.1 Example Spreadsheet

Date	Day	Casino	Shift	Win/Loss	Totals	Remarks

Recording the date, day, casino, and shift will allow you to spread future plays over different days of the week or times of the day when casino personnel are different. Noting the casino you played in will allow you to sum your total win for each house. Since you took the Burbank

Boat for so much money last time, perhaps on this trip to that general area you should hit the Grand Veronica instead. You'll be surprised to find how quirky probability can be when you later examine overall results for certain casinos versus overall results at others. The win/loss per session will allow you to figure out how many sessions you left as a winner, and how many as a loser—as well as information like average win and average loss per session. You'll see bunches of negatives and bunches of positives that seem about as predictable as red and black on one of those electronic roulette displays. Finally, the most important column of all: the total plus/minus. This allows you to instantly know your bottom-line result, which of course allows you to revel a little in satisfaction, depending on how successful you've been. It also allows for accurate reporting to the Internal Revenue Service, which is a requirement by law for all income made from gambling. The "Remarks" column can be used to record anything of relevance. For example:

"Heat from Fred Zaitz, swing shift manager at the Monte Carlo."

"Penetration here not as good as last month."

"Phenomenal shoe to end session. Spread $10 to $100 without a second look."

"Met Patricia Farley, day shift pit boss usually in the bac pit. We both have one daughter and one son. Very nice lady."

"Horrible cards overall, even through positive shoe."

"No heat, and comp dinner to boot. Excellent filet mignon at The Winstead Steakhouse."

Using a graph is especially helpful if you are unfamiliar with probability in general, or with the mathematical principles relating time to some function involving number of trials, a given advantage, and how much variance can occur from the expected result. I honestly believe that not enough card counters understand this concept—one critical to playing at the professional level and knowing in advance what to expect and what not to expect.

Take a moment and look back again at the graphs shown in Figure 15.1. Then develop your own. Let the "x" or horizontal axis represent time, and the vertical or "y" axis represent total plus/minus. Pick increments relative to your betting level and plot your results. Study the hills and valleys that accumulate, noting what seems to be a bunch of random points that magically start to trend upward in time. Get accustomed to how volatile this game can be, and how your results can skyrocket or plummet in the short run. In many cases, a picture is, indeed, worth a thousand words.

On Making It a "Life Game"

If you're not playing regularly, the result will be fewer hours logged for a given period, which makes you a lot more susceptible to the negative fluctuations common to playing blackjack with only a 1.5 percent advantage. And if you're behind for an extended period, you may become somewhat disheartened. So it's essential to grasp this meaning of the long run of time, and know that results over the short run can be somewhat misleading.

As mentioned in Chapter Fifteen, four hundred hours is a span of time that could, in a general sense, be considered as the long run. To put this in perspective, four hundred hours is reached in about twelve months by a part-time serious player logging eight hours per week.

Remember that winning takes a while—so make it a life game if you can't play with any kind of regularity. And thinking in a bottom-line sense will make things like breaking even over an extended period a little easier on the psyche. Also keep in mind that as time goes on and your win column gets higher, any single loss should have significantly less meaning from the bottom-line perspective.

On Admitting You're a Card Counter

Never do. No matter whom you're talking to or what's implied, said, or suggested—never, *ever* admit to being a card counter while inside a casino. It does nothing for you, yet provides confirmation for them. Play dumb instead—say you only wish you could do that. Imply your skepticism. Use your imagination, and be creative: "How could a system that assigns a positive to high cards and a negative to low cards possibly help me draw a 5 when I have a total of 16?"

On Viva Las Vegas

If you're not plying your trade here for at least a few days annually, then you're not taking part in the convention that will help you become a more informed and experienced player. Consider card counting in Las Vegas as continuing education credits.

Not every counter gets to Mississippi, Minneapolis, or Monte Carlo. But every professional-level player does get to Vegas, sooner or later. Consider Sin City as the standard by which to measure all other blackjack rules, penetration, heat, crowds, and conditions. And have fun while you're at it.

Epilogue

As with any endeavor, the greatest experience comes with getting out there and doing for yourself. Hopefully the pages of this book have provided the tools necessary for you to take your game to the highest level.

And your timing is perfect. At present, the popularity of casino gambling is at an all-time high, as evidenced by the continuous expansion of casino gambling and the recent explosion of Native American and riverboat casinos throughout the United States. Not to mention the magazine articles, television shows, coffee shop conversations, and other aspects of life this now widely accepted form of entertainment has managed to penetrate. So what better time than now to take a game like blackjack and master it such that you, and not the casino, are holding the mathematical advantage?

Begin your odyssey and you'll find a thrill ride to last a lifetime. It really does provide everything: mental challenge, financial gain, suspense, elation, sorrow, comedy, travel, exercise, free room and board, a cat-and-mouse game, and a chance to meet some really interesting characters. And when I say "characters," I mean that only as a compliment, of course.

It's all there for you to experience. So enjoy it. And I'll be there too—right alongside you at the nearest blackjack table.

Remember? I'm the guy in the picture on the back cover of this book.

Appendix One:
High-Low Numbers Matrix

Stand, double down, split or surrender if the true count is equal to or greater than the number in the table. Hit (do not double down, split, or surrender) if the true count is less than the number in the table.

Insurance
Insure all hands when the true count equals or exceeds +3

Hitting and Standing

PLAYER'S HAND	DEALER'S UPCARD									
	2	3	4	5	6	7	8	9	10	A
17										-7
16	-9	-11	-12	-13	-14	10	8	5	0	9
15	-5	-7	-8	-9	-10	12	11	8	4	10
14	-3	-4	-6	-7	-8					
13	0	-1	-3	-4	-5					
12	4	2	0	-1	0					
A,7										1

Hard Doubling

PLAYER'S HAND	DEALER'S UPCARD									
	2	3	4	5	6	7	8	9	10	A
11	-13	14	-15	-16	-17	-10	-7	-4	-4	1
10	-9	-10	-11	-13	-15	-6	-4	-1	4	4
9	1	0	-2	-4	-6	4	8			
8	15	10	7	4	2					
7			14	11	11					

Soft Doubling

PLAYER'S HAND	DEALER'S UPCARD				
	2	3	4	5	6
A9	11	9	7	5	5
A8	9	6	3	2	1
A7	1	-2	-6	-8	-10
A6	2	-3	-7	-11	-14
A5	16	5	-2	-6	-13
A4		8	0	-4	-9
A3		8	2	-1	-4
A2		8	3	0	-1

Splitting Pairs (doubling after splitting not allowed)

PLAYER'S HAND	DEALER'S UPCARD									
	2	3	4	5	6	7	8	9	10	A
A,A	-13	-14	-14	-15	-16	-11	-9	-8	-9	-3
10,10	12	9	7	5	5					
	2	3	4	5	6	7	8	9	10	A
9,9	-1	-2	-3	-5	-5	7	-8	-10		3
8,8										
7,7	-9	-12	-14	-16						
6,6	2	0	-3	-5	-7	-13				
5,5										
4,4			15	9						
3,3	9	4	0	-3	-12	13				
2,2	8	3	-2	-6	-10					

Splitting Pairs (doubling after splitting not allowed)

PLAYER'S HAND	DEALER'S UPCARD									
	2	3	4	5	6	7	8	9	10	A
A,A	-13	-14	-14	-15	-16	-11	-9	-8	-9	-3
10,10	12	9	7	5	5					
9,9	-3	-4	-5	-7	-7	4	-8	-9		3
8,8										
7,7	-11	-13	-14	-15			2			
6,6	-2	-4	-7	-9	-12	-16				
5,5										
4,4		8	3	-1	-2					
3,3	-1	-6	-9	-10	-15		4			
2,2	-3	-6	-7	-9	-14		6			

Conventional Surrender

PLAYER'S HAND	DEALER'S UPCARD				
	7	8	9	10	A
17			15	14	
16	13	5	0	-2	-1
15	13	7	2	0	1
14		13	7	3	6
13			14	8	16
12				14	
8,8			8	1	

Appendix Two:
Uston APC Numbers Matrix

Stand, double down, split or surrender if the true count is equal to or greater than the number in the table. Hit (do not double down, split, or surrender) if the true count is less than the number in the table.

Insurance

Insure all hands when the true count equals or exceeds +3

Hitting and Standing										
PLAYER'S HAND					**DEALER'S UPCARD**					
	2	**3**	**4**	**5**	**6**	**7**	**8**	**9**	**10**	**A**
17										-7
16	-10	-12	-14	-17	-16	14	13	6	0	10
15	-7	-8	-10	-12	-12	18	19	11	4	12
14	-3	-4	-6	-8	-8			19	9	14
13	0	-1	-3	-4	-4					
12	4	2	0	-1	0					
A,7										1

Hard Doubling

PLAYER'S HAND	DEALER'S UPCARD									
	2	3	4	5	6	7	8	9	10	A
11	-13	-14	-15	-18	-19	-11	-8	-5	-4	1
10	-11	-11	-13	-15	-17	-8	-5	-1	5	5
9	1	0	-2	-5	-7	5	12			
8	16	11	7	5	2					
7			17	14	14					

Soft Doubling

PLAYER'S HAND	DEALER'S UPCARD				
	2	3	4	5	6
A9	13	11	8	7	6
A8	9	6	4	2	1
A7	1	-1	-5	-8	-8
A6	1	-2	-5	-10	-13
A5		4	-1	-6	-11
A4		6	0	-4	-8
A3		8	2	-2	-5
A2		9	4	0	-2

Splitting Pairs (doubling after splitting not allowed)

PLAYER'S HAND	DEALER'S UPCARD									
	2	3	4	5	6	7	8	9	10	A
A,A	-14	-15	-18	-19	-20	-11	-9	-8	-9	-4
10,10	14	11	8	6	6					

PLAYER'S HAND	DEALER'S UPCARD									
	2	3	4	5	6	7	8	9	10	A
9,9	-1	-2	-4	-6	-5	10	-13	-13		6
8,8										
7,7	-8	-9	-12	-14						
6,6	2	0	-3	-6	-7					
5,5										
4,4										
3,3	10	4	0	-4	-7					
2,2	8	3	0	-3	-6					

Splitting Pairs (doubling after splitting not allowed)

PLAYER'S HAND	DEALER'S UPCARD									
	2	3	4	5	6	7	8	9	10	A
A,A	-14	-15	-18	-19	-20	-11	-9	-8	-9	-4
10,10	14	11	8	6	6					
9,9	-3	-4	-5	-7	-7	5	-11	-10		3
8,8										
7,7	-12	-11	-11	-14	-18	-18	2			
6,6	-1	-3	-11	-12	-15					
5,5										
4,4		10	3	-1	-4					
3,3	0	-3	-5	-7	-10		5			
2,2	-4	-6	-7	-9			6			

Conventional Surrender

PLAYER'S HAND	DEALER'S UPCARD			
	8	9	10	A
17				
16	7	0	-3	-2
15	10	3	0	2
14	13	7	3	6
13		12	7	12
8,8		9	1	

Glossary

Action: Bets that are dependent on the outcome of an event soon to happen, such as a hand of blackjack or a roll of the dice. In a more general sense, a player's "total action" equals the cumulative amount bet over a given period of time.

Bac Pit: Short for "baccarat pit," where often higher-limit blackjack tables are found.

Back Counting: Card counting by standing behind a table, before playing.

Backed Off: Being told by casino management that you are no longer allowed to play blackjack, but are still welcome to participate in any other game.

Bank: A player's total stake.

Barred: Being escorted off the premises and permanently prohibited from reentering, after being read the Trespass Act.

Basic Strategy: The most advantageous way to play each hand, based on computer simulation or combinatorial analysis, and before card counting techniques are applied.

Big Player: In team play, the player who is called into a game by a spotter to play for larger amounts during favorable counts.

Black Action: Any bet involving black chips, valued at $100.

Breaking: Another term used to describe busting, or exceeding 21.

Bubble: The outer covering of a ceiling-mounted surveillance camera.

Burn: To "burn a card" is a blackjack tradition that involves the dealer's removing the first card from the deck or shoe following the shuffle and placing it in the discard tray.

Busting: To go over or exceed 21.

Camo: Short for "camouflage," which in the world of advantage blackjack means anything done in an attempt to hide the fact that you're counting cards.

Card Eating: To spread to two or more hands in an effort to use up cards at a faster rate.

Cashier's Cage: The area where chips may be exchanged for cash.

Casino Manager: The top-ranking decision maker among casino floor personnel.

Checks: Casino language for chips.

Color Up: To exchange chips for higher denominations upon leaving a table.

Comp: Short for "complimentary," such as dinners, rooms, drinks, or show tickets provided to certain customers by the casino.

Day Shift: The shift for casino personnel that runs from about noon to 8:00 P.M.

Dealing Seconds: Dealing not the next card, but the one below it.

Double Exposure: A variety of blackjack in which both of the dealer's cards are visible to the players.

Doubling for Less: Doubling down for any amount less than your original wager.

Eighty-sixed (86'd): Being barred by a casino.

Expected Value (EV): The average of all possible outcomes.

Eye in the Sky: Casino surveillance from cameras positioned at the ceiling level.

First Base: The first seat at a blackjack table, to the dealer's extreme left.

Flat Bet: To bet the same amount hand after hand (or "flatline"), usually the table minimum.

Floorperson: A games supervisor.

Glam Palace: A large, opulent casino.

Graveyard: The shift for casino personnel that runs from about 4:00 A.M. to noon.

Grind Joint: Usually a smaller-sized casino that hangs on the outcome of larger action.

Hand Held: The name given to single- and double-deck games that are dealt by hand, and not by using a shoe.

Hard Hand: A blackjack hand without the presence of an ace, or with any number of aces all being totaled as 1.

Heads Up: To play head on or one-on-one against the dealer.

Heat: Scrutiny of one's play that's likely to result in a casino countermeasure.

Hit: To request an additional card. A player may "hit" more than once.

Hole Card: The dealer's card that is not visible to the players.

Host: The casino representative responsible for keeping certain customers happy.

Marker: An amount drawn against a player's credit on deposit with a casino.

Multi-Level Point Count: A card-counting system that uses point count values in addition to -1, 0, and 1.

Natural: A blackjack, consisting of an ace and any 10-valued card dealt on the first two cards.

Nickels: $5 chips.

Off the Top: A phrase used for the first hand dealt after the shuffle, usually pertaining to the amount bet on that hand.

One-Level Point Count: A card-counting system in which card values are either -1, 0, or 1.

Paint: A jack, queen, or king.

Pat Hand: A hand totaling 17 through 21.

Penetration: How far into the deck or decks the dealer deals.

Pit Boss: The person in charge of a specific gaming pit.

Push: A tie between a player and the dealer.

Pressing: Adding more to an existing bet.

Quarters: $25 chips.

Resplit: To split a hand a second or successive time, such as when dealt an 8 on the first card after splitting two prior 8s.

Risk of Ruin (ROR): The likelihood expressed in percent of losing one's entire stake. Synonymous with a player's "element of ruin" percentage.

Rated: Getting "rated" is when a player gives his name or casino-issued players card to a floor person so that the player's bets and time at the table can be recorded. "Freebies" such as complimentary rooms, meals, etc. are awarded to players based on prior "ratings."

Round: A complete hand of blackjack, from start to finish, dealt to all players at a table.

Running Count: A cumulative count based on preassigned values given to each card.

Shoe: A device used by the dealer to hold decks of freshly shuffled cards. Shoe games usually involve four or more decks.

Shuffle Tracking: A method that tracks cards or clumps of cards through a shuffle and into the next shoe.

Snapper: A blackjack, or natural.

Soft Hand: A hand in which the ace is counted as 11.

Spotter: In team play, a card counter used strictly to identify positive counts and relay this information to a "Big Player," who may then enter the game.

Spreading Horizontally: Playing more than one hand, such as two or three.

Spreading Vertically: Increasing your bet on one hand, usually dramatically.

Stand: To stand or "stay" on a hand is to decline additional cards.

Standard Deviation: A way of describing in mathematical terms how far from our expected outcome our results are likely to fall.

Steaming: Losing control and over betting. Advantage players may appear to "steam" when attempting to use this kind of behavior as camouflage for betting large at opportunistic points in the deck.

Stiff: A hand totaling 12 through 16.

Suits: Casino personnel such as floor supervisors or others involved with casino management.

Surrender: An option in which the player may give up on his hand, and in doing so must forfeit half of his original bet. Two varieties exist. Early surrender allows the player to take advantage of this option before the dealer checks for blackjack. Late, or conventional surrender, is the ability to bow out only after the dealer checks for blackjack.

Swing Shift: The shift for casino personnel that runs from about 8:00 P.M. to 4:00 A.M.

Tap Out: To lose all of one's playing capital.

Third Base: The last seat at a blackjack table, to the dealer's extreme right.

Toke: A tip.

Trespass Act: The name given to the statement read by casino personnel to advantage players that prohibits them from reentering the premises.

True Count: The running count divided by the number of decks or half decks remaining, depending on the system used.

Unit: Used to describe a player's minimum bet, such as $5.

Upcard: The dealer's card that is visible to the players.

Washing: Randomly mixing brand-new cards prior to shuffling them in a traditional fashion.

Whale: A term usually used by casino personnel for a player who gambles for very large amounts.

Selected References

Andersen, Ian. *Burning the Tables in Las Vegas.* Las Vegas: Huntington Press, 1999.

Griffin, Peter A. *The Theory of Blackjack.* Las Vegas: GBC, 1979; fifth edition, Las Vegas: Huntington Press, 1996.

Malmuth, Mason. *Blackjack Essays.* Henderson, NV: Two Plus Two Publishing, 1987.

Mezrich, Ben. *Bringing Down the House.* New York: The Free Press, 2002.

Perry, Stuart. *Las Vegas Blackjack Diary.* Pittsburgh: Conjelco, 1997.

Revere, Lawrence. *Playing Blackjack as a Business.* Secaucus, NJ: Lyle Stuart, 1971: last revised, 1980.

Schlesinger, Don. *Blackjack Attack.* Oakland: RGE Publishing, 1997: third edition, 2005.

Snyder, Arnold. *Blackbelt in Blackjack.* Berkeley: RGE Publishing, 1983; third edition, New York: Cardoza Publishing, 2005.

Thorp, Edward O. *Beat the Dealer.* New York: Random House, 1962; revised, New York: Vintage Books, 1966.

Uston, Ken. *Two Books on Blackjack.* Wheaton, MD: The Uston Institute of Blackjack, 1979.

———. *Million Dollar Blackjack.* Hollywood, CA: SRS Enterprises, 1981.

———. *Ken Uston on Blackjack.* Fort Lee, NJ: Barricade, 1986.

Wong, Stanford. *Professional Blackjack.* La Jolla: Pi Yee Press, 1975; last revised 1994.

Index